CONVERSATIONS ABOUT THE END OF TIME

*Umberto Eco // Stephen Jay Gould*
*Jean-Claude Carrière // Jean Delumeau*

# CONVERSATIONS ABOUT THE END OF TIME

*Produced and edited by Catherine David, Frédéric Lenoir
and Jean-Philippe de Tonnac*

*Translated by Ian Maclean and Roger Pearson*

ALLEN LANE
THE PENGUIN PRESS

ALLEN LANE
THE PENGUIN PRESS

Published by the Penguin Group
Penguin Books Ltd, 27 Wrights Lane, London W8 5TZ, England
Penguin Putnam Inc., 375 Hudson Street, New York, New York 10014, USA
Penguin Books Australia Ltd, Ringwood, Victoria, Australia
Penguin Books Canada Ltd, 10 Alcorn Avenue, Toronto, Ontario, Canada M4V 3B2
Penguin Books (NZ) Ltd, Private Bag 102902, NSMC, Auckland, New Zealand

Penguin Books Ltd, Registered Offices: Harmondsworth, Middlesex, England

First published 1999
10 9 8 7 6 5 4 3

Original text copyright © Librairie Arthème Fayard, 1998
Translation copyright © Ian Maclean and Roger Pearson, 1999

Set in PostScript Linotype Sabon and Trade Gothic
Typeset by Rowland Phototypesetting Ltd, Bury St Edmunds, Suffolk
Printed in England by The Bath Press, Bath

A CIP catalogue record for this book is available from the British Library

ISBN 0-713-99363-4

# Contents

Foreword                                                                ix


*Stephen Jay Gould*
**Time Scales and the Year 2000**

*Introduction*                                                          1
The Delights of the Calendar                                            4
The Oddities of Zero                                                    7
A Thousand Years are as One Day                                        12
The Ravages of Hope                                                    15
The End of Time Has Already Taken Place                                18
What Evolution Teaches Us                                              27
The Threats to Our Existence                                           33
A New Vision of the Past                                               39
In Search of Other Life Forms                                          42


*Jean Delumeau*
**Back to the Apocalypse**

*Introduction*                                                         45
The Test of Time                                                       49
Evil and Suffering                                                     53
The Judgement of the Individual and the Last Judgement                 58
Jesus's Inauguration of the End of Time                                64
A Thousand Years of Happiness on Earth                                 70
Millenarianism's Finest Hours                                          78
The Fear that the World Would End                                      87
The Regaining of Hope                                                  91

Jean-Claude Carrière
**Answering the Sphinx**

Introduction                                                    95
The Time of Kali                                                99
Vishnu's Sleep                                                  104
Getting Ready for the Night of Nights                           107
The Dizzying Perspectives of Time                               115
The End of Time, or the End of Times?                           121
Oedipus at the Gates of Thebes                                  127
The Blind Man and His Daughter                                  130
The Watchmakers' Secret                                         137
The Age of Lawyers                                              140
Withdrawing from the World                                      143
Space and Time: A Very Old Couple                               151
The End of the Human Race is Not the End of the World           158
In Praise of Slowness                                           164
Dreams are Our Real Victory over Time                           167

Umberto Eco
**Signs of the Times**

Introduction                                                    171
The Myth about the Panic Terror of the Year 1000                173
Paranoiac Visions                                               175
All Men are Mortal                                              179
Time is an Invention of Christianity                            184
The Millennium Bug                                              187
Funes or Memory                                                 189
The Myth of the *Tabula Rasa*                                   197
'If I Were an Elephant, I Would Have Tusks'                     199
The Time of Repentance                                          203
For an Ethics of Negotiation                                    205
Tragic Optimism                                                 213

## Conclusions

*Stephen Jay Gould*    217
*Jean Delumeau*    220
*Jean-Claude Carrière*    223
*Umberto Eco*    226

# Foreword

By the time the year 2000 finally arrives, Hollywood producers will no doubt already have presented us with every possible doomsday scenario. After the return of the dinosaurs, the arrival of the aliens and a meteorite impact, we can hardly wait for the nuclear apocalypse, for the earthquakes and the giant tidal waves . . . And yet most of the film-goers crowding into darkened cinemas for the thrill of seeing fireballs rushing at them are the very same people getting ready to celebrate the turn of the millennium in the best restaurants on the planet. Indeed, apart from a few cranks, the members of apocalyptic sects and the terminally neurotic, no one is seriously expecting the world to end on 31 December 1999. Many have even forgotten the significance of the date, and will be celebrating the arrival of three noughts rather than the 2,000th birthday of Christ. But that's what it's about, and all it's about in fact – even if, to make a pernickety historical point, we're actually a few years into the third millennium already. It seems that the experts are agreed that Jesus was born five or six years before the Christian era officially began.

The year 2000 is a date to conjure with and hence an excuse to market the Apocalypse in an extraordinary fashion. But perhaps it can also serve, less frivolously, as an occasion to reflect on the notion of the end of time, and beyond that, on the philosophical meaning of time itself. Hasn't the moment also come to take stock of 2,000 years of Christian history and to think about what the key issues are in a society that is undergoing profound changes? With this in view, we three journalists decided to question four speakers of widely different backgrounds and exceptional intellectual range: the American scholar Stephen Jay Gould, the French historian Jean Delumeau, the French author and screenwriter Jean-Claude Carrière and the Italian novelist and semiologist Umberto Eco. Thus this book was born.

As Jean Delumeau here shows us in detail, the idea of the 'end of time' comes directly out of the Bible which, in contrast to the thought of Ancient Greece and the East, invented the notion of linear time, with a beginning and an end. Incidentally, we will see how this conception of time influenced the whole development of Western thought, even in its most secular form. If the book of Genesis sets out to tell the story of the origin of the world, the

different eschatological narratives of the Bible – among them the famous
Apocalypse, or Revelation of Saint John* – are devoted to describing the end
of time. This astonishing Book predicts, without giving precise dates, a
certain number of events, most of them momentous in character, which will
punctuate human history up to the day of the Last Judgement, when God will
interrupt the course of history and judge all creatures according to their
deeds. The Book also speaks of a period of a thousand years, preceding the
end of time, when the devil will be bound in chains and the triumph of Christ
on earth will be seen. Jean Delumeau and Stephen Jay Gould recall in this
regard the degree to which this prediction has affected minds throughout the
last 2,000 years; so-called 'millenarian' hopes have created more
disturbances and stirred up more passions than the turn of the first
millennium which, contrary to popular belief, left many Christians unmoved.
As for the hopes and fears associated with the end of the world, these
developed mainly during the Renaissance, a period of anguish, during which
every unusual event was interpreted as a sign that one of the prophecies of
the Book of Revelation was being fulfilled.

These characteristically religious beliefs and fears faded from the
imagination of people in the West with the decline of the Christian world and
the secularization of society. Yet, as Umberto Eco is at pains to point out, 'A
preoccupation with the end of the world is nowadays more a feature of the
secular than the Christian world. The Christian world turns this prospect into
an object of meditation, and the secular world pretends to ignore it, while
being haunted by it.' In other words, no one interprets the 'signs of the times'
as signs of the end of the world, as does the hero of Umberto Eco's novel *The
Name of the Rose*. No one is afraid that the 'stars will fall on his head', that
'the Beast will rise up out of the sea' or that 'locusts will swarm up out of the
bottomless pit'. However, the secular world is facing other eschatological
fears, alien to any religious agenda, but no less terrifying: the nuclear threat;
the hole in the ozone layer and all the other possible ecological disasters; the
resurgence of fundamentalism and the threat of sectarianism; the North–
South divide; the fear of economic meltdown; the possibility of another
collision with a meteorite; and so on.

* Hereafter this text will be referred to as the Book of Revelation to avoid confusion
with the wider connotations of the word 'Apocalypse'. Biblical quotations have been
taken from the Revised Standard Version. The phrases '*la fin des temps*' and '*la fin du
temps*' have been variously translated in these conversations as 'the end of time', 'the
end of the world', 'the end of Time' and 'the end of times' according to context
(translator's note).

What each of our four speakers reminds us of in their own way, is that every troubled age produces its own phantasms of annihilation. Indeed, we remain unavoidably marked by the stamp of the Judaeo-Christian conception of 'time's arrow', the directionality of history and the end of the world. Jean-Claude Carrière is careful to remind us that people in the East view time as cyclical, and to explain that if, as the Hindus believe, we are living through a period of destruction – the *Kali Yuga* – this is also the prelude to a new Golden Age. None the less it remains true that many of our contemporaries have the sense that they are living through an age of unpredictability, and that they dread, some more consciously than others, the coming of a great catastrophe. The number of reprintings of Nostradamus's prophecies which predict the end of the world in July 1999; the fear which the announcement of a solar eclipse on 11 August 1999 has provoked; the world-wide success of *The Bible Code,*\* which predicts that the Apocalypse will occur at the turning of the century; the enormous viewing figures for disaster movies such as *Armageddon* (a biblical expression which means 'the end of time') are all signs of this inarticulate fear. Humanity has begun to question the fabulous technological advances in which it used to place all its hopes; won't these in the end cause its destruction? At bottom, even if hardly anyone really dreads the arrival of AD 2000, many would not be surprised to see our proud ship suddenly hit an iceberg. The modern myth of the *Titanic* expresses perhaps better than anything the hidden terrors of our age.

What remains indisputably striking is the coincidence between this period of great upheaval and the change in the millennium. This coming together in time, whether significant or fortuitous, has provided us with an excuse for a fascinating discussion with some of the great minds of our age. For a year we have been busy conducting these conversations in Paris, New York, Milan and Brittany. Each of our four authors has carefully read all the interviews and has reacted to the texts of the other three, thereby broadening the debate. We also asked each one for a conclusion; these are to be found at the end of the book. Four major themes provide the unifying threads which run through these conversations: the year 2000, its meaning and the questions about the calendar which are related to it; the notion of the 'end of time', with its double resonance, both religious and secular; the philosophical and scientific dimensions of the question of time itself; finally, our own age, what is specific to it, what is seen as important and what are the future threats or good things to come. All these themes intermingle and echo each other throughout the

\* Michael Drosnin, *The Bible Code*, Simon and Schuster (1998).

discussions. Each conversation has nevertheless its own unique tone, linked to the personality of the speaker and his special area of enquiry. As readers will be able to observe, there is a great diversity in the views and intimate convictions expressed here. They will also note, however, many points at which these converge, suggesting a certain shared outlook on the part of all four men. Ultimately, Stephen Jay Gould, Jean Delumeau, Jean-Claude Carrière and Umberto Eco (in the order of their appearance in this book) are agreed on the importance of a number of key issues: liberty, lucidity, reason, responsibility, a sense of humour.

# Time Scales and the Year 2000
*Stephen Jay Gould*

## *Introduction*

It is impossible to reflect on the end of time without taking into
account the 'deep time' of palaeontologists and geologists, a
dizzying telescope pointed back towards time s beginnings.
According to Stephen Jay Gould, the discovery in the eighteenth
century that the history of the universe was to be counted not in
thousands but in thousands of millions of years troubled scholars
deeply and constituted the greatest intellectual revolution of
modern times. Thanks to the books of Stephen Jay Gould, we
have learnt that the 'end of the world' has already occurred, on
many occasions, after every great catastrophe that struck the
planet  we are in fact the survivors and beneficiaries of these
instances of widespread extinction, and we owe our existence to
the sequence of 'ends of the world' which can be traced
throughout the history of life – not only the one which witnessed
the disappearance of dinosaurs 65 million years ago, but also
the extinction of 95 per cent of the species on the planet which
occurred at the end of the Permian age. And if things had
happened differently, we wouldn't be here to talk about them.
For Stephen Jay Gould, evolution is grounded in contingency and
punctuated by unpredictable apocalypses.

Wind back the film and start from the beginning; this is the
desire which Stephen Jay Gould felt stirring in him when he was
about five years old, at the moment he met his first dinosaurs.
He realized a few years later that he had had the good fortune to
be born in an age in which for the first time science could offer
reliable instruments to effect this extension of the imagination,
to stage this epic production of the mind. So he became a
palaeontologist. But in the United States, university disciplines
are less rigidly compartmentalized than they are in Europe; so

his enthusiasms include geology, biology, astronomy, philosophy and history (as well as classical music and baseball, as it happens). All these disciplines feed into his teaching in Harvard's zoology department and add spice to it, as well as enriching the many publications with which he delights his readers.

So, as the third millennium dawns, there is nothing surprising in the fact that an encyclopedic mind like his, accustomed to changes of scale, should leave the confines of his speciality to enquire into the measurement of time, which rules our society and our lives, and especially into the history of the calendar and the eschatological theories that are linked to it. One will not be surprised either to discover the philosopher peeping out from behind the historian. Gould's crusade is that of a scientist who refuses to see man's appearance on earth as a result of some intentional act but rather as an epiphenomenon of evolution. How are we to assess the dangers which are threatening us today? Where does the fascination of human societies with predicting apocalypses come from? From excessive clearsightedness based on real dangers, or from a morbid delight in the sensational and the tragic? Gould puts these questions with a mixture of erudition and humour, but always in a rigorous and responsible manner. His historian's vision is wide-ranging, extending from deep time right up to the posturings which characterize today's marketing of the Apocalypse.

**As a child you used to delight in the fact that you would probably be alive at the turn of the next millennium. Not out of reverence for the number 2000, but because you knew that on that one day everybody on planet earth was going to be thinking about the same thing. Should we be afraid of this non-event or just quietly wait for it to happen?**

There isn't anything to fear, nothing special's going to happen! That's just what's so funny. In the past, in religious civilizations, people had a real, profound terror of apocalyptic catastrophes. What frightens us in our secular age is the computer breakdown that'll occur if computers interpret the oo of the year 2000 as a return to 1900. But no one dreams of claiming that this threat to computers will be an Apocalypse in the biblical sense.

No, I can assure you, nothing special's going to happen. People will have parties, there'll be a few more deaths on the roads, a few drink-driving accidents, and maybe we'll see a few new cults of the 'Heaven's Gate' variety. Other people will pour scorn on the party-goers and remind them that the date is arbitrary and trivial, but in the end there'll just be one big party, with people all over the planet kissing each other. And that'll be that.

**Can you calm people's anxieties just by telling them that a date is arbitrary?**

You think lots of people are afraid of the end of the world? In this godless age? No, I think people exaggerate. The year 2000 is a very special date, it's true, but for reasons that have to do with the history of the calendar. We're going to have the very rare opportunity, you know, not only of witnessing a change of millennium but a change of century with a 29 February in it. Because the year 2000 will be a leap year.

**Sure, like 1996, since leap years fall every four years . . .**

Don't you believe it! In our present calendar the leap year is omitted every hundred years, on the boundary between each century. But every 400 years 29 February is restored at the turn of the century, and 2000 will be one of those exceptions. So that year we'll have the privilege of enjoying an extra day that comes round only once every four hundred years, and which has occurred only once before, in the year 1600, shortly after the Gregorian calendar was adopted in 1582.

## The Delights of the Calendar

**Why all these adjustments? Couldn't they think of a less crazy system?**

The problem, you see, is that nature doesn't produce regular astro-nomical patterns of the sort that would allow us to create simple numerical cycles. The earth doesn't go round the sun in 365 days, nor in 365 and a quarter days, but in 365 days, 5 hours, 48 minutes and 45.96768 . . . seconds. All civilizations have had to contend with this problem. Which shows, what's more, that the calendar isn't fundamentally arbitrary since it's based on planetary motion.

**What do you mean?**

Nature has given us three principal cycles: the earth's rotation on its own axis, which determines the length of the days; the moon's rotation round the earth, which determines lunar months; and the earth's rotation round the sun, which determines the length of a year. These three forms of calculation are necessary; societies that hunt and farm need to know the seasons, fishermen and navigators need to know the tides. Why have calendars at all? In order to predict the regular patterns of nature. In an agricultural society you need a solar calendar to know when best to sow your crops. In a society that lives by fishing you need a lunar calendar to know the tides. Yet it's impossible to establish a simple arithmetical relationship between the two that would bring them into harmony. That's why we have so much trouble calculating the date of Easter, for example. Easter is a particularly complex case because its date is fixed with reference to both calendars, the solar and the lunar. It falls on the first Sunday after the first full moon (in the lunar cycle) following the vernal equinox (in the solar cycle) and so requires the two cycles to be co-ordinated. The relation-ship between the calendar and astronomical cycles is not false, but it can't be expressed in simple mathematical terms. The problem arises from the way nature functions.

**And weeks don't correspond to any natural cycle.**

That's right. The earth's rotation dictates a division of time into days, but arranging these days into groups of seven represents an arbitrary decision, particular to certain cultures. Because 365 is not exactly divisible by fifty-two, there's an extra day each year which puts the weeks out. That's why a Tuesday in 1997 will be a Wednesday in 1998, a Thursday in 1999, etc., except for leap years.

**What exactly are leap years?**

In 45 BC Julius Caesar reformed the Roman calendar and adopted the principles of the Julian calendar, based on a year estimated at 365 and a quarter days. Caesar took no account of the extra hours and minutes and restored three-quarters of the missing day by providing every four years one year of 366 days – called a 'bissextile' year because of its two sixes. The system works reasonably well, except that it quietly adds eleven minutes and fourteen seconds to the length of each year. Over the centuries these extra minutes add up to days – about seven each millennium.

**So the Julian calendar was bound to become less and less accurate as time went by.**

That's right, and in the sixteenth century, at the time of Pope Gregory XIII, it had accumulated ten extra days. By that stage the small difference was beginning to create practical problems for priests and astronomers, in particular when it came to fixing the dates of equinoxes and solstices. In 1578 Gregory XIII appointed an eminent Jesuit mathematician, Christopher Clavius, to devise a new system that stuck more closely to the astronomical facts. The new calendar was proclaimed in 1582. On the one hand, it eliminated ten days from the current year: in 1582 the days from 5 to 14 October inclusive disappeared. That year, the day after 4 October was 15 October!

**That's what you call killing time!**

In a manner of speaking! Of course, the whole thing was quite arbitrary. Time didn't simply stop in 1582; the days continued to go by quite normally. It was just that Clavius put the clocks right. Incidentally, Russia only made this adjustment in 1918, which is why the so-called October Revolution of 1917 actually took place . . . in November, according to the Gregorian calendar. But it wasn't enough simply to adjust the calendar by ten days. It was also necessary to ensure that the inaccuracy of the Julian calendar was not repeated over the coming centuries. So what was to be done?

**Play around with the leap years . . .**

Exactly. The leap years in the calendar are like the jokers in a pack of cards. You can put them in or take them out as the need arises. So Clavius replaced the 365 and a quarter days the Julian calendar was based on with something much closer to reality: 365.2422 days. In order to match this he decided to eliminate one leap year every century, but then to restore it at the turn of every century divisible by 400.

**Which still leaves a tiny discrepancy.**

Yes, at the moment the discrepancy is 25.96 seconds, which makes one day too many roughly every 2,800 years. You can't eliminate it completely. Plus the fact that you need to make the lunar and solar cycles coincide. Societies that both hunt and fish need to reconcile the two cycles. The moon goes round the earth in 29.5 days (or, to be more precise, 29.53059 . . . days). The lunar year of 354 days (twelve moons) is shorter than the solar year by eleven days. How can they be reconciled? The so-called Metonic lunar calendar is an attempt to fit in with the solar calendar: it consists of ordinary years of 354 days and then occasionally some exceptional, long years of 384 days. The Metonic cycle lasts nineteen years, and adds a thirteenth month in seven of these nineteen years. The Hebrew calendar intercalates a thirteenth month of thirty days into the third, sixth, eighth, eleventh, fourteenth, seventeenth and nineteenth years of a Metonic cycle. That's why the dates of feasts in the Hebrew lunar calendar seem to go backwards or forwards depending on the year. As for the Islamic calendar, it takes no account of the Metonic adjustment: hence the fact that Ramadan always seems to be falling earlier and earlier in the Gregorian calendar.

The complexity of the calendar is a permanent challenge to human ingenuity. That's why we say: if God exists, either he's got a sense of humour or he's a lousy mathematician . . . or else he just can't be understood by the human mind.

## The Oddities of Zero

**Why does the number 2,000 mean so much to us? Because we've all got ten fingers?**

The year 2000 would occur in the history of the world even if we had a different system of calculation. But we give it psychological significance, for whatever mysterious reason, because the human mind seems to need cycles that have meaning within a mathematical system. In our system, hundreds and thousands only have the meaning we give them. When we talk about the nineteenth century or the twentieth century we are giving a meaning to arbitrary categories.

The year 2000 seems special to us because our system of arithmetic is based on the number ten. Ten is an excellent basis for calculation, with many advantages. There's nothing to prove that its choice is in any way related to the fact that we all have ten fingers, but I would be surprised if there were no connection.

**We could have had six or eight, as you say in your book _Eight Little Piggies_.**

That's right. The accidents of evolution could have given us a different number, one that would have been just as functional. The earliest vertebrates had six, seven or eight fingers on each limb. Pentadactylia has probably not been a universal stage in the evolution of terrestrial vertebrates. We could just as well have thought of taking mathematics forward using base eight . . . though it would have caused pianists and typists a few problems! However, having ten fingers is no guarantee that you'll end up with a decimal system. The Mayas counted in twenties – they probably counted on their fingers _and_ their toes! Theirs was a good mathematical system, with complex cycles analogous to our own, cycles of 1,600 and 2,400 years. In a system like that, of course, the number 2,000 has no particular significance. For us, yes, sure, it's the product of a mathematical logic, but the numbers we choose to mark the beginning and end of the cycles are arbitrary. Having said that, these numbers have to be chosen from a narrow range. The mind doesn't work well with big numbers. I doubt if we'd find a numerical system that counted in 250s. The Aztecs counted in fifty-twos, which is really big.

**And then there's the old chestnut that keeps coming up every hundred years. Does the new century begin in the year 0 or the year 1? The beginning of our century was celebrated on 1 January 1901, but it seems highly likely that the celebrations this time are going to take place at the turn of the year 2000. So we could say – as you have suggested – that our century will be only ninety-nine years long.**

We could indeed say so. It's an excellent solution to a debate that's been going on for several centuries, and certainly since the turn of the century from 1599 to 1600. It's a trivial and meaningless debate in fact, but everybody gets very excited about it. And there's a very curious reason why this problem of calculation came about, a ridiculous but fascinating reason.

**What happened?**

We have to go back to the sixth century, to when the modern calendar was established – well before Clavius' day – by the monk, Dionysius Exiguus, or Dennis the Short. Pope John I asked him to draw up a Christian chronology of human history, based on the date of Christ's coming. Following the practice of the day, Dennis was accustomed to dating events *ab urbe condita*, from the founding of Rome. So that was the basis on which he fixed the date of Christ's birth as 25 December 753 AUC. Then he made the Christian era begin one week later, 1 January 754 AUC – the date of the circumcision of Christ, who was then one week old. The first of January was also – and this was no coincidence – New Year's Day in the Roman calendar. At the time this was a perfectly legitimate decision, given the information

Dennis had at his disposal in the sixth century, but it was to cause endless hassles for future generations.

## Why?

We mustn't blame him, there was nothing else he could do, but Dennis didn't use zero. Hence all the problems. When we made time begin again on 1 January 754 AUC, that day became 1 January in the year 1. And that's why our centuries begin with 01 and not with 00. If Dennis had called this founding date 1 January in the year zero, there would have been no reason for all these arguments about when centuries and millennia begin.

## He didn't think of it?

He couldn't think of it. In his day Western mathematics hadn't yet developed a working concept of zero. The Egyptians had used it, but only sporadically; the Chinese had the concept, but not the numeral; the Mayas knew about it, but didn't use it. Our own idea of zero came from Hindu and Arabic mathematicians only in the late eighth or early ninth century. The choice of 1 January in the year 1 is simply a convention, it's neither true nor false. But what one's got to realize is that the choice of convention, whatever it may be, has long-term consequences. If you decide you are one year old at the end of your first year of existence, you'll be 100 years old at the end of your hundredth year on earth, which means that at the beginning of the hundredth year you're only ninety-nine. If you make the calendar begin on 1 January in the year 1, and you're determined that a century absolutely must last 100 years, then the century ends only after the hundredth year. The following century begins at the start of the year 101. That's the mathematically correct way of looking at things.

On the other hand, given the way we write our numbers, with a mathematical base of ten, the number 100 looks much more interesting than the year 101, and 1900 is more interesting than 1901. Between 1899 and 1900 you change all the numbers except the first. Between 1900 and 1901 you change only one. Between 1999 and 2000 you change all the numbers. Between 2000 and 2001 you change only one. You may say that this is nonsensical, of no importance, that it's trivial, all in the mind. But my answer would be that that's just what a calendar is, a set of small calculations that serve to create a convention that's valid for all of us. And there's no harm in being interested in it.

**So each new century doesn't begin in 0, as our intuition suggests, but in 1 as arithmetic demands.**

Yes, and that's where the endless arguments begin. On the one hand, there are those who want to make the change of century coincide with the change in the numbers and, on the other, those who care about mathematical precision. It's a slightly absurd debate, but also very funny, because it shows us the foibles of human reason. Some people get so worked up about the problem that they fail to understand an obvious truth: the reason why no one has managed to solve the problem is that there isn't a solution. Both responses to it are right, but each one's founded on different premises. It all depends on what you think is essential. If you tell me that the century must begin in 1901, or in 2001, because every century has to have a hundred years, my answer is: fine, that's our usual way of understanding the matter, but it's an arbitrary code. I'm totally free to choose a different code. I can decide that the first century only had ninety-nine years. That may seem odd, but the calendar hadn't yet been invented then anyway, so what does it matter?

What interests me in all this is that we're on the brink of a historic change in the history of the calendar, because it's the year 2000 we're going to celebrate and not the year 2001.

**And for the first time.**

Yes! Previously, at each turn of the century, the people wanted to choose the year 0 but the experts of the time insisted on the year 1. The first great debate on this subject took place at the time of the transition from the seventeenth to the eighteenth century. Then Judge Samuel Sewall of Boston hired four trumpeters to announce the entry into the new century at dawn on 1 January 1701 – not 1700. By the end of the nineteenth century the debate had become an international one and clearly reflected a division between high and vernacular cultures. Kaiser Wilhelm II, like Sigmund Freud, had a preference for the year 1900. But all the public celebrations took place in 1901;

all the big magazine feature articles were published that year.

This distinction between popular culture and the élite's conception of things runs like a continuous fault line through European civilization. At the beginning of our century cultivated people – journalists, writers, teachers, anyone with a voice that could be heard – were in favour of choosing 1901, and they won. But today, a hundred years later, the age-old distinction between two cultural worlds has largely vanished, at least in the United States. Pop culture has spread everywhere, beginning with jazz, and the élite is no longer in a position to impose its preferences in the face of what the majority of people want. These people want to see the new millennium celebrated in the year 2000, and celebrate it they will. So that's why, as you were saying, our century will only have ninety-nine years. That's just a joke, of course.

**And what's going to happen in 2100? Do you think they'll wa t till 2101 to start celebrating?**

Neither of us is going to be there! And very few of today's babies will witness that great date.

**Isn't it also said that Dennis got the date of Christ's birth wrong?**

Yes. Not having the information, he situated the birth of Christ four years after the death of King Herod, which doesn't fit with the story told in the Gospels. We don't have any historical sources for the birth of Christ, but we do know the date when the famous Herod died: 750 AUC or 4 BC. Well, Herod and Jesus must have spent some time together on this earth, otherwise the stories in the Bible don't make sense any more. Remember the massacre of the Innocents, and the Magi returning into their own country? If Herod was in power when Jesus was born, then Jesus must have been born in the year –4 or earlier. What's to be done?

At any rate, it was on the basis of this historical discrepancy that Archbishop James Ussher, the Primate of All Ireland, calculated in his famous chronology published in 1650 that the creation of the world had taken place in –4004, on 23 October, at noon, and that the end of the world would therefore happen on 23 October 1997, at noon, i.e. exactly 2,000 years after the birth of Christ, and 6,000 after the Creation.

## A Thousand Years are as One Day

**In your latest book, *Questioning the Millennium*,* you show that millenarian ideologies derive from the theological interpretation of a remark by Peter, in his Second Epistle (3:8): 'One day is with the Lord as a thousand years, and a thousand years as one day.'**

That's the real question, in fact. Why do we attach so much importance to the number 1,000? As we've just seen, it has no special significance from the point of view of natural cycles. Its symbolic charge depends entirely on the fact that numerous passages in the Bible make an analogy between a thousand years for us and one day for God. For those who wrote the Bible I think these passages weren't intended to designate a precise length of time but rather were a way of exalting the glory of God. You have to remember that in classical Christian theology the millennium doesn't designate a period in human history but a kingdom of happiness on earth that shall last a thousand years, from the return of Christ until the Last Judgement. The coming of this millennium begins with the Apocalypse, so it's important to know when it's going to happen so that we can prepare for it. The whole thing is all the more difficult because Jesus himself clearly proclaimed the imminent arrival of the Kingdom. The time is nigh, and it's hard not to believe that the great event is going to take place during the lifetime of those listening to him preaching the Sermon on the Mount. And then . . .

**And then nothing happened!**

The way reality proves predictions false is a constant pattern in human history, and the only certainty we have about the Apocalypse. Well, if the event you were waiting for doesn't come along, you've got a choice. Either you renounce your belief, or you touch up the photograph: I didn't understand things correctly, my calculations were false. And you work wonders trying to reinterpret the message so as to discover the real date. That's why there's been

* Jonathan Cape, 1997.

an endless succession of new prophets throughout the course of history.

**All these prophets were wrong by definition, since we are here to talk about them.**

Yes, even the excellent Ussher we were talking about a moment ago. And yet he was a very rigorous man. It's just that he was living in a mental universe where the history of mankind was the one related in the Bible. At that time most people 'knew' that 6,000 years were to elapse between the Creation and the Second Coming – the beginning of the millennium. God created the world in six days and on the seventh he rested, and that meant symbolically that the world would last 6,000 years. The seventh day corresponded to the millennium, which was to bring a thousand years of blissful repose.

**That corresponds to the Shabbat.**

Yes, one long Shabbat.

**These people seem to have conceived of a well-organized god who didn't get his zeros wrong.**

Yes, everything was basically fairly straightforward. To calculate the end of the world all you had to do, therefore, was calculate the date of its Creation by tracing things back through biblical history. That's why Ussher devoted his life and thousands of pages to this research. He was a man of great learning, capable of carrying out complex calculations, and with a knowledge of Latin, Greek and Hebrew. In order to go back in time and to estimate how long had elapsed since the Creation, he used a multiplicity of sources: the Old Testament, of course, but also Babylonian documents, the history of Rome, the Gospels. According to Ussher, Solomon's temple was built halfway through, 3,000 years after the Creation, and Jesus was born exactly a thousand years later, in the year 4000 following the Creation. Between the birth of Christ and the beginning of the millennium, of the Seventh Day, there would therefore be exactly 2,000 years.

**Ussher didn't take the risk of seeing his prediction falsified during his lifetime. But others have been more daring.**

Oh, indeed, the list is long. In fact the prophets have never quite managed to agree on the 'real' date! In 1525 Thomas Müntzer, the Anabaptist, convinced that he was living at 'the very end of all ages', led a peasants' revolt in Thuringia and was decapitated. In the 1840s the Adventist William Miller, with a following of a hundred thousand disciples, expected the world to end on 21 March in either 1843 or 1844. Then he set a later date of 22 October 1844. But it took more than that to put the Millerites off. Numerous Protestant communities in the United States and Canada, notably Seventh Day Adventists and Jehovah's Witnesses, originated in apocalyptic sects of this kind. Jehovah's Witnesses had to revise their teaching: their founder, Charles Taze Russell, predicted that the world would end in 1914.

**He wasn't far wrong . . .**

But it wasn't the end of the world! It was a good year for assassinating archdukes but not for the troops of Armageddon. Waiting for the final cataclysm can have explosive effects on society; it can lead to the collapse of all taboos. The fact is, if we've only got one week to live, why obey the laws? Why be afraid of the powerful? And then what happens? How do you keep on living? There have been occasions when frustrated expectations of the Apocalypse have carried over into dramatic social conflicts. As far as the true believer is concerned, either he looks to join another sect, or he gets depressed and never recovers, or he becomes even more dogmatic and does his sums over again. The majority of sects survive very well despite being repeatedly proved wrong like this.

**And what's the truth in the end about the 'panic terror' of the year 1000? Myth or reality?**

I've had the greatest difficulty in coming to my own opinion on that subject. The so-called 'panic terror' of the year 1000 has been a political football in university circles for the last two centuries. The Romantic historians of the nineteenth century loved the idea; the Rationalist historians hated it. And they were always crossing swords. In the end my colleague Richard Landes convinced me that there was in fact a certain measure of millennial stirring in France and in what was to become Germany. But these movements don't seem to have assumed any great proportion, since, for example, Pope Sylvester II, who reigned from 999 to 1003, makes no reference to them, and nor do royal chronicles. There doesn't seem to have been any widespread panic, just a certain amount of unease.

**Perhaps people didn't know what the date was?**

I've long asked myself that question. In those far-off days did people even know that the year 1000 was approaching? But actually, according to the historian Richard Landes, whom I consulted, it does seem in the end as though they did in fact know. Dennis the Short's system of dating events from the year 1 of the Christian era had been widely popularized thanks to the famous chronology drawn up by the Venerable Bede, a learned English monk of the eighth century. The monk Raoul Glaber was predicting that 'Satan will soon be unleashed because the 1,000 years have been completed.' He later claimed that the building of cathedrals had begun immediately after 1000, when people had realized that the end of time had been postponed. 'Three years after the year 1000, the world put on the pure white robe of churches.' Then Glaber announced that the end of time would come at the millennium of Christ's Passion, in 1033.

### The Ravages of Hope

**Are apocalyptic predictions a way of dealing with our own personal anguish about the approach of death?**

In a certain sense, yes, one can say that all religions derive from the awareness of death. But it's more complicated than that. In most cases the eschatological doctrine contains a promise of resurrection. You're going to come back, you'll be able to sort things out for your friends and your children. Imagine the joy of seeing your dear departed ones again on the day of the great revelation! And then it's such a comfort to know one's going to come back to life, even after being dead for a long time. Millenarianism isn't just about being afraid; we mustn't underestimate the hopes to which apocalyptic doctrines give rise. Remember this, they say: there's no reason to despair, the end isn't the end, but the beginning of a shining future, the salutary destruction of our wretched world! It's that kind of hope that does the damage. It can be so strong that a people gives up looking after itself and its own country. That's why the Xhosa in South Africa allowed themselves to be reduced to slavery without protest: they were waiting for the return of their ancestors and for the arrival of a new order.

**That's terrible, the suicide of an entire community by its own consent.**

Yes, and it's happened more than once. Our society is paying a very high price for the consequences of these beliefs. The members of the 'Heaven's Gate' cult believed they were departing to eternal life. They had constructed an explosive mixture of traditional Christian millenarianism and pop culture myths of science fiction, in particular ufology. They believed themselves to have been sent by the 'Level Above Human' and to have 'come from distant space to offer a doorway to the Kingdom of God at the end of this civilization, the end of this millennium'. A spaceship was waiting for them behind the tail of the Hale-Bopp comet to take them 'home'. They carefully packed their bags for the journey ... and they're all dead. One remembers also those Iranian soldiers, during the Iran–Iraq War, who went off to get killed with the key to paradise round their neck.

**Whereas in our Western societies the threat is more that of despondency. Don't you think that this is one of the main dangers of our time?**

The danger has always existed; maybe it's greatest among Parisian intellectuals. Sorry, I'm joking, but it's true that the tendency to see the bad side of everything is perhaps the symptom of hyper-sophisticated societies who've lost the naïve enthusiasm of children. It's also a question of temperament; there are people who are naturally depressed.

**Do you think some periods in history are more receptive than others to apocalyptic tensions?**

Yes, of course. The second century AD, for example, which saw the rise of gnosticism and the Montanist heresy. In 156 a certain Montanus went into trances and predicted the imminent return of Christ. The Heavenly City of Jerusalem was to descend to earth and establish itself upon the Phrygian plain. Although the predicted Apocalypse was late, yet again, the Montanists remained strong for several centuries. And as everyone knows, predictions flourished in Europe at the time of the great plagues and the Crusades. But what one has to realize is that apocalyptic movements are generally social movements.

**You write in *Questioning the Millennium* that 'Apocalypticism is the province of the wretched, the downtrodden, the dispossessed, the political radical, the theological revolutionary, and the self-proclaimed saviour' [Vintage (1998), p. 45]. In other words, for all those who do not accept the world as it is, those for whom the earth is a vale of tears.**

That is in general why the powers that be, whether spiritual or temporal, are hostile to apocalyptic movements and actively combat them. Prophets are seen as revolutionaries.

**Do you think humanity has reached an advanced stage in its evolution?**

That's a question we can't answer. We have no idea what we are capable of on the basis of our genetic make-up. After all, we haven't been around very long, the human race is very young, about 200,000 years only. From the cultural point of view we are scarcely more than 5,000 years old. Language and technology are only just beginning, the most surprising, terrifying, exciting things can still happen, we haven't yet begun to explore the possibilities of social and technological organization. Most scenarios, it's true, are probably more terrifying than inspirational. But what of it? Perhaps you've noticed: we're not very good at making predictions! On the other hand, we are very good at forecasting catastrophes for the wrong time.

**Does humanity need great moments of crisis in order to progress?**

Perhaps it doesn't really. We've succeeded in surviving so far! But I have noticed that we only decide to do something when we're forced to it. We only begin to find solutions to famine when lots of people have died of hunger, we wait for genocide to be committed before denouncing it, we take steps against overpopulation when there is a threat of famine . . . Why? I don't know. It's probably a deep-rooted tendency in each of us. It's difficult to change, and changing society is even more improbable than transforming one's own self. The people in power want to stay there, and that desire is a powerful factor in creating inertia. It's often necessary to attack the powers that be in order to change things. But things are not as dramatic as they might be . . . I'm always surprised that there aren't more automobile accidents, given how many irresponsible people there are driving. A catastrophe is really quite a rare event.

**You seem almost optimistic.**

Let's just say that I tend to be prudently optimistic. I don't predict that things are going to get better, but at least I have the certainty that we have the means of putting up a fight. That's probably the best we can hope for.

## The End of Time Has Already Taken Place

**For a palaeontologist 7,000 years is really a very short period of time, isn't it?**

Hardly more than the twinkling of an eye.

**Of God's eye?**

No, geology's eye. It's an incredibly short period. So short that we can't even measure it with the tools we've got.

**It was in the nineteenth century that scientists discovered the 'deep time', which you've written a book about.\* They realized then that the world hadn't been created a few thousand years ago but that we had to think in terms of millions or thousands of millions of years.**

In fact that revolution took place at the end of the eighteenth century. At the beginning of the nineteenth century educated people already knew that time is long. The London Geological Society was founded in 1807, on the basis of time's immensity. People then were just beginning to measure the scale of geological time and to become aware of the reality of evolution.

**What was the spark that led to this discovery?**

It was simply an effect of scientific development. Once you have a general research method for the investigation of efficient causes and you have a global vision of the mechanisms at work in the universe, the old ways of explaining things no longer make sense. Once they understood fossils were in fact organisms, it became obvious that they couldn't all be the result of one single event, whether or not that was the Flood! They understood that these traces were evidence of an immense length of time. As soon as you attempt to explain natural phenomena on the basis of the laws of nature, the examination of geological archives leads you almost automatically to that conclusion. However, it took almost a century for people to accept the idea that we were faced with the traces of a history that stretched over an immense distance. Of course, you may be convinced that the earth today is identical to how it was in its original state, you may believe that miraculous events can suspend the course of natural laws, and you may mix all these ideas together to show that what seems to us the product of a long history is simply the result of a miraculous event which we are incapable of understanding. Or that it's God's doing.

The baroque age liked flamboyance and catastrophes, whereas the Age of Enlightenment was devoted to rationalism, to the reasoned setting-up of systems and orders; whence the idea that evolution is necessarily something orderly and systematic. The understanding of

\* *Time's Arrow, Time's Cycle*, Harvard University Press (1980).

deep time is the result of what happened in Western culture and, notably, in science.

## Who are the heroes of this new continent of knowledge?

There's no one single hero, each country has its own. The English always cite James Hutton, who lived around 1780. In Italy there were a number of people who studied the subject, and the French cite Buffon, particularly *Les Epoques de la nature*. Buffon was a great Newtonian and a distinguished mathematician, although he had more or less given up doing mathematics in his middle age. He was one of the first to attempt to calculate the age of the earth. By taking the example of a ball of metal of the same size as the earth, he tried to calculate how long it would take to cool down and to pass from its primary, elastic state to the point where it formed a crust able to support life. He made it 75,000 years, which is a poor finding from our point of view. But Buffon was making his calculations at a time when the majority of people still blindly believed in the biblical chronology.

## Newton himself thought that the world was 6,000 years old.

There were great debates about this question. Geology was fashionable in England. In 1691 a friend of Newton's, the Reverend Thomas Burnet, an Anglican priest who championed reform and was an ardent anti-Papist, published *The Sacred Theory of the Earth*. Burnet took up the theory of 6,000 years, but with the intention of reconciling it with a natural explanation of the formation of the earth. He didn't contest the biblical chronology, any more than Newton did. But he was looking for a law of nature. He was trying to understand how so many events could have happened in such a short time. His theory seems crazy to us: he imagines that all the water on the planet had collected beneath the earth's first crust. Then one day there was an explosion, and all the water came gushing out. And that was the Flood!

## Burnet and Newton were still trying to reconcile the two views of the world.

Yes, but by starting with the laws of nature. Even though Burnet, for example, firmly believes that the Bible is a historical narrative, he's convinced that his mission as a scientist is to explain everything by the laws of nature. He's not looking for any miracle.

**We talked about the arbitrary nature of the calendar. But aren't geological eras just as arbitrary?**

No way! That's just what is so remarkable about the scales of geological time – the fact that they're not arbitrary. Every year I make my students commit the sequence of geological eras to memory. All the teaching staff do the same, and the students complain. Why, they ask, are you making us learn these arbitrary names, these divisions of time, by heart? But I tell them that these distinctions aren't arbitrary, quite the reverse. When the geological scale was established in the nineteenth century, the boundaries were placed between eras which corresponded to mass extinctions. Not because scientists had a theory about these decimations, but because, empirically, the major changes in the fossil archives coincide with the time when they took place.

In my laboratory at Harvard University there are drawers full of the fossils of animals that lived before the great extinction at the end of the Permian age. They're very easy to recognize. Once you've seen them, you can never again confuse them with the fossils of organisms that lived after that extinction. In fact the destruction was so radical at that particular moment that the form of what we find later is totally different. You only need to open those drawers the once to understand that these boundaries are not arbitrary; they are the great rifts in evolution. The last great boundary is between the Cretaceous and the Tertiary, and bears the trace of the impact from some huge, extra-terrestrial object. We know that the fall of this asteroid caused the extinction of the dinosaurs. And in the end, the reason why we're sitting here talking like this is that an asteroid struck the earth, wiped out the dinosaurs, and spared a few little mammals. Darwin thought that the mass extinctions were human inventions resulting from the incompleteness of fossil archives. Today we know that they were real enough: the history of life has been punctuated by several massive and brutal decimations. Evolution is not one long, sleepy river! Take, for example, the mass extinction at the end of the Ordovician, 438 million years ago; or the one at the end of the Devonian, 367 million years ago. But the worst was the one at the end of the Permian, 250 million years ago. It wiped out, at one go, almost 95 per cent of all invertebrate marine species. Finally, we have the extinction of the dinosaurs, on the boundary between the Cretaceous and the Tertiary, 65 million years ago, triggered by the impact of an extra-terrestrial object containing iridium.

**We know that great catastrophes have occurred, that innumerable ends of the world have taken place. Consequently we know that it can happen again. Is this not where we should look if we're seeking a rational basis for our eschatological fears?**

No, because when eschatological predictions began spreading through Europe, no one knew that the earth had had such a long and dramatic history. The Bible mentions neither geological eras nor extinctions. True, there's the Flood, but that particular myth couldn't have originated in knowledge of the real history of the planet because the authors of the Bible didn't have access to such knowledge.

**But what did people say back then, whenever they found a fossil?**

In Antiquity they believed that fossils were the remains of antediluvian animals or human beings, the remains even of mythological heroes like Antaeus, Polyphemus or the giants mentioned in the first chapter of Genesis. In 413, in *The City of God*, Saint Augustine tells of a gigantic molar, the size of a hundred human teeth, that was found not far from Carthage and put on display in a church: 'These ancient bones,' he writes, 'show clearly, all these centuries later, how large primitive bodies were.' For a long time people thought human beings had become smaller in the course of history, it was a commonly held opinion among ancient writers. In the seventeenth century collectors made much of the giant shoulder-blades and teeth displayed in their cabinets of curiosities. Yet as early as the end of the fifteenth century Leonardo da Vinci was saddened to see these crazy notions still current, and he declared himself convinced of the organic origin of fossils.

In any case, it takes more than just finding one isolated fossil in order to conceive of mass extinctions. A fossil is simply the trace of a particular animal's stay on earth. You need prior knowledge in order to understand that they represent periods in the history of the living. Up until the nineteenth century nobody had such knowledge. The first dinosaur bones were found in 1825. No one knew of their existence.

**The dragons in myths are sometimes disturbingly like dinosaurs.**

That proves nothing, any number of living reptiles could have served as a model.

**In the long run we are the beneficiaries of their extinction.**

In the short run, you mean! We're the immediate beneficiaries!

**And we're also the only ones who are aware of the fact. All other living species benefited too, but they don't know they did.**

Quite right. All that proves is the extent to which consciousness is something rare and unforeseeable.

**People have tried to find regular patterns between the dates of the mass extinctions.**

There doesn't seem to be a regular pattern but there are clearly identifiable moments in the history of life, geological instants during which great transformations in the fauna took place. As I was saying, whether it's the extinction of the dinosaurs 65 million years ago, or the great catastrophe of the Permian 250 million years ago, these great rifts meant that the structure of living beings, during the period that followed, was determined by the groups that survived. So the principal pattern of the continuity of the living necessarily assumes the form of a tree of life.

**How long does it take life to recover after an extinction?**

It takes 5 million to 10 million years for it to reassert itself properly. Of course, it never starts over again from nothing; 65 million years ago, the mammals survived. Ten million years later they were flourishing. Evolution can be quite rapid on occasions.

**As Paul Valéry said: 'The rest of us civilizations now know that we are mortal.' Today we know that our species is mortal, just as all species are. You've written that 'extinction is the normal fate awaiting all species'. Basically, survival is the exception, and disappearance the norm.**

But that doesn't necessarily mean that extinction is a solution to the dangers currently threatening us. People who don't want to face up to the reality of the situation sometimes tend to use the discoveries of palaeontology to say: everything's going to disappear anyway, so what does it matter, why worry about the ecosystem? They even end up becoming advocates of the worst-case scenario; since new species have developed after every mass extinction, why not wish for a new extinction that will be even more productive? It's a quite unjustified line of argument, because it's irrelevant to the scale of human life. We can't apply the criteria of geological time to our destiny which is counted in days, weeks, months, generations, centuries . . . not to mention the largest category, millennia! It's a question of temporal scale, of proportion. Imagine you're a tyrannosaurus. You're living at the end of the Cretaceous, and here comes this asteroid. For you it's an unmitigated disaster, you're going to die just like the rest of your species. Nothing could be more tragic. From your point of view the fact that life will re-establish itself 5 million or 10 million years later is no consolation. The possibility of an extinction concerns us, and quite rightly, but at our own level, not at the level of the whole earth. From that point of view we're no different from the tyrannosaurus. The earth itself isn't in any danger. It's already experienced great explosions that were much more powerful than anything all our bombs are capable of producing. And it recovered from them, even if it did take millions of years to do so. But for us human beings that time-scale is irrelevant. Our temporality is the length of our lives, of our parents' and our children's lives. What is a millennium? For a geologist it's the twinkling of an eye, but in human experience it's a gigantic, almost inconceivable length of time. When the year 2000 comes, there'll be very few people alive who were around at the turn of the last century. No one on this earth was alive in 1800.

**Our minds have difficulty in apprehending periods of time that have no common measure with the time of our own lives. But at the same time we are quite capable of juggling all these millions of years.**

Our minds have varying capabilities. We're not very good at calculating probabilities. When it comes to concepts like the infinite or eternity, we are completely incapable, we haven't the faintest notion.

**And yet we use them, don't we?**

Yes, we use them when we're left with no choice. Since we can't imagine how phenomena originated, we talk about eternity. Since we can't conceive of space having an end, we talk about infinity. But we don't really understand what that means.

**We are prisoners of our own scales of time and space.**

I wouldn't say we were prisoners. It's just that we have the scale that suits us.

**But geology allows us to transcend this scale by thought, it's a privilege.**

Yes, it's the privilege of consciousness.

**Where is the dividing-line between man and animal? Is it language, tools, the capacity to plan ahead, the awareness of death?**

All these things are the multiple manifestations, consequences, of the phenomenon we call consciousness. Everything depends on what you mean by it. Even if you define consciousness as an aptitude for conceptualizing and using logic, you'll find animals who are capable of that, however rudimentarily. If consciousness is the capacity to recognize someone, to feel compassion for one's friends and relatives, dogs have it. If it's the capacity to use language in an abstract manner, then we are the sole conscious beings. But all this debate about logic and concepts is not as interesting as people imagine. In reality, whatever your definition of consciousness, the way the human mind manifests itself is radically different from everything that has ever existed on this planet; our mind gives us such immeasurable power and influence. Indeed, one can regard the emergence of human consciousness as the most sensational invention in the history of human evolution. An accidental invention, unforeseeable in my view, and perhaps never to be repeated, but that's not the issue. Even if it was an accident, its impact has been enormous. So, how shall we define consciousness? We can talk about language, the awareness of death, certainly, but we mustn't look for one single determining factor, there's a large number of criteria.

**In *Life's Grandeur* you talk about how bacteria see us as great mountains full of seams to be mined.**

I was speaking metaphorically, of course! In talking about the universe of bacteria in that book my objective was to put human arrogance into perspective. Bacteria let us think that we rule the world, but they were here long before us, they will certainly outlive us, they thrive in tiny spaces inside rocks three kilometres underground. So then people tell me they're not conscious, and that's why we're superior to them. We don't really know to what extent bacterial life is in fact dominant on earth, in the universe even. We've no idea what they're really capable of. It's a question of criteria. If you value consciousness, you make man the master of the world. But if you value long-lastingness and big numbers, then bacteria unquestionably have it over us. Among mammals the most thriving species are currently the antelope, the rat, the bat.

**This has the appearance of being a scientific debate, but in fact you're posing ethical questions. You're trying to cut our human pretensions down to size.**

Yes, that's right. It's a philosophical debate, laced with scientific questions. Eco tackles it in a particular way in *The Name of the Rose*. He's got a very subtle sense of this principle of differing temporal perspectives. The story is set bang in the middle of the huge dispute over the two popes, at the time of the great quarrel between Avignon and Rome. When the murders start happening, everybody's convinced they're connected with all the intrigues going on because of this major controversy, and that seems a reasonable theory. Of course, in the twentieth century, most people don't even know that there were popes in Avignon. In the United States, at any rate, 99 per cent of students are completely ignorant of that famous episode. Eco has the measure of this phenomenon, and his detective, William of Baskerville, realizes that the murders have nothing to do with current events but are linked to the fact that the monastery library contains the only surviving copy of Aristotle's *Treatise on Comedy*, thought to have been lost. Now, it takes a broad vision, one that can span the centuries, to be able to realize the importance of a fact like this. 'Today this book is of no importance, nobody's interested in it any more, but in the fullness of time it will be infinitely more important than all the ephemeral events of history': the only ones to realize this are Baskerville and the thief who's trying to destroy this work – and that's why Umberto Eco's 'bad guy' is so interesting. He's a scholar, and he can't stand the idea of destroying the text. If he had no scruples, he could easily take it away and burn it, but he can't, you can't ask a scholar to do that, so he tries to eat it!

**To embody it.**

Yes, exactly. Ha, ha! He can't bring himself to destroy it, but he doesn't want the text made public because its content is revolutionary. It's absolutely great.

## What Evolution Teaches Us

**What is your definition of life?**

I can't give a definition. All we've got, you see, is this one example on earth. One can only define it as a historical phenomenon deriving from the appearance on earth thousands of millions of years ago of a system for reproducing DNA, a system prone to error and which confers its attributes on the living: evolution by natural selection, population formations, metabolic transformations . . . But, as I say, that's all we know. If one day we were to find other systems that share the characteristics of the living . . . But then how are we to define these characteristics? Should we fix chemical criteria?

## Motion, growth?

I'm not one of those who tries to find a unique formula, a key definition. Key definitions are applicable to objects that human beings have defined for their own use. We know how to define an automobile because we made it. But life on this planet has a historical origin, and if there were other forms of it, they have died out. All living forms that exist today are descended from that one single origin. So all you can do is tell the story of this unique phenomenon, but that doesn't give you a category.

## One can contrast the living with the inanimate, with minerals . . .

One can contrast it with everything else, I suppose. Living creatures have to have some form of historical continuity, to grow and to reproduce, to inherit the characteristics of their ancestors. But artificial systems exist, and ones which are capable of behaving in the same way. The only reason we refuse to say they're alive is that they're not historically linked to what we call life.

## And that's a long story.

Our planet is 4,500 million years old, but its surface was molten during the first stage of its history, the heat made the atmosphere unbreathable, and countless isotopes generated even more heat. Then the whole thing cooled down. If primitive forms of life did appear before the cooling, they were swept away by the storms. The rocks dating from the period when the earth's crust formed, about 3,700 million years ago, were subsequently given such rough treatment by the heat and the pressure that no fossil evidence remains, only carbon isotopes, which can indicate the presence of life. These are the oldest traces of life on earth. And what's most interesting about them is precisely the fact that they indicate the presence of life about 3,700 million years ago.

When I was a student, it was faculty dogma that the emergence of life was a highly improbable phenomenon. In his articles on the origins of life, George Wald wrote that the only reason this phenomenon had eventually occurred was that the earth was so old: 'In time the impossible becomes the improbable, and the improbable becomes the almost certain.' And that's right, but basically it was his whole perspective that was flawed. For now we have fossils that come from the oldest rocks, and today we can say that life appeared as soon as it was possible for it to do so, it could not have been older than it is. Because the oldest rocks capable of containing it do in fact contain it. And this simple fact obliges us to reconsider the whole question.

If life appeared as soon as it could, you may conclude to the contrary, that its appearance is predictable, that it is the logical result of the way organic chemistry and the physics of self-regulating systems function. But it doesn't prove it! You have to bear in mind that even a very improbable event can happen very quickly. In the same way, you could get a coin to fall tails up 100 times in a row. It's possible but improbable. Hence this early emergence of life is not a proof, but a clue. So we know that life appeared on earth very quickly, but we shouldn't immediately jump from the fact that its origin seems to have been inevitable to the notion that its evolution, or its gradual complexification, was equally inevitable. Let's say that I'm ready to accept the idea that the appearance of life is almost inevitable, because here we're in the domain of chemistry, but the theory of evolution is a quite different matter.

**Because of the diversity of possible evolutionary paths?**

Once living creatures appear, the choices made point to a contingent history. One day you have a hundred possibilities, the next day one of them has been chosen, the one which will be realized in the history of life. Only chance decided the way in which living forms deployed themselves across this planet. Chance, circumstances. Whoever we are, we owe our existence to a series of chance occurrences that have happened in the history of life since the beginning. To those who think that there are reasons to believe in a pre-established plan leading necessarily to increased complexity and to the appearance of man, I say that the great patterns in the history of life largely contradict such a theory. You see, half the history of life is the history of unicellular organisms, the prokaryotes. It was only 1,800 million years ago that another form of unicellular life, the eukaryotes, emerged. Then, if you look closely, you'll probably find multicellular algae about 1,500 million years ago. All these organisms are only aggregates of cells, they still don't have anything to do with the evolution of animals, which began very late. And there go five-sixths of the history of life before it was even remotely a question of some form of animal life. And then, all at once, in a geological twinkling of an eye, the first animals appeared – the ones found in Ediacara – 600 million years ago. They look strange to our eyes, they bear pretty little resemblance to modern organisms, to such an extent that some people think that maybe they're evidence of some separate evolutionary experiment which failed. At any rate most of them are not related in any way to present living creatures.

**What's so different about them?**

They look like flat pancakes, and many of them are rooted in the soil.

**You're sure they're not plants? Mushrooms?**

No, it's quite clear that they're animals, but they don't seem to be connected to the great branches of today.

**What period are we talking about?**

Between 600 million and 543 million years ago. In the Precambrian. Then came the explosion of the Cambrian. The great animal branches of today all appeared at this time, within a period of about 10 million years, which is amazing. With one exception, a small group that almost nobody's heard of nowadays, called Bryzoa, which seems to have appeared during the next period. But it's possible that we just haven't found the older fossils. And then you have 500 million years of the history of animals, punctuated by mass extinctions, and overall showing no particular direction, no interesting pattern. It's really a strange history, very surprising.

**In *Wonderful Life* you wrote that there hasn't been any new branch in the history of the living since the great explosion of the Cambrian.**

Yes, it's a big mystery.

**What is a 'branch'? A biological structure?**

In principle branches correspond to basic anatomical structures. In fact there is a degree of subjectivity in the definition of branches, because species are the only objective units, they're populations of organisms. Taxonomy has generated orders, classes, but all these distinctions remain arbitrary since our fossil archives are full of gaps. The majority of lines that ever existed have disappeared, and the ones that have survived are very old.

In the tree of evolution only a few branches have survived, with enormous gaps between them. What is objective is the tree-like shape of evolution, and the existence of branches. It is clear to everybody that echinoderms – starfish, sea-urchins, crinoids – are markedly different from all other species, so it's logical to class them in the same category. It's clear that all vertebrates have common characteristics. A fish scarcely resembles an elephant, but they both have a spinal column and structural homologies. So the branches are basic anatomical units in the history of life. But you can decide that such and such a species is a branch; it's a question of definition. It's we who decide how many subsidiary branches belong to the same branch or to the same order, and where the dividing-lines fall.

**Which is more important? To explain the extinctions or to explain why certain species have survived?**

Both! What we are trying to explain is how the history of the living works. A species that dies out leaves no record. If you want to know why one group survived, you have to understand why, case by case. The basic problem is that each of these mass extinctions is unique, there's no law of nature, for example, that says that in the course of the next catastrophe all animals weighing more than 20 kilos will die! The causes of a species dying out are various and particular, they don't follow any general law, any regular pattern. There have been only five mass extinctions after all.

**Isn't that enough?**

It's very few if you want to establish a serial pattern! You know, we're very lucky that no mass extinction ever wiped out life altogether.

**Could that have happened?**

I imagine so, but we wouldn't be sitting here talking about it! At the end of the Permian we came very close to total destruction, about 95 per cent of species.

**But you were saying that life, at the beginning, appeared as soon as it found a favourable environment. Isn't it possible to think that it would have begun again anyway? It's what the old scientist in *Jurassic Park* keeps saying: 'Life will find a way . . .'**

It might have found a new origin, I don't know. As I say, we only have the one example.

**In the end, as a palaeontologist, you have to be a geologist and a biologist as well.**

Palaeontologists work in an area which, by its nature, is split between those two disciplines. They need geological tools to find the fossils, but most of fossil analysis belongs to the area of biology and derives from the theory of evolution. By its very nature palaeontology is interdisciplinary. In fact, the way the study of it is organized in the United States, it doesn't much matter whether you're a geologist or a biologist. The university syllabus consists of a mixture of the two disciplines, and the students put them together however they like. You can get a diploma in geology having done a lot of biology and vice versa. Study programmes are more rigid in Europe, I believe.

**Why did you take up science? Was it because you were looking for answers to questions about existence?**

I was five years old when I decided to do science. I don't know if one asks philosophical questions at that age.

**You think children aren't philosophical?**

Oh sure, of course, just like everybody else! If I try to remember what fascinated the little boy I was then, I immediately think of fossils, these marvellous things that were once alive but aren't any longer. I just loved fossils, I loved the idea of those wonderful animals that had lived so long ago, animals that were truly wild and strange . . . It made me happy to learn that life had a history and that our existence, our human existence, was the immensely complicated product of that history. And yes, of course, I asked a child's questions, I still do: about eternity, infinity and lots of essential things about which we have no certain knowledge. At the time I don't think I'd heard about the theory of evolution. When I studied it, later on, I discovered new reasons for staying on the same track.

**In the end you became a historian.**

That's right. In one way it's regrettable that palaeontologists are always posted to scientific departments. They ought to be part of history departments. A lot of our work is much closer to the historian's than the physicist's.


## The Threats to Our Existence


**You have called for the implementation of an ecological ethics. What do you understand by that?**

It seems to me important to insist on the fact that the human time-scale is the only one we ought to take into account in our ecological or ethical discussions. Proper ecological ethics mustn't look to the far-off future of life on other planets, it's got to concern itself with the quality of our life and the life of other species in the here and now. There are also extinctions of which we are the unwitting cause. On many occasions we've wiped out entire habitats without even realizing it, and exterminated the species unfortunate enough to have set up home there.

**Is it important in your view to become more attentive, more aware of the way things are?**

That's what biologists are trying to do. Most people are totally unaware of the effects of our manipulation of the environment. Just being aware of them wouldn't be enough on its own to halt the destruction, but it would be a first step.

**Do you worry when you think of the nuclear waste which has been buried deep underground, and which will remain active for hundreds of thousands of years?**

Longer than that!

**Does it worry you?**

It is of no great significance in terms of the earth as a whole. Sure, it would be bad news if in 2,000 years' time somebody dug a trench right through the middle of a large nuclear waste dump. What I mean is that we should not worry about what's going to happen to our planet. We should not be big-headed about it, we've poisoned it but it will survive. Having said that, however, nuclear waste is a problem. We have to store it somewhere, and even the place which seems to us the best protected perhaps isn't, on the geological scale of things.

**Which species seem to you the most urgently in need of protection?**

Let's save them all, if we can; I have no particular priorities. I place my trust in one general principle: we shouldn't let any species disappear if it's in our power to prevent it. Nevertheless, we've altered local climates and environments so profoundly that it is inevitable that some extinctions will occur. The second principle is that we must never regard some little beetle that nobody's ever heard of as unimportant. That may be true on the aesthetic level, but not on the pharmacological.

**Do mass extinctions provide us with a workable model for the nuclear winter that may be threatening us?**

After they came up with the theory that the impact of an extraterrestrial object was responsible for the extinction of the dinosaurs, the Alvarezes (father and son), who had invented this asteroid theory, developed a model according to which the cause of the extinction was a cloud of dust spreading across the whole planet after the impact and interrupting the process of photosynthesis. People haven't quite realized that this would be a risk in the case of nuclear war.

**What are your thoughts about the hole in the ozone layer and the greenhouse effect?**

Everything depends on what we do in the future. This brings us back to our discussion about time-scales. I am prepared to believe that the greenhouse effect poses no major danger to the planet itself, at least not the greenhouse effects that we are capable of causing. It will warm the planet up to temperatures that it has already experienced several times in the past. So it isn't a danger to the planet, but it is a danger to us. If the poles begin to melt, our towns and cities will be flooded, our lives will be severely disrupted. But the earth itself will simply have slightly bigger oceans, that's all.

**That happened at the time of the single continent, the so-called Pangaea.**

It's happened several times. One can't extrapolate from the present curve, for the following reasons: if the level of carbon monoxide increases alarmingly and there's further global warming, we'll take steps to bring it under control. We'd even be able to reverse the trend. Everything depends on human will, on our intelligence, on our capacity to co-operate, on our politicians. The dangers are real, the anxieties legitimate. Some people think the present trend is bound to continue and will lead to disaster. But in fact there's nothing inevitable about it, and we can even hope that we'll be smart enough to reverse it. Which brings me back to what I was saying about taking the tragic view. Often we're a bit slow to realize what's actually happening, by which time many people are already dead and the irreparable has already occurred. But that's better than never realizing at all.

**As a scientist and a man of good sense, you don't believe in predictions, and yet you predict an increase in the number of books about the year 2000.**

Ha! Ha! I can predict that one with confidence!

**You have also predicted that the sun will explode in 5,000 million years.**

Yes, but that's different – that's scientific.

**So it is possible to anticipate the future to a limited degree?**

It's possible to foresee a general pattern. Events that are the results of the regular laws of nature have a certain coefficient of probability. We know how long next year will last, we can be sure that the sun will rise tomorrow, we can predict an eclipse of the sun . . . On the other hand, we scarcely have the means to anticipate the future in terms of the chance occurrences of historical evolution. Human history is the most unpredictable of all, not because it's illogical or a matter of chance, but because it's not governed by the laws of nature.

**You've just defined human freedom.**

We are free to choose from among hundreds of thousands of possible directions. And our choices are perfectly interpretable, but only once we've made them.

**That's the theory of contingency that you develop in *Wonderful Life*. Things could have happened differently, so one mustn't attribute meaning in retrospect. Here we are again in the middle of a philosophical debate.**

I agree. Our evidence is in part scientific, though. If the world had been constructed differently, if life were as regular as the periodic table, you could think that all species living on the earth were different categories founded on the same structures. Which is not the case. The philosophical problem, to my mind, is this: I have no means of knowing if contingency is the result of our ignorance of determinisms at work in the universe, or if it manifests itself because chance actually exists in nature. You French have in your pantheon Pierre Simon de Laplace, the most determinist of all scientists in history. Laplace said: give me the position and motion of every particle in the universe at a given moment, and I shall be able to predict the future with certainty. And yet we also know that Laplace invented the theory of probabilities. If everything is determined, why did he need one? His answer would have been: everything is determined, but we cannot know everything. We shall never be able to know the position and motion of all particles existing in the universe at a given moment. So, even if the universe is determined, we cannot verify the fact. Consequently, we are incapable of predicting what will happen, and probability theory offers us the best mental instrument for looking into the future.

**A scientist like Ilya Prigogine is convinced that determinism is an illusion that we must outgrow.**

I tend to believe, as he does, that the course of things is not determined. I am ready to bet that the universe is not determined, and that contingency is not the result of our ignorance of the determinist nature of things. I am ready to bet that somewhere out there there is an indeterminacy, some essential freedom. But that's a philosophical question to which one cannot offer a scientific reply.

**If we were determined entirely, as we seem so desperately to want to be, we would presumably have succeeded in proving the fact!**

Don't you believe it, there's just no way of knowing. In Laplace's system, even if the universe is entirely determined, in order to know what's going to happen, you need a complete description of the past, which is not available to us.

**You've referred elsewhere to the dangers posed by the electronic revolution.**

I'm not the person you should be asking about that. I haven't got a computer, I still use my old typewriter. However, it's clear that this revolution has brought about a whole host of changes. Faced with the phenomenon, we're a bit like the scholar living in the middle of the fifteenth century wondering what consequences the invention of printing would have for intellectual study. He had no means of imagining where it would lead us! He couldn't have foreseen magazines and comics! That's roughly where we are with computers. What will happen in fifty years' time? What skills will be necessary? Will there still be books? I'm sure there will be, people will always buy a novel before getting on an airplane, but . . .

**Do you think that, with the advances in genetic engineering, humankind is now on the verge of modifying evolution itself?**

There's a philosophical error in that question. How can one say that human beings are interfering with evolution?

**Thereby forgetting that they themselves are part of it!**

Exactly. Asking a question like that implies that there's a sort of pre-established programme of nature which is taking its course and which we're intruding on and disrupting. Whereas we are part of this process, even if we modify it. The history of life as a whole is simply the interaction of certain forms of life with others. Would you say, for example, that insects disrupted evolution when they began to fertilize flowers? That plants have disrupted evolution by transforming different soils? No, I think that human beings are interacting with the life process to a degree that has so far been unparalleled. The only thing that does seem as though it could accelerate the process is genetic research, but it's the same as with computers, we're right at the start of the adventure, it's much too early to predict anything. And then, there will be limits, laws . . .

**It seems that experiments are underway to try and combine several species and create hybrids or chimeras.**

You can introduce the genes of one species into another species, but creating a hybrid out of a cat and a rabbit, say, is unthinkable. They develop in completely different ways, their chromosomes are different. You can't just take the maternal genes of a rabbit and the paternal genes of a cat and cross them, it simply won't work, the chromosomes won't match, you won't get the programme up and running. What *is* possible, on the other hand, is to introduce genes from one species into another. The effects of these manipulations are powerful, and they have potential benefits in agriculture and medicine. You can't just ban them wholesale. If you discover a gene that allows maize to resist the cold better and you get two harvests instead of one, how – in these days of food shortages – can you not exploit that discovery? On the other hand, if some crazy madman decides to manufacture 10,000 absolutely identical soldiers, all very strong and very stupid and trained to obey orders ... Basically, I think that if we'd got that far, if someone really did have the means to do something like that, then we'd be done for anyway, but for other reasons. This is a political question, not a matter of scientific debate.

## A New Vision of the Past

**What will archaeologists say in the year 3000 when they discover our great computerized libraries? Will they still be able to make electricity work so they can use our machines? Will anything be left that is still consumable, still comprehensible? In the case of Aristotle's *Treatise on Comedy* the thief could still read it and even still consume it, but all this virtual information stored on the Web can surely vanish in the twinkling of an eye?**

Well, one hopes not. Our age wants to collect together all the archives of the past. Perhaps it's an illusion, but I hope that we'll be able to cover ourselves and leave enough indestructible copies. Of course, when you come to think of it, the major part of ancient Greek culture has disappeared. We were lucky to have saved Aristotle and Plato, but often there is no more than fragments left of the texts of the pre-Socratics. We've certainly lost more than we've saved.

**What sort of fossils are we going to leave to our descendants?**

Darwin said that our fossil archives are like a library of which only a few pages, a few words, a few letters, have survived. It's a striking image, don't you think?

**We evolve in an ocean of oblivion.**

Everything depends on an unforeseeable historical continuity. But if we succeed in developing our culture while continuing to respect our past, we have a chance of preserving it. Culture is so fragile . . .

**You have devoted a lot of effort to preserving the memory of the lost ages.**

Yes, I'm conscious that it would only take a terrible war to wipe out the history of our culture entirely, even if our species were not destroyed. I'm aware of it, I know that such a thing can happen, it's already happened in the past. And yet, I think that we are probably smart enough to find ways of protecting it all. After all, lots of things have already come down through the centuries in miraculous fashion. Think of the paintings in prehistoric caves. Thanks to them we now know what certain prehistoric mammals looked like!

**But for you, 35,000 years ago is like yesterday!**

Yes, but those paintings preceded the invention of writing by 30,000 years! Those people left us what are veritable archives of the fauna of their time.

**In *Wonderful Life* you describe the multicellular fauna of the Cambrian, and then you say: 'These little creatures are like the Ancients, and they're trying to tell us something.' You're fond of referring to messages like this that travel across time.**

Clearly we are ignorant about most of what has existed. Instead of lamenting the fact, let's be thankful that by some miracle we've discovered as much as we have.

**The past is not what it was . . .**

We've reinterpreted it. In the library of the history of palaeontology one can find hundreds of men and women, throughout the world, who have devoted their lives to cataloguing and preserving the archives of life. The truth is, our work is fragile and our species corrupt, but in this respect we have done our best. Our intellectual history is a wondrous thing!

**Has your vision of the past evolved much?**

Of course. When I came into this field, I had a much more simplistic vision. I was still hoping to find some general laws that would allow us to predict almost all phenomena. I thought that all this history, despite the fact that it seemed confused and tortuous, would one day be reducible to an elementary chemical formula. Today, it's not that I believe things are inexplicable – I haven't become a mystic – but I think that the history of evolution is just a story, impossible to repeat or to reproduce, something for historians and not a series of logical consequences deriving from a law of nature. Wind back the film of life and play it again. The history of evolution will be totally different.

**So your vision has become more complex.**

I always knew that extremely complex issues were at stake, whether or not there were any simple, underlying laws that might allow us to explain everything. There is complexity in every domain, even in the experiments of classical physics. And there are always lots of factors that we overlook or ignore so that we can still proceed. What's particular to the history of life is that every detail seems essential to us. It's a question of point of view. Even chemistry isn't simple; each quartz crystal is different from all the others, but we don't investigate these differences. We look at the crystals and we say: they've all got the same chemical structure. But we can't do that with people, you see. We can't say: they've all got DNA. What we say is that John is different from James, and it's this difference that interests us. Again it's a question of scale.

**Are you interested above all in diversity?**

What interests us is human history. We'd like to understand ourselves better. We know we're not simply the product of our genes or how our parents brought us up, we know we're largely determined, and yet . . .

**We can choose . . .**

And even change, if we want to.

*In Search of Other Life Forms*

**We have the sense that we're living at a very special time, at a decisive moment in human history. But in the end, all human beings, in all ages, must have had the same feeling, don't you think?**

Look at the literature of the turn of the century: it was a high-point of optimism! Alfred Russel Wallace, the co-inventor of the theory of evolution, wrote a book called *The Wonderful Century*, in which he said that he was living in the most inspiring of epochs, and he sang the praises of new things like trains and telephones and the telegraph. On the other hand there have been periods of stagnation. The twentieth century has been pretty awful, with dreadful wars. And today we have technological progress that has unforeseeable consequences. Nobody today knows where the computer and biological revolutions are taking us. When I think that DNA was discovered only in 1953 . . . I was twelve years old!

**Would you say it was more important than managing to walk on the moon?**

Walking on the moon wasn't important in itself, but if that first step leads to the exploration of distant planets . . .

**Do you think it will?**

It's possible. One thing I'd really like to see is them sending a palaeontologist to look for fossils on Mars. Mars had running water during the first thousand million years of its history, life could very well have developed there.

**If there was running water, there must have been life!**

No, no, that's not at all certain, we just can't tell. As far as we know, there is no life without water. But there can be water without life. After all, as I said, we only have the one example to work with:

planet earth. On earth there was water, and life appeared. That's just one event. I don't know if life appears every time the right conditions are in place, or one in three times, or one in ten ... All we know is that it happened at least once. But it's possible that it may have happened elsewhere.

**Do you think that human beings will visit other stars?**

It's possible in theory. The problem is that human beings don't live very long and the stars are so far away that it would be difficult to reach one in the course of a human life. If Einstein is right, we shall never be able to travel faster than the speed of light, and it would take us a very long time to get there. But perhaps he's wrong. Perhaps there is a way! That's why science fiction has based so many of its plots on the holes in time.

**How do you see the earth looking in a thousand years' time?**

I don't see it. The things one can actually predict are not very interesting. The sun will continue to shine ... But the history of human beings – and that's what your question is about – consists only of unpredictable events. What we are least well-placed to predict is technological evolution. I can't predict what will happen in fifty years, let alone in a thousand ... Culture evolves in a Lamarckian way, in that it allows the transmission of acquired characteristics. We directly transmit what we have learned to subsequent generations, which is why technological evolution is ultra-powerful, cumulative, directional ...

**So in fact, what you, too, find interesting is human history. By putting bacteria at the centre of the picture, you've chosen a provocative vision.**

Yes, but from a planetary point of view bacteria are more important than us! We're back to the question of scale. I don't know if human action will leave a profound mark on the planet. I've no idea what will become of technology in the future. But I do know that we have more chance of destroying ourselves than of upsetting the ecosystem. From the point of view of the earth, where bacteria have been around for 3,500 million years, why worry about some strange species that's been around for only 200,000 years?

**In *Life's Grandeur* you talk of bacteria being found buried deep within the earth and at the bottom of the oceans. You conclude that this may indicate that life exists everywhere in the universe, inside planets. Bacteria would thus be the universal life-form. Would you like to see this theory confirmed?**

Oh yes, I'd love it! We could send a spaceship to Mars and bring some back. That would be fabulous.

**Basically, what has always excited you, your main object of study, has been life itself.**

That's the fundamental issue. As I've already mentioned, life on earth is the result of a unique event, with a unique origin and unique mechanisms for repeating and replicating itself. But as far as the phenomenon of life itself is concerned, there is no replication, we don't know any other forms of life, which is why it would be so exciting to go and visit other worlds. All life forms on earth are based on DNA. But that doesn't prove it's the only possible way of doing things. Who knows? To be able to answer that question, you'd have to find a life-form endowed with a separate origin, on another world, and then analyse its biochemical make-up in order to compare it with the one we know. Then you'd have your replication of the phenomenon of life itself.

**But if they find life on Mars, it may have the same origin . . .**

That's right. Martian meteorites fall on the earth and vice versa. Planets can inseminate each other reciprocally. So let's put the matter another way. If you find life on Mars and it's configured exactly like life on earth, you'll have proved nothing. But if we find life and that life is very different from ours, then things are going to get really exciting.

*Conversations held in New York on 6 and 7 May 1998*

# Back to the Apocalypse
*Jean Delumeau*

## *Introduction*

No one is better qualified to assess the historical significance of
the eschatological fears and hopes of our contemporaries than
Jean Delumeau, who has made such fears and hopes the subject
of his research. In the eyes of this eminent historian and
professor at the Collège de France, who is considered to be one
of the leading specialists in the history of mentalities in Western
Europe between the fourteenth and eighteenth centuries, the
end of time is in the first place one of the recurrent themes of a
vast body of apocalyptic literature, and the spark which ignited
the powder-keg of millenarian movements over the centuries.
Indeed, from the time when time's arrow was introduced to the
human mind by Judaeo-Christian thought, it had seemed logical
to think about the date of the end of the world, and hence of
creation itself. Such unimpeachable logic gave rise to learned
calculations and long treatises, which in turn provoked
passionate debates. But why is it that there has been from the
beginning of the Christian tradition a persistent confusion of the
millennium with millenarianism? What role does the Book of
Revelation play in the periodical upsurge of eschatological fears?
What is the theological meaning of the millennium? Why did
Saint Augustine declare that the millennium was already with
us? And how did it come about that dashed millenarian hopes –
since the end of the world had not occurred on the dates
predicted – could have been succeeded in so tragic a way by the
disappointments born of the coming into being of the Marxist
utopia?

Jean Delumeau is a scrupulous scholar and lover of broad
historical frescoes; his approach is to think about history over
long periods of time. His well-established reputation in university

circles is reflected in a Festschrift written in his honour entitled *Homo religiosus*, published by Fayard in 1997. He has become known to a wider public through a series of forty-six television programmes on the theme of men and their religions, brcadcast on French television. He is an ecumenical Catholic whose loyalty is to a Church that has rehabilitated Galileo, accepted the theory of evolution, recognized its Jewish roots and organized at Assisi in 1986 a meeting of representatives of different religions.

After the completion of his famous comprehensive study of fear in Western Europe* and several books on the history of the material and spiritual scourges which have overwhelmed the West since the Renaissance, Jean Delumeau investigated the ways in which men sought grounds for reassurance; the progress of this research was marked by the publication *Reassurance and Protection: The Feeling of Security in Western Europe of the Past*.† Thereafter he was inspired to write two long studies on the history of paradise. One can sense that the successive central themes of Jean Delumeau's work are related not only to the logic of historiographical research but also to a personal odyssey. After fear came consolation, and then hope. Whether the dreams of mankind take the form of the expectation of the second coming or of a fear that the sky will fall on our heads, Jean Delumeau has never forgotten that people's dreams, which are central to his work as a historian, contribute in the same way as their acts to the making of their destiny.

**Is the religious notion of a beginning and an end to time an invention of the Bible?**

There is certainly an important difference between the Judaeo-Christian tradition and a certain number of others. Hinduism, in particular, and Buddhism in its wake, harbour a belief in a sort of cyclical course of affairs. At the end of a certain number of centuries or eras there will be a return to the point of departure. This is also how the Greeks conceived of things.

---

* *La Peur en Occident.*
† *Rassurer et protéger: le sentiment de sécurité dans l'Occident d'autrefois.*

In the Judaeo-Christian tradition, on the other hand, history has been looked upon as a vector. There is a beginning and an end. God has created the world, life and mankind, and thereafter mankind is subject to time. One day God will decide to bring the cosmic story, the story of terrestrial life, to a close, and that will be the end of the world, the end of history, the end of time – all of which come to the same thing. I think that the Jews of, what we call for convenience's sake, the Old Testament – although this is just a Christian designation of the Bible of the Hebrews – at first did not imagine very clearly what the end of history might be. But after the exile in Babylon, they conceived of their national story as one directed towards the coming of a Messiah who would liberate them as a Saviour. I am not well enough informed to be able to tell you what they envisaged would happen after the Messiah had come, but it has been noted by others that around two centuries before Christ there arose the idea of a judgement of the dead, with a reward for the righteous and a punishment for the wicked. Such an idea implies a sort of survival and a final resurrection, without making it formally explicit. It is worth recalling in this respect the amazing vision of the prophet Ezekiel to whom God revealed how he would revivify dry bones and resurrect the dead:

> Thus says the Lord God unto these bones . . . I will lay sinews upon you, and will cause flesh to come upon you, and cover you with skin, and put breath into you, and you shall live . . . And you shall know that I am the Lord, when I open your graves, and raise you from your graves, And I shall put my spirit within you, and you shall live (Ezekiel 37: 5–6, 13–14).

Here one can see the idea emerging among the Jews of a judgement and a horizon beyond death with an eternal reward. Christianity finds its place in the continuity of this intuition. Jesus promises and proclaims that the end of time has been ordained by God, with the resurrection of all the dead, followed by a general judgement. It is solemnly affirmed in all the gospels that there will be something beyond death, and therefore something beyond history, and an eternal life. In this respect, it seems to me that Christianity defined with far greater sharpness the idea that was in the process of being formulated in Judaism during the last centuries before the Christian era.

**For the Hebrews, even in later Judaism, Messianic hope was not necessarily associated with the coming of a man; it could just be hope for the coming of the kingdom and for peace on earth.**

Indeed. It was the hope for a kingdom which would eventually encompass all creation. It has also been said that in Jewish thought, the kingdom of God could not be in a higher world, but would be the renewal and recreation of our own, a new earth under the exclusive and boundless sovereignty of God. This is particularly clear in the words of the prophet Isaiah: 'For, behold, I create new heavens and a new earth; and the former things shall not be remembered, or come to mind . . . No more shall the voice of weeping be heard in Jerusalem, and the cry of distress . . . The wolf and the lamb shall feed together, the lion shall eat straw like the ox' (Isaiah 65:17, 19, 25).

### Is the Christian vision identical?

Ancient Judaism envisaged, at the end of history, the coming of an earthly kingdom or, more precisely, it prophesied that the earth would be radically transformed by God. Christianity took up this theme, notably in the Book of Revelation (Chapter 21), but in the gospels Jesus always pointed to a kingdom which was not of this world, which was beyond this world, and which was, as it were, the transfiguration of the one in which we live.

### What about Islam?

As a religion of the Book, Islam has a place in the same tradition as Judaism and Christianity. From this point of view, it is purely and simply the heir to the Judaeo-Christian tradition; it formally postulates an end of time, a resurrection and a last judgement, and an eternal afterlife of bliss or punishment. In world history one can therefore isolate the group of three religions of the Book which believe in a vectorial conception of time, with a beginning and an end, as opposed to the cyclical conception of Greece and Asia.

### So the biblical notion of 'the end of time' is equivalent to the notion of 'the end of history'?

Absolutely. The end of time, especially in Christian thought, means the end of history. Humanity has played out its part, whether for good or for evil. An account is drawn up, and eternal life begins. It's the end of time. It's also the end of time in the sense of temporality. But it isn't the end of mankind. On the contrary, mankind finds its complete fulfilment in eternity.

**You mean that the end of time, in the sense of the end of the world and the end of the created universe, implies the 'end of Time', that is to say, the end of the condition of being in history?**

Yes, the end of time is the end of Time. One can as it happens translate this equivalence into Augustinian terms. A fundamental idea in Saint Augustine's *City of God* is that time is the site of insecurity. It is dangerous because it offers the possibility both of improvement and of corruption. It is the site of a hazardous transition in which anything – the best and the worst – can happen. But once time has stopped and history has come to an end, sinning, evil-doing, and making amends are no longer possible. That is the meaning of the end of time. Time has vanished. It has been replaced by eternity.

## The Test of Time

**The whole story of freemasonry is also conceived of symbolically as the search for the lost word: from the moment we are cast into the world and into time, the word is, as it were, in suspension.**

I would be happy to associate myself with this point of view in the sense that time, especially in Augustinian thought, never stops corrupting and destroying. As a result it is impossible to see how the eternal word could express itself fully through it; it can only express itself through it in a veiled way. One has to wait for the end of time for revelation wholly to make itself known and let itself be understood. This is, I believe, wholly consistent with Judaeo-Christian thought.

**From the point of view of the believer, should the end of time –
which allows for the transition of time into eternity – be an ardent
hope and not an anguished expectation?**

Indeed, it is the hope of emerging from darkness and entering into
the light of total revelation. As Saint Paul says, what is hidden will
become plain. Now we see, he says, 'as if in a mirror dimly'; then we
will see 'face to face'. What, in the Christian terms of any age, is
heavenly bliss, if not seeing God 'face to face'? We will see Him
before us, in all His immeasurable love, splendour and beauty. That
is why the expression 'face to face' has consistently been used in
Christian theology to signify the greatest heavenly bliss. There will
be other, peripheral joys, but they will all flow from this one. Human
life and the adventure of being human are thus conceived of as a
journey; and this journey has a destination. That doesn't stop there
being trials and tribulations of all kinds, as well as the feeling of the
absurd or the insurmountable which we may experience from time
to time. But for the believer, the journey, whether tortuous or not,
ends in absolute and perfect bliss. I should repeat that in contrast to
Greek or Asiatic beliefs in reincarnation, the journey never starts
again.

**Don't the mazes that one finds in some great cathedrals symbolize
the journey of initiation which constitutes all human existence?**

Quite so. Mazes, especially the maze of Chartres, are illustrations of
Augustinian thought. Life is difficult, complicated and tortuous.
There is the constant risk of taking the wrong path and of going up
blind alleys. But in the end there is one way – and only one way –
out.

**Aren't the biblical accounts of the flight from Egypt and the
wanderings of the Hebrews in the desert the great metaphor of time
and of the story of the human race?**

André Caquot, my colleague at the Institut de France and probably
the leading Hebrew scholar in France, tells me that for the Jews –
and this is also true for Christians and for Muslims – life is a
pilgrimage. As we have just said, a pilgrimage is a journey with a

precise goal which implies a quest of some sort. For the Jews, the pilgrimage ends in the promised land. Christians borrowed this image from the Old Testament, and the Church Fathers often compared human life, human history and the progress of the Church to a difficult pilgrimage in the wilderness. We are on a journey, but the journey has a clear destination. So we mustn't look at what is going on on either side of the path, or let ourselves be distracted or discouraged. We know where we are going, in the complete trust that God will lead us safely to harbour, in spite of the trials which we encounter and also in spite of the occasional apparent absurdity of our situation. Such is the central idea of Saint Augustine in his *City of God*: time is a trial. We are wholly steeped in time, but we look forward to the moment when we shall escape from it. The end of time is truly the moment of transition; suddenly we end up in another form of reality which has no time and which is called eternity. It's a haven, if you like, and we will not travel beyond the harbour, whether it is a haven of happiness or sorrow. During the whole voyage, mankind is sustained by a hope which will be realized when time comes to an end.

**So can one say that in this biblical vision, the more history unfolds, the more it progresses towards completion and perfection, or isn't this necessarily the case?**

Certainly in the case of Christianity and, I believe, also in that of Islam, nothing is written which says that humanity will get better and better. What is said is that at a precise moment in time – which God alone knows – history will come to an end and God will come to judge all mankind and separate the wheat from the chaff. But nowhere is it said that we are getting better and better. However, this idea is present in the works of certain Greek Church Fathers – I'm thinking particularly of Saint Irenaeus – who took into account the salvation brought by Christ, and believed that humanity from thenceforth would develop and fulfil itself. This notion is, however, altogether absent from Western theology which is deeply influenced, as you know, by Saint Augustine; and he didn't have an optimistic view of mankind. Another thesis developed by Saint Augustine in his *City of God* is that good and bad are inextricably bound up with each other in human history and that this state of affairs will only end at the Last Judgement. Or to put it another way: anything can happen for good or for ill as long as human history, with its unpredictability, proceeds to unfold over time. Until the end of time, as I have already said, no outcome is decided, and there is no security nor any certainty as to the destiny of mankind in general or each human being in particular.

**So, basically, Christians do not expect a form of earthly paradise to come about; they ground their hope in the destiny of each individual after his or her death, and on something which is beyond history.**

Indeed. I would say that in general all religions, but perhaps Christianity more so than the others, start from the premise that in life there are more tribulations than there are moments of joy. Life is difficult and will remain so, in spite of all the ways one may be able to make it more bearable. Mankind has to draw from this both the consequences for itself and a discipline for daily existence, a spiritual life which copes with tribulation, and reaches out for a kind of happiness which can never be totally achieved on this earth. Personally, as a Christian, I am convinced that there will never be a paradise on earth, but that all suffering, inequality and evil will cease one day after time has come to an end. That will be a 'utopia' [no-place] in the strong sense of the word. On the other hand, we have seen what atrocities result from utopias, whether religious ones or atheistic ones like Marxism, when they have striven through deliberation and design to bring about a perfect world here on earth. I simply believe that we must make the best of our human condition.

**Does this mean that you would give up trying to improve humanity and to make this world a more humane and fraternal place?**

Not at all! The whole message of Christ encourages us to relieve the suffering of our fellow men. I merely want to say that I do not believe that life on earth can ever be free from evil and suffering. Such a conviction does not stop thousands of Christians from devoting themselves to the service of their neighbour and making, as you say, the world a more fraternal place. Look at Mother Teresa. She said again and again that she was not involved in social work and that her objective was not to eliminate all misery from the world. Her aim was rather to love the poorest of the poor as Christ would have loved them. As she used to say, 'I am not in the business of transforming the whole of humanity, but of loving each individual human being I come into contact with.' On the other hand, I am very suspicious of those ideologists who set out to change humanity and who proclaim a better world, yet do not look after those who are nearest to them. The Christian message, which is certainly a message of brotherhood and love, speaks only of personal love, engaging every individual with one another. If humanity is transformed thereby, so much the better! But that is not its foremost purpose. Of course that doesn't stop Christians from active engagement in the course of the affairs of this world.

## Evil and Suffering

### Does suffering have any meaning?

For me, life has meaning. And if life has meaning, suffering also has meaning, even though it may appear repulsive or even incomprehensible. What Jews, Christians and Muslims believe is that suffering and death will not have the last word. This is a thought common to the religions of the Book. Let's be very clear about this: unlike other philosophical or religious systems, the Bible does not offer an explanation for the problem of evil, but it does bring the hope that all the forms of evil, including pain and suffering, of course, will be eliminated once and for all at the end of time.

### And only then will men understand the meaning of suffering.

Exactly. For as long as we are living in time, we are not able to understand the reason for the colossal enigma of a child's suffering (in my own view, an enigma beside which all other mysteries pale). It's incomprehensible. The Bible, especially the Book of Job, dissuades us from looking for reasons for the existence of evil. There are none which can be formulated within the context of time in terms which we can understand.

**Isn't the theory of original sin supposed to supply an explanation for the problem of evil, at least from the ethical point of view?**

I am very uncertain about this. The story in Genesis of the sin of Adam and Eve in paradise lost is, of course, not historical. It's a myth . . . and it's worth being clear about this. Don't forget that in certain fundamentalist circles, especially in the United States, the story of Genesis is still taken literally. But in fact we know perfectly well, from a scientific point of view, that humanity took hundreds of thousands of years to evolve and become what it is. I do not see how one could situate at the very origins of humanity a fantastical piece of wrongdoing which, on top of everything else, is said to have had repercussions on the whole subsequent destiny of humanity. On the other hand, wherever one looks, one sees men engaged in fighting each other. As soon as a human being worthy of the name developed, there was malice, jealousy, pride and murder. So sin existed in the first human being; that's perhaps what the myth of original sin means. But I should add that love and goodness also certainly existed from the beginning. Happily, human history does not just consist of evil! But we are more aware of evil than good because good does not blow its own trumpet and call attention to itself. It takes 2,000 years to build a city, but nowadays it can be destroyed in two minutes.

**You have rightly stressed the fact that monotheistic religions have no answer to offer to the problem of evil. Isn't that one of the very reasons for the growing success of eastern religions, notably Buddhism, in the West, which offer explanations for the problem of evil, of suffering and of inequality?**

I quite agree. But if I must express my deepest thoughts on the matter, I would say that I find such explanations rather simplistic. Broadly speaking, people receive in their next life the reward, in happiness or misery, for how they have lived in their previous existence. To put it another way: if a person is blind, handicapped or dies in a tragic manner, that person is paying for evil acts committed in a previous life. So they don't have to revolt against the conditions of their present existence; they have deserved them in an earlier life. This explanation may reassure some people, but personally, I find the causality which is derived from the universal law of karma unsatisfactory. Judaeo-Christianity and Islam do not argue in this way.

## How do they argue?

As is their practice in other cases, they refuse to proffer a rational or simplistic explanation for evil, and in an act of faith they leave the matter to God. When speaking to his apostles, who believed that a person born blind had been punished for the sins of his parents, Jesus declares: 'Neither did this man sin, nor his parents' (John 9:3). This shows clearly that he both refuses to give an explanation for the cause of sin, but also, that he doesn't at all believe in any kind of theory of karma or reincarnation, as certain people nowadays would have us do. He expresses exactly the same opinion about the victims on whom the tower in Siloam fell and about the Galileans massacred by Pilate (Luke 13:1–4). The question of evil and suffering is at the heart of a gripping Old Testament book, the Book of Job, to which I have already alluded. Job is presented as a righteous man who is suddenly assailed by all sorts of trials. The 'sages' (his 'comforters') are convinced that he is being 'punished by God' because of his 'great malice and countless faults'. This is his karma, as we might say today. But Job, confident in his rightness, answers back: 'I hold fast to my righteousness, and will not let it go: my heart does not reproach me for any of my days' (Job 27:6). Indeed, from the beginning of the book, God had declared to Satan: 'Have you considered my servant Job, that there is none like him in the earth, a blameless and upright man, who fears God, and turns away from evil?' (Job 1:8). God allowed all these calamities to happen to him to test his belief and his faithfulness, not to punish him for his sins, as the 'sages' think.

In other words, this text recommends that we should have the humility not to offer an explanation where one doesn't exist. We all find ourselves at some time or another in Job's situation, and it is in all of our interests to remember this essential text. God replies to Job's persistent questions about the misfortunes which rain down upon him with a non-answer: 'Where were you when I laid the foundation of the earth? Can you bind the chains of the Pleiades, or make the signs of the Zodiac appear in their due season? Do you know the ordinances of the heavens? Shall a faultfinder contend with the Almighty? He who argues with God, let him answer it' (Job 38:4,

31–3; 40:2). These are powerful replies which highlight the unfathomable mysteries of the universe and the incomprehensible character of suffering. And so Job submits: 'I know that thou canst do all things, and that no purpose of thine can be thwarted. Who is this that hides counsel without knowledge? Therefore I have uttered what I did not understand; things too wonderful for me, which I did not know' (Job 42:2–3). And Jesus, following on from the Book of Job, refused to link sin to punishment in the form of illness, ruin and so on.

**Quite unlike certain fundamentalists who look upon Aids as a divine punishment . . .**

It's worth repeating, I think, that Jesus offered no explanation for evil and misfortune. But having said that, believers suppose that everything will appear clear and simple once they have passed into eternal light. But for the time being, as far as evil and misfortune are concerned, they just don't know.

**At a slightly different conceptual level, isn't there, at least as far as Christianity is concerned, a stress on suffering as a condition of salvation, which thereby gives religion an essentially sacrificial and masochistic image?**

It is true that at certain times, and above all in the West, Christianity laid great emphasis on the redemptive role of pain, sacrifice and suffering. That much is undeniable, and it's notably the theme of my book *Sin and Fear*.* Over time there occurred what I would be inclined to call a drift. But one must clearly realize that this drift towards a culture of pain stands in contradiction to the life and words of Jesus. For if one looks again at the gospels, at Jesus at prayer in the Garden of Olives on the night before his death, just before he is arrested, he says to his Father: 'Could not this cup pass from me?' He didn't at all want to have to undergo suffering. But he then added: 'Thy will be done'; in other words, if my death is inevitable (as a logical consequence of his preachings, which were so disturbing), I accept that I must die to remain faithful to my message till the very end. The problem is that Jesus's death has often been interpreted in

* *Le Péché et la peur.*

a sacrificial sense, with God the Father requiring the blood of His son to be shed to save mankind. But if we look closely at the gospels, we see that Jesus never sought either death or suffering. What is more, he was accused at the time of not being ascetic.

**Indeed, he was accused of drinking with his disciples, of being invited to feasts . . .**

Quite so. He went to feasts. At the wedding feast at Cana we are even told that when the wine ran out, he changed water into wine: not an everyday thing for a prophet to do! At the house of Lazarus, Martha and Mary, who were well-to-do people, he was received in lavish style. Yet the gospels report that before beginning on the public phase of his life, he spent forty days praying and fasting in the desert. So he did go through an ascetic period. All the great religions on the planet, particularly Buddhism, recommend this type of spiritual retreat which allows for the purification of body and soul. But such an experience, limited as it is in time, is in no way masochistic.

So if it is true that Jesus accepted to undergo suffering without having sought to do so, then Christianity witnessed very early on a drift towards a culture of pain, which has admittedly lasted a very long time, but is now beginning to disappear.

**Did this drift towards a culture of pain consist of attaching value to suffering as such?**

It consisted of seeking out suffering and thinking: 'The more one suffers, the more Christian one is.' From the first centuries after the death of Jesus, a certain number of ascetics or Christian athletes thought that there was no suffering great enough to expiate their faults. This resulted from an acute sense of sin.

**For centuries Christian iconography represented Christ as risen and glorious. Then representations of Christ suffering on the cross spread across the West. Why did this change of image occur?**

It is true that a transformation happened in this respect in Latin Christianity, especially from the thirteenth century onwards, probably under the influence of Saint Francis of Assisi and the Franciscans.

Francis of Assisi tried to identify himself with the suffering Christ
and received the marks on his hands and feet of the nails of Christ's
passion. These are known as the 'stigmata'. Francis of Assisi had an
enormous reputation in the Middle Ages; he was even known as 'the
other Christ' or 'the new Christ'. For people at that time, he was the
greatest saint since Jesus. He had a sensitive and affectionate nature,
and wanted to suffer for Him whom he passionately loved. So as
Franciscan spirituality spread throughout all of Christendom, it produced more and more images of the suffering Christ, as opposed to
the Christ in glory of an earlier age. But all Christianity is not to be
reduced to this drift towards a culture of pain, which took different
forms at different times and in different places. The Christian who
is faithful to the spirit of the gospels is someone who says to himself:
'If suffering and pain occur – which God forbid! – well, one has to
make the best of it for oneself and for others.'

## The Judgement of the Individual and the Last Judgement

**Isn't there, at least in Christianity, a distinction between the
particular judgement of a soul which occurs after death and the
collective judgement of humanity which will take place at the end
of time?**

Traditional Christian theology, especially in the Middle Ages and
during the modern era, indeed distinguished between the judgement
of individuals, which takes place immediately after their death, from
the general judgement of mankind.

**And this would occur after the end of time?**

Exactly, at the end of time, when God decides to stop the passage of
time and bring history to a close. According to the Synoptic Gospels
(Matthew, Mark and Luke), what will then happen is a cosmic event
called Parousia. This is the return of the risen and glorious Christ

who will come to judge the living and the dead. Jesus proclaims this very explicitly:

> But in those days, after that tribulation, the sun will be darkened, and the moon will not give its light, and the stars will be falling from heaven, and the powers in the heavens will be shaken. And then they will see the Son of man coming in clouds with great power and glory. And then he will send his angels, and shall gather his elect from the four winds, from the ends of the earth to the ends of heaven (Mark 13:24–7).

### Who will the elect be?

I have no authority to speak on this matter. But I think that it is important to turn to Chapter 25 of Matthew, where we read that the criterion of judgement will not be a theological criterion, or a criterion of faith or belief, but a criterion of love and service to one's fellow human beings. It is worth recalling this famous text, which lies at the heart of what we are talking about:

> When the Son of man comes in his glory, and all the angels with him, then he will sit on his glorious throne. Before him will be gathered all the nations; and he shall separate them one from another, as a shepherd separates the sheep from the goats, and he will place the sheep at his right hand, but the goats at the left. Then the King will say to those at his right hand, 'Come O blessed of the Father, inherit the kingdom prepared for you from the foundation of the world; for I was hungry, and you gave me food; I was thirsty, and you gave me drink; I was a stranger and you welcomed me, I was naked, and you clothed me, I was sick, and you visited me, I was in prison and you came to me.' Then the righteous will answer him, 'Lord, when did we see thee hungry, and feed thee, or thirsty, and give thee drink? And when did we see thee a stranger, and welcome thee, or naked, and clothe thee? And when did we see thee sick, or in prison, and visit thee?' And the King will answer them, 'Truly I say to you, as you did it to one of the least of these my brethren, you did it to me.' (Matthew 25:31–40).

**Seeing that this judgement which will occur at the end of time will concern each individual, how will the sentence be different from the particular judgement of the soul after death?**

There will be no change in the sentence. But the particular judgement, as its name indicates, is addressed to the person who has just died, whereas at the end of time, a sort of general recapitulation will occur at which the whole of humanity will be assessed. On this topic, however, the theological issues were hotly debated in the first centuries of the Christian era and in part of the Middle Ages. It was especially discussed whether individuals would have full access to the joys of paradise after their death but before the Last Judgement; or whether there wasn't some sort of time and place of waiting. This notion was rejected by the Catholic Church during the period in the fourteenth century when the Popes were in Avignon. It is also important to point out that historically speaking preachers began by stressing the Last Judgement. Then, as pastoral care and the practice of catechism developed, more and more emphasis was laid on the judgement of the individual. Thus in the sermons of the seventeenth, eighteenth and nineteenth centuries, much more is said about the judgement of individuals than about the Last Judgement. Nowadays these distinctions have become much more fuzzy. I would even go so far as to say that preachers practically do not speak about them any more.

**It seems to me that one debate which still troubles Christianity is that which concerns bodily resurrection. Isn't it said that after death, the soul will have to wait until the last judgement to be united with a 'glorified body'?**

In the Christian creed – first in the Apostolic creed, which is the older, and then in the Nicene creed of AD 325 – it is said: 'I believe in the resurrection of the body and the life everlasting.' This is how the creed ends; it is its last episode. I must say again that I am speaking here as a historian; I am not speaking of my personal beliefs. I am talking about traditional ideas. The judgement of the soul constitutes particular judgement.

**You have written several works on paradise; could you tell us in a few words what the Jewish, Christian and Muslim visions of paradise consist in?**

I am not a specialist in Judaism or in Islam, so I shall be cautious in replying to your question. It seems to me that ancient Judaism stressed the Messianic dimension, through which creation would no longer be separate from the divine world. Adoration of the one God and universal fraternity would mark the end of the vicissitudes of history. What is more, Ezekiel's prophecy of the resurrection of the dry bones may have been understood to be the proclamation of rebirth to eternal life. That this would come about seems to have been believed by most Jews at the time of Jesus, with the exception of the Sadducees. Otherwise, broadly speaking, there does not seem to me to have been much of an emphasis in Judaism on a paradise beyond this world.

There is more of an emphasis in the Koran, which in many verses confirms that there will be a Last Judgement with an eternal reward for the righteous and a definitive punishment for the evil-doers. The paradise beyond this world is always described as a regained garden of Eden with very concrete pleasures. Sura 14 provides the following elucidation:

> The righteous will be in a place in which they will feel safe. They will find themselves in the midst of gardens and fountains of living water. They will be clothed with clothes of fine silk and brocade, and lie face to face on couches. So will it be. And we shall have married them to virgins having dazzlingly white eyes and wide black pupils. They will ask for, and be assured of, every sort of fruit. They will not taste of death again, after they had died the first time, and God will have preserved them from the torments of Gehenna.

Before Islam, Christianity proclaimed in the most unequivocal way the Last Judgement and the 'resurrection of the flesh', which Christ's resurrection made possible. Hence this prophecy by Saint Paul in Romans 8:11: 'If the Spirit of him that raised Jesus from the dead dwells in you, he who raised Christ Jesus from the dead will give life to your mortal bodies also through his Spirit which dwells in you.' On the other hand, if we set aside the depictions of the heavenly Jerusalem which we find in the Book of Revelation, we have to say that the gospels and the other texts of the New Testament have no description to offer of paradise. Later, the Church Fathers, and also Saint Benedict in the rule he wrote for his monks, never tired of applying to the joys of eternity what Saint Paul says in 1 Corinthians 2:9: 'We speak of . . . what no eye has seen, nor the ear heard, not the heart of man conceived, what God has prepared for those who love him.' I should like to stress the discretion shown by Christians towards the mystery of what lies beyond this life.

**And what about hell?**

As far as Catholicism goes, the traditional teaching, that of Saint Augustine, postulates the existence of a place of eternal suffering for those who perpetrated considerable evil in this life and never repented of it. Nowadays in the Catholic Church there is much debate on the subject of hell, even if it is not an official tenet. I'm the first to have doubts about it.

**What is your own point of view?**

For me, hell is the 'second death' of which Saint John speaks. I believe that when we die there is indeed a reckoning and that we shall have to answer for what we have done during our lives. More will be expected from those who have been better endowed than others and who have received more gifts and greater powers. But we shall all have to give account of ourselves, at least in so far as we have been responsible for our lives.

How could those who have committed real and serious wrongdoing accede to eternal bliss? To my mind they will be sent to a 'second death'. I'm not talking about a place or a state of endless suffering – I find the idea of this intolerable – but to eternal punishment none the less: a definitive death penalty.

**Do you mean that they will return to nothingness?**

They will be condemned to nothingness: that will be their punishment. While the righteous will, after their resurrection, be summoned to eternal bliss. In other words, those who have been rejected will see at the moment of resurrection the joy of the elect, a joy which they know will endure for ever and then they will understand that they are condemned, without the chance of appeal, to eternal death.

**So you do believe in the notion of eternal punishment?**

I do, but not in eternal suffering. The whole Bible proclaims to us that 'God is justice and mercy.' This is the common belief of the three religions of the Book. Now if God's justice demands punishment for grave wrongdoing, His mercy prevents me from believing that this punishment could take the form of eternal suffering. That is why I associate myself with the solution of 'second death', which is a definitive annihilation. It's not a solution of my own invention; it was that of Saint Irenaeus, for example, who lived in the third century after the death of Christ. Saint Irenaeus effectively said that if inveterate, obdurate sinners have cut themselves off from God, they have cut themselves off from life as well. And if they have cut themselves off from life, how could they continue to exist? This is Saint Irenaeus's line of thought, which I personally share.

**But what if they ask for forgiveness?**

You are right to ask this, because I believe that God's forgiveness is infinite; I am speaking of those who are obdurate to the point of refusing to ask forgiveness.

**What about purgatory?**

Purgatory is another solution which was thought of at the time of the Early Church. It's notably the solution of Origen. But the expression is not a happy one, and as the historian Jacques Le Goff has clearly shown, both the word and the place emerged only in the twelfth century. On the other hand, the notion of a purgative period of punishment is very ancient and existed before the place and the name. According to Origen, all of sinful humanity, except for the saints who will go directly to paradise, will be subjected after their death to a sort of recycling, to a series of purifications which will be accompanied by a degree of suffering, but also by the hope, as something to aim for, of eternal bliss. Some people will go through the various stages of this process without difficulty, while others will have to make a great improvement in order to reach the state of eternal bliss. But everyone will get there in the end. Then all possible forms of hell will cease to exist. Christian theology quickly thought up two possible solutions, that of Irenaeus and that of Origen, to dispense with the idea of a place of eternal suffering. I would say that of these two solutions, I prefer that of Saint Irenaeus; it accords better with the scenes of the Last Judgement to be found in the gospels. But that's only a personal opinion.

To come back to the end of time, there is clearly a movement from history to eternity in all these cases, whether you take the solution of Saint Irenaeus, of Origen or of Saint Augustine.

## Jesus's Inauguration of the End of Time

**In many places the New Testament presents the coming of Jesus as the inauguration of the end of time. According to Saint Paul, for example, Jesus will come 'in the fullness of time'. What does that mean?**

In the eyes of the authors of the New Testament, without a shadow of a doubt Jesus inaugurates the final age and begins to fulfil the eschatological promises – those which concern man's and the world's ultimate destiny. The formula 'in the fullness of time' means that humanity is entering the final age of its history and that the definitive end of history is drawing near. The kingdom is in the process of coming. Christians distinguish between Christ's two comings: the first was the birth of Jesus, the incarnation of the 'Word of God'. The second will be, as I have already pointed out, the Parousia, that is to say, the return of the risen Christ in glory, coming to judge the living and the dead. With the first coming, we entered into the last age of history, and this will reach its end with the ultimate coming of Christ.

The second Epistle General of Saint Peter in the New Testament (3:8–13) is particularly illuminating about the expectancy and impatience felt by the first Christian communities with respect to the last age. Let me read you a passage from it:

> But, do not ignore this one fact, beloved, that with the Lord one day is as a thousand years, and a thousand years as one day. The Lord is not slow about his promise as some count slowness; but is forbearing toward you, not wishing that any should perish, but that all should reach repentance. But the day of the Lord will come like a thief, and then the heavens will pass away with a loud noise, and the elements shall dissolve with fire, and the earth and the works that are upon it

will be burned up . . . But according to his promise, we wait for the new heavens and a new earth, in which righteousness dwells.

In the course of our conversation I shall certainly have to come back to the complication in eschatological expectations produced by the Book of Revelation. For the moment, let me just say that it produced a second version of them, in proclaiming first Christ's glorious return to reign over the earth for a millennium, and thereafter the coming of the final form of Jerusalem in heaven.

**Could you say something about the two mysterious Old Testament figures, Enoch and Elijah, who, it is said, will come again just before the end of time?**

Enoch is one of the most enigmatic figures in the Bible. He is one of those descendants of Adam and Eve, one of the patriarchs from before the flood who lived a very long time. According to Genesis – which, I repeat, I take to be a myth – Enoch lived altogether 365 years, and did not die. We are told by the Bible that 'Enoch walked with God: and he was not; for God took him' (Genesis 5:24). As for Elijah, he was a great prophet of Israel who is said to have lived about the ninth century before Christ. According to the Bible, he didn't die either, but was taken up into heaven in a chariot of fire as his amazed disciple Elisha looked on: '. . . and as they still went on and talked, behold, a chariot of fire and horses of fire separated the two of them. And Elijah went up by a whirlwind into heaven' (2 Kings 2:11). What these two figures have in common, then, according to the Bible – and I think that they are the only two of which this is the case – is to have been taken up into heaven by God without having experienced death. An apocalyptic tradition then grew up among the Jews around the idea that these two figures would come again at the end of time to prepare the way for the Messiah. Around the time of Jesus, which was an age marked by strong Messianic expectations, many Jewish religious groups expected the coming of Enoch and more especially that of Elijah. That is why the emissaries of the chief priests asked John the Baptist, as he was baptizing in the river Jordan; 'Are you Elijah?' (John 1:21). It's also why many religious Jews believed Jesus to be Elijah (Mark 6:15).

**Is there a connection between Enoch and Elijah on the one hand and the famous 'two witnesses' we read about in the Book of Revelation on the other?**

Yes, indeed. John's Book of Revelation, which is the last book in the New Testament, takes its inspiration from the Jewish apocalyptic tradition, and picks up from there the theme of the two prophets of the end of time. According to the Book of Revelation, a great eschatological battle will precede the second coming of Christ. In the course of this struggle, God will send two witnesses who will testify to the Truth and then will be killed by the 'Beast', a sort of incarnation of evil. But the Book tells us that 'after the three and a half days a breath of life from God entered them, and they stood up on their feet; and great fear fell on those who saw them. And they heard a loud voice from heaven saying unto them, "Come up hither!" And in the sight of their foes they went up to heaven in a cloud' (Revelation 11:11–12). Enoch and Elijah are not mentioned explicitly by name, but the Christian tradition, especially in medieval iconography, often assimilated them to these 'two witnesses' of the end of time. For example, maps of the world were represented with the Garden of Eden at the top and the east, with Adam and Eve on either side of the tree, and symmetrically, in the west, Enoch and Elijah, placed there to proclaim the end of time. In this way even cartography began with the Garden of Eden and finished with the Last Judgement. Such was the vision of history and of humanity for Christians of the time.

**As we are speaking about the Book of Revelation, can you tell us in what way it speaks about the end of time? What will be the signs presaging the end of the world and the Last Judgement?**

The Book of Revelation attributed to Saint John is not the only New Testament text to speak about the end of time. In the Synoptic Gospels, Jesus sometimes speaks in eschatological terms. In his day, it was a very common literary genre. The main idea was that mankind would not reach the eternal and celestial Jerusalem before there had been a definitive battle between Good and Evil. This was already a widespread idea; it found its full expression in the gospels and the Book of Revelation. Looking back over the gospels, we can point to a certain number of signs which Jesus presents as harbingers of the end of time: there will be wars and earthquakes, signs in the heavens, the powers of the heavens shall be shaken, men shall be in anguish, evil will be widespread. Even Jesus asks: 'Will there still be faith on earth?' But he points out in another place that 'this gospel of the kingdom shall be preached in all the world ... And then shall the end come' (Matthew 24:14). This is one of the reasons why Christopher Columbus was certain that he was living in the last age of the world when he discovered America, because the gospel was going to be proclaimed to peoples who, up till then, had been unknown. And there is also Jesus's prophecy of the imminent destruction of the Temple of Jerusalem (a destruction which was to occur forty years after his death) and His disturbing words about the destiny of the people of Israel: 'They will fall by the edge of the sword, and be led captive among all nations; and Jerusalem will be trodden down by the Gentiles, until the times of the Gentiles are fulfilled' (Luke 21:24). With this verse in mind, certain people have gone on to interpret the recent return of the Jewish people to Israel as one of the signs proclaimed by Jesus of the imminence of the end of time.

**But throughout history, the people of the West have not stopped interpreting the extraordinary or dramatic events of their own time as signs of the end of the world.**

Of course! Especially particularly tragic happenings – the outbreaks of plague, the great schism of the end of the fourteenth and the beginning of the fifteenth centuries, the wars of religion – all of which have been thought to be signs of the end of the world. Without doubt these dramatic events have been seen through the prism of apocalyptic literature. People found no difficulty in believing that these eschatological 'days of reckoning' – an expression I am deliberately using in this context – were imminent. Such days of reckoning could either mark the end of time, or the transition to a thousand years of happiness on earth. For there are these two sorts of eschatological days of reckoning.

**You have alluded to the millenarian beliefs which were inspired by the Book of Revelation. Before discussing them, tell us something about this text which has left so deep a mark on the history of the West. Who wrote it?**

By tradition this book is attributed to Saint John, the 'much loved' disciple of Jesus, who is also said to be the author of the fourth gospel and of several epistles. Many modern interpreters reject this attribution, and tend to think of the work as a collective enterprise emanating from the Christian circles in Ephesus who considered themselves to be the heirs of Saint John's teachings. I can offer no opinion on this subject, which lies beyond my competence. What is a bit more certain is that the Book was composed at the end of the first century, in about AD 90, at the time of the persecutions of Domitian. The apocalyptic prophecies which it contains were designed to restore the morale of those being persecuted. In the eyes of most commentators, the 'Beast' or the 'Dragon' who figures throughout the Book is undoubtedly Rome – the Rome which engaged in persecution. It was broadly a matter of giving Christian victims of persecution the following message: you are suffering now because of your faith, but stand fast, because Good will surely triumph over Evil.

### What does 'apocalypse' mean?

'Revelation'. It is the Book of 'revelations', revealing what is hidden. Incidentally, the book begins in this fashion:

> The Revelation of Jesus Christ, which God gave him to show his servants things which must soon take place; and he made it known by sending his angel to his servant John, who bore witness to the word of God and to the testimony of Jesus Christ, even to all things that he saw. Blessed is he who reads aloud the words of the prophecy, and blessed are those who hear, and keep what is written therein: for the time is near.

### What is the framework of the book?

In the beginning, the Book of Revelation addresses seven named churches in Asia. It foretells the Last Judgement of mankind, but this is to be preceded by three phases. First, an age of long and painful trials; cataclysms, catastrophes and the like. Then a period of world peace lasting a thousand years, during which the Devil will be in chains. Finally, a last brief but very terrible period, that of the final battle between Good and Evil, coming immediately before the end of time, the Last Judgement, and the final inception of eternity, during which the elect will be gathered around the Throne of the Lamb, this figure representing Jesus Christ.

**So you can set our minds at rest: it's certain that Good will triumph.**

There's no doubt about it at all: history will finish well. We must read and re-read the splendid pages which bring the Book to a close. They take their inspiration first and foremost from the visions of the prophet Isaiah, and describe the 'new heavens', that is to say, eternity, thus:

> Then I saw a new heaven and a new earth; for the first heaven and the first earth had passed away, and the sea was no more. And I saw the holy city, new Jerusalem, coming down out of heaven from God, prepared as a bride adorned for her husband; and I heard a loud voice from the throne saying, 'Behold, the dwelling of God is with men. He will dwell with them, and they shall be his people, and God himself will dwell with them; and he will wipe away every tear from their eyes, and death shall be no more, neither shall there be mourning nor crying nor pain any more, for the former things have passed away.' And he who sat on the throne said: 'Behold I make all things new.' Also he said, 'Write this, for these words are trustworthy and true.' And he said to me, 'It is done! I am the Alpha and the Omega, the beginning and the end. To the thirsty I will give from the spring of the water of life without payment' (Revelations 21:1–10).

Next, taking his inspiration from the visions of the prophet Ezekiel, the author describes the holy city in which the elect will live: '[The Angel] carried me to a great, high mountain, and showed me the holy city Jerusalem coming down out of heaven from God, having the glory of God, its radiance like a most rare jewel, like a jasper, clear as crystal' (Revelations 21:10–11). The city 'has no need of sun or moon to shine upon it, for the glory of God is its light, and its lamp is the Lamb. By its light shall the nations walk, and the kings of the earth shall bring their glory into it, and its gates shall never be shut by day – and there shall be no night there' (Revelations 21:23–4). The Book ends with these words of Christ: 'Surely I am coming soon!'

**Umberto Eco points to the fact that one instinctively thinks of the Book of Revelation as a book of malediction, whereas in fact it is a book of hope.**

He is quite right! It is a book of consolation as well as of hope. The book was read in a dramatic way when people focused attention on its catastrophic episodes. But in the end it was a matter of telling the persecuted Churches of Asia: You are going through a period of trial, but it will soon end. Then will come unending joy, and evil will be once and for all defeated.

## A Thousand Years of Happiness on Earth

**It is also a unique feature of the Book of Revelation that it brings the New Testament to a close: it's the last of the 'revealed' books.**

Indeed, but it is important to note that the West had some difficulty in accepting the Book of Revelation as one of the canonical books precisely because of the question of millenarianism, and those famous thousand years of happiness on earth. The religious authorities thought that a millenarian interpretation of the Book ran the risk of deflecting the faithful from concentrating on spiritual matters, and it took several centuries for the Book to be adopted into the canon of the Bible.

**Haven't you recently published a whole book devoted to the fascinating question of millenarianism?**

In 1992 I published the first volume of a *History of Paradise* entitled *The Garden of Delights.** In this book I tried to conjure up the nostalgia for a lost paradise in the way this has been expressed in our Western civilization. It followed naturally that I should write a second study – to which I gave the title *A Thousand Years of Happiness*

* *Histoire du Paradis: Le Jardin des délices.*

*on Earth** – in the enduring hope of rediscovering in the future the original earthly paradise. This hope can be called a 'nostalgia for the future'. In composing this new work, I did not stray from the same broad plan on which I have been working for twenty years which is designed to explore in succession the past fears of our civilization and its need for security, and then to recall its dreams of happiness. The American historian Marjorie Reeves rightly stated that 'men's dreams constitute a part of their history and explain many of their actions'.

**When people talk about millenarianism, they are generally thinking about the expectation of the catastrophes which will mark the year 1000 or 2000. But, as Stephen Jay Gould has made clear in this book, that is not at all what it is about; it is rather the belief in a thousand years of earthly paradise.**

As we are getting close to the year 2000, there is indeed a constant confusion between the fear of the end of the millennium and millenarianism, the hope for a thousand years of earthly happiness, the figure 1,000 having been sometimes understood across the ages in a strict sense, sometimes in a symbolic way. The nostalgia for a country or a world without evil and unhappiness has existed in many cultures, such as in that of the Guaranis; my own study, however, has been confined to Western civilization.

**Do millenarian beliefs stem from the Book of Revelation?**

Certainly in the case of Western Christianity. But it is important to stress again that the Apocalypse is rooted in a very vigorous Jewish tradition. Many were the prophecies of the Old Testament which told of a radiant future for the Jewish people when they were in danger or persecuted or exiled or humiliated. The most uplifting of these have been attributed to Isaiah:

> The wolf shall dwell with the lamb, and the leopard shall lie down with the kid; and the calf and the lion and the fatling together; and a little child shall lead them. The cow and the bear shall feed: their

---

* *Mille ans de bonheur.*

young shall lie down together; and the lion shall eat straw like the ox. The sucking child shall play over the hole of the asp, and the weaned child shall put his hand on the adder's den . . . and the Lord God will wipe away tears from all faces; and the reproach of his people he will take away from all the earth: for the Lord has spoken (Isaiah 11:6-9 and 25:8).

Among the texts of the Old Testament to have profoundly influenced Christian millenarianism we must also mention the famous dream which Daniel interpreted for Nebuchadnezzar. A statue made out of four substances of diminishing value was knocked over by a rock that mysteriously broke loose from the mountainside. According to Daniel, the statue symbolized four kingdoms which would collapse in succession and which would be replaced by a fifth which would have no end. In the sixteenth century, the revolutionary figure Thomas Müntzer produced a commentary on this text in the presence of the princes of Saxony, and in the seventeenth century, English millenarians called themselves 'Fifth Monarchy Men'.

But, of course, it was the Book of Revelation attributed to Saint John which provided the main basis for Christian millenarianism; the expression 'a thousand years' is explicitly found in it. Indeed, the author sees in his vision an angel coming down to earth and binding the Dragon, that is to say, evil itself, in chains 'for a thousand years'. Then the martyrs and all those who refused to worship the Beast and its image 'came to life and reigned with Christ a thousand years'. This is the first resurrection . . . 'And when the thousand years are ended, Satan will be loosed from his prison, and will come out to deceive the nations' (Revelation 20:1-7). Then will occur God's final battle against evil, after which comes the general resurrection – for, during the thousand years, only the righteous were raised from the dead – and finally the Last Judgement. The basis of millenarian belief is therefore the conviction that there will be an intermediary period of peace and happiness on earth between the times in which we are now living, with their evil and their crime, and eternity, which will come after the Last Judgement. Christ will reign at this time with the resurrected 'righteous'. This reign will be preceded and followed by periods during which cataclysms and wars will succeed one another; the second period being shorter than the first, as I have already said.

**From what historical date does one find traces of millenarian beliefs among Christian communities?**

There seems to me to have been widespread adoption of millenarianism among Christians of the first centuries of this era: this is what one would expect in times of persecution. Martyrs were encouraged, mainly from their reading of the Book of Revelation, to believe that their death would be swiftly followed by their resurrection, as a result of which the tables would be completely turned and they would reign with Christ over the world that had martyred them. In the group of these Christian millenarians of the first centuries of our era we may single out Papias, the Bishop of Hieropolis in Asia Minor, who had sat at the feet of Saint John; Saint Justin, a Palestinian martyred in Rome around 165; Saint Irenaeus, the Bishop of Lyon who died in 208; Tertullian who died in 222; and after the 'Peace of the Church', the great Christian writer Lactantius.

According to Saint Irenaeus, this is how Papias, whose writings have been lost, described the millennium: 'The day will come when vines will grow and bear 10,000 stocks, and on every stock there will be 10,000 branches, and on every branch 10,000 bunches, and in every bunch 10,000 grapes, and every grape will yield twenty-five measures of wine when crushed.' The same applied to cereals, fruits and all other seeds. 'All animals will enjoy this earthly food, and will live in peace and harmony with each other and be wholly under the power of man.'

As for Justin, he declared that in the glorious Jerusalem of the millennium 'the voice of crying and of wailing will no longer be heard; no child will be born premature, no old person would not see out his full measure of years . . . People would build their own houses and live in them, and they would plant vines and consume their fruit.' Procreation would continue to occur, but it would produce a race of blessed people. We can tell that millenarianism was more or less an official doctrine from another of Justin's statements: 'For me, and for wholly orthodox Christians, in so far as they are such, we know that there will be a resurrection of the flesh for a thousand years in a Jerusalem rebuilt, beautified and extended, as the prophets Ezekiel, Isaiah and others have foretold.'

For Saint Irenaeus the rebuilt Jerusalem of the millennium would prepare the way for the definitive heavenly Jerusalem, but would not be the same as it. The Bishop of Lyon declared that 'such events could only occur in supercelestial places ... But they will occur during the time of the kingdom, when the earth shall have been renewed by the Lord and Jerusalem rebuilt in the image of heavenly Jerusalem.' In this way the first holy city will prepare the way for the second. Finally Lactantius, a pagan rhetorician who was converted to Christianity and became the tutor to Constantine's son, pointed out:

> After the resurrection, the son of God will reign for a thousand years among men and his government of them will be a very just government. Those alive at this time will not die, but will beget a countless multitude ... Then will the sun be seven times hotter than it is now. The earth will show forth its fertility and will spontaneously produce plentiful harvests. Honey will stream from the mountains. The streams will flow with wine. The earth will be joyful, and free from the reign of evil. Animals will no longer feed on flesh.

**You said that the Church had some difficulty in accepting the Book of Revelation as one of its canonical books because of its millenarianism, but as I listened to you, I got the impression that the Early Church was won over to the idea.**

There was always fierce opposition to the theory of the millennium; Saint Augustine was the one who did most to reverse the tide of millenarian beliefs, to which, incidentally, he had himself at first subscribed. He refused to express his approval of visions of the future that seemed to him more carnal than spiritual. So he put forward a symbolic interpretation of the Book of Revelation and taught that the birth of Christ marked the beginning of his thousand years of earthly rule, which would be directly followed by the Last Judgement and the coming of the celestial city. So there wasn't an intermediary period to be expected. Thereafter the official organs of the Church ratified the Saint Augustinian interpretation of the Book of Revelation. As a result, the famous decree of Pope Gelasius at the end of the fifth century, which distinguished between canonical and apocryphal books, kept the Book of Revelation in the first category, but cast suspicion on the millenarian writings of Tertullian, Justin, Lactantius and others. The refusal by the Church to sanction a literal reading of the twentieth chapter of the Book of Revelation perhaps explains why over the ages the iconography of the Book of Revelation most often omitted to depict the thousand years of Christ's reign on earth. Moreover, the Orthodox Church took much longer to accept the Book of Revelation as part of the canon. This wasn't done until the fourteenth century, and even then not without considerable misgivings. So millenarianism has been marginalized since the fifth century – this doesn't of course mean that it had no historical importance.

**In your book you show how millenarianism came back to prominence in the twelfth century with the Calabrian monk Joachim de Fiore.**

Without ever using the term 'millennium', Joachim de Fiore indeed foretold the coming of the age of the Spirit during which humanity would live in holy poverty, piety and peace. For him, history fell into three periods: the 'time before grace', the 'time of grace' and the 'time we are expecting, which is close at hand'. In other words: the time, before Christ, of Mosaic law – the age of the Father; the time marked by the coming of Christ and the writings of the gospels – the age of the son; and the time now close at hand in which 'spiritual intelligence' will reign – the age of the Holy Spirit and of the 'eternal gospel'.

In his best-known work, the *Concordia Novi et Veteris Testamenti* (*The Concordance of the Old and New Testaments*), Joachim wrote:

> The first state was that of knowledge (that is to say, the state in which mankind had to learn); the second is that of wisdom; the third will be that of the fullness of intelligence. The first was one of enslavement; the second is one of dependence as of a child on his parent; the last will be one of liberty. The first took place under the whip; the second, under the banner of action; the third will be under that of contemplation. Fear characterized the first; faith, the second; charity will mark the third. The first was the age of slaves; the second, of freemen; the third will be that of friends. The first was the time of old men; the second, of young men; the third will be that of children. The first took place under the light of the stars; the second is the moment of dawn; the third will be that of broad daylight.

Joachim, who died in 1202, thought that a critical period was on the point of beginning and that it would last until about 1260; after this turbulent age, 'monastic religion' would bring peace to the world. He only describes this period of future spiritual, if earthly, happiness in very sober terms. What is important is that he broke with the Augustinian interpretation of the official Church and went back to the eschatology of the first generations of Christians – that which interposed a period of rest on earth between our tormented human history and the Last Judgement. His message had been called 'the return of the repressed eschatological message'.

**Why did this peace-loving monk give rise to a later revolutionary movement, which became sometimes very violent?**

I can see two reasons why. First, he prophesied that the Church of the contemplative orders – monks, all of them poor – would succeed that of the clerical orders. This unintentionally struck a blow at the institution of the Church. Second, he often used the evangelical form of words 'the last shall be first', to which he gave substance by the statement I quoted above, according to which the age of old men and adults would be followed by that of children: the 'parvuli' would reign over the earth and would confound the proud and the mighty. These forms of words explain the role played by the poverty-loving Franciscans in the diffusion of Joachite ideas. They explain also why less irenic souls than Joachim transformed his thought into a radical and violent millenarianism. But his influence went beyond extremist circles, and even beyond Christian ones. Dante called him a 'prophet'. Christopher Columbus and Campanella (1568–1639) quoted him on more than one occasion. In the nineteenth century, Hegel and Auguste Comte revived his division of history into three periods. George Sand put him at the centre of her novel *Spiridon*, which describes the coming of a religion of humanity. Michelet saw in him the harbinger of an 'age of the free spirit and of science'. As late as 1921, we find the German Marxist Ernst Bloch placing him in the ranks of those who have 'lit the burning spark which will never die'.

**Was the famous prophet Nostradamus, the protégé of Catherine de Medici, whose famous *Centuries* proclaim the coming of a 'great monarch' who will reign over the earth, also influenced by millenarian Joachite theories?**

I don't know the work of Nostradamus at all well, and to be perfectly frank, I am not much interested in him. But an important historical fact which must be stressed is that Joachim de Fiore's message, whether well grasped or less well understood, was linked from the thirteenth century onwards with another more ancient eschatological tradition. In the fourth, and then again in the seventh centuries, the prophetic texts known as *Sibylline Oracles* were put together. These prophesied that for about one hundred years (a hundred years seemed much longer to people in the past than it does to us) a Christian king or emperor, enthroned in Jerusalem, the sovereign of the 'last days', would unite under his sceptre all of the inhabited earth, would bring it peace, and would convert all of humanity to the Christian religion. At the end of his reign, he would deposit his crown on the hill of Golgotha. Thereafter would ensue the last attack of the Antichrist, and then the end of the world. The *Sibylline Oracles* circulated throughout the Middle Ages and were printed at the end of the fifteenth century. Like traditional millenarianism, they carried the message that before the Last Judgement there would be a Christian Golden Age. Hence the amalgamation which occurred between these two eschatological visions. It is very likely that the 'great monarch' of whom Nostradamus speaks is this sovereign of the last days.

**Wasn't the hope of seeing the sovereign of the last days reign in Jerusalem part of why the Crusades were undertaken?**

Indeed. Thereafter the kings of France, the emperors of Germany, the Spanish and the Portuguese monarchs tried either at the same time or one after another to harness this hope for their own ends. The hope was alive in the entourage of Charles VIII of France, and explains at least in part his campaign in Italy of 1494, which was to be succeeded by the reconquest of Jerusalem. That same hope was one of the guiding thoughts of Christopher Columbus. His plan was always to accede to the lands – notably China – thought to be rich in gold, silver and precious metals, by a westerly route and, with the riches thus obtained, to finance the reconquest of Jerusalem by the kings of Spain, who would thereby become the sovereigns of the last days.

⌐ *Millenarianism's Finest Hours*

**Millenarianism and violence have frequently been linked. I'm
thinking here of Norman Cohn's book *The Pursuit of the Millennium*.**

It's a remarkable book. Throughout history certain groups of people
have indeed tried to impose the millennium by force. The most violent
examples of such revolutionary millenarianism are the radical Czech
movement of the 1420s, the Thuringian 'peasants' revolt led by
Thomas Müntzer in 1525, and the occupation of the city of Münster
in 1534–5 by fanatical Anabaptists who thought that Christ was
going to come down to earth there to found the new Jerusalem.

**Isn't that the episode described by Marguerite Yourcenar in her
book *L'Œuvre au noir*?**

That's right. There were also plots hatched in England in the middle
of the seventeenth century by the 'Fifth Monarchy Men'. I discussed
all these events in my book, and notably referred to documents about
the fifteenth-century Czech extremists which have hitherto not been
known about outside Bohemia. I was also able to provide a detailed
analysis of a strange work entitled *The Book of a Hundred Chapters*
which was composed about 1500 by an anonymous Alsatian fanatic
who has come to be known as 'the revolutionary of the Upper Rhine'.
None the less, I wanted above all to demonstrate the importance and
variety of millenarianism well beyond the examples supplied by
seditious egalitarian movements.

**Which countries were the most affected by the millenarian utopia?**

Outside Portuguese-speaking countries it is not well known that from
the fifteenth century to the seventeenth century inclusive, powerful
currents of millenarianism swept through Portugal; it is impossible
to make sense of the history of this country without being aware of
them. Historians have thereby been able to claim that in Portugal
'the persistence of Messianic thought which animated the outlook of
the people for so lengthy a period and with such consistency of

expression is a phenomenon without parallel in history, with the exception of that of the Jewish people'. Recent research has shown that the plans and overseas expeditions of Manuel [the Happy] must be given an eschatological meaning. He was dreaming of a sort of universal Messianic sovereignty, Daniel's fifth empire, which would see Portugal bringing the Christian religion to all non-Christian nations. What is unique to Portugal are the *Trovas* (songs), notably those of the visionary cobbler Bandarra, which were composed between 1530 and 1546, and which proclaimed the imminent coming of a king who was still hidden from view but who would be the saviour of the world. The hope that King Sebastian, who disappeared during a battle against the Moors in Morocco in 1578, would reappear, forms part of this tradition. In the seventeenth century, Sebastianism was transformed into an authentic version of millenarianism, thanks specially to Antonio Vieira.

Antonio Vieira (1608–97) was a Jesuit, the most famous Portuguese preacher of his day, and one of the great names of baroque literature in his country; he was also an authentic millenarian. He was born in Brazil, spent part of his life there and died there. He was a tireless defender of the Indians. He was a supporter of Portugal's independence from Spain; he hailed John IV of Braganza as the restorer of the fatherland and saw him as the 'hidden king' proclaimed by Bandarra's *Trovas*. Aside from his eschatologically inspired sermons, Vieira expressed his millenarian ideas in three main works: *Esperanças de Portugal* (1659); *Historia do futuro*, probably begun in 1649 and never finished; and the *Key to the Prophecies*, written in Latin, which he first mentioned in 1663 and which is also an incomplete work of which only fragments survive.

In his books Vieira spent much time in establishing that the prophecies of David, Isaiah and Daniel foretold the fifth empire of the world; in his voyages of discovery which took him to the ends of the earth, he saw proof that this empire was beginning. Having demonstrated that there would be a fifth empire, he asked the question: Would it be in this world or the next? His reply was categorical: 'It is the common belief of the saints, accepted and followed by all their exegetes, that the reign and empire of Christ foretold by Daniel is an earthly empire in this world.' According to Vieira's idea, Christ would not reign directly over a regenerated world, but would exercise his sovereignty through two representatives, the Pope and the King of Portugal, the Church having by then reached its ultimate state of perfection. Jerusalem would be restored in all its glory. Sin would disappear through the conversion of the heathen and the expected death of those sinners who refused to be converted. Under this fifth empire, life would continue as now with agriculture, industry and commerce, but there would be no war. This state of perfection would last one thousand years, until the return of the Antichrist to earth. Lisbon would be the centre of this Christian empire on earth, because it is, as he said, 'the best-proportioned and best-suited place for the purpose which the Supreme Architect chose . . . Set between her two promontories, which are like open arms . . . She awaits the willing obedience of all the nations who will discover there their solidarity, even with people from as yet unknown lands which will lose the stigma of this epithet.' While the Pope would be the sole spiritual pastor of humanity, the King of Portugal, having become the Emperor of the World, would be the universal dispenser of justice. He would bring to an end all conflicts through which the nations were destroying one other, and he would 'keep the whole world in the peace of Christ of which the prophets sang'.

**Apart from Portugal, were there other European countries deeply affected by millenarianism?**

Many people in France, even in Protestant circles, are not aware that Jurieu, the great Calvinist adversary of Bossuet and the orchestrator of resistance to Louis XIV from Rotterdam, was a millenarian. As for seventeenth-century English history, it is incomprehensible unless one gives eschatological hopes their rightful place. Across the channel millenarianism played an important role during the time of Cromwell. In a more general way, the birth and development of Protestantism allowed millenarian currents of thought to manifest themselves more openly and more widely than before, even though it is true that the great reformers Luther and Calvin stuck to the Augustinian interpretation of the Book of Revelation. There has always been a link between millenarianism and heresy. The arrival of America on the scene gave a new impetus to millenarian hopes. The French historians Marcel Bataillon and Georges Baudot have clearly shown that the first Franciscans to arrive in Mexico in 1524 were deeply imbued with Joachite ideas, and that they believed that the 'last age of the world', that is to say a period of peace, reconciliation and general conversion to Christianity preceding the end of history, was close at hand. Motolonia and Mendieta, the two best-known Franciscans involved in the 'spiritual conquest' of Mexico in the sixteenth century, shared the conviction that they would be able to recreate the golden age of the Early Church in the new world, far from the corrupt Christianity of Europe, among the indigenous Indians, in their simplicity and poverty. Mendieta dreamed of making the natives of New Spain live 'in virtue and in peace, in the service of God, as though in an earthly paradise' – terms to which one must give their eschatological sense. This was also the hope of the Jesuits when they created the so-called '*reducciones*', or settlements, in Paraguay for the Guaranis.

**You have also said that the first puritans who went to live in America believed that it was the place from which the universal reign of Christ could spread.**

I did, and it's something that is not sufficiently known here in Europe. When, in 1628, those leaving for America from England were being dissuaded from setting sail, one of the pioneers of the project declared: 'Do not set back the time of your departure . . . know that the Lord will create over there a new heaven and a new earth, new Churches and a new Commonwealth.' In the eyes of John Cotton, a theologian who emigrated to America in the seventeenth century, New England occupied 'an unprecedented situation in history'. Its inhabitants constituted a society 'freed from the Beast'. For him, America 'could be read in the promises', that is, in the prophecies of the Old Testament. In 1652, John Eliot, the first Protestant missionary to the Indians, declared that the kingdom of Christ was 'being established in the Western parts of the earth'.

But the most striking expression of millenarianism linked to North America is found in the works of Jonathan Edwards, the pioneer of the Protestant 'great awakening' of the years 1740–44. He declared most notably:

This new world is probably now discovered, that the new and most glorious state of God's church on earth might commence there; that God might in it begin a new world in a spiritual respect, when he creates the *new heavens* and the *new earth*. God has already put that honour upon the other continent, that Christ was born there literally, and there made the purchase of redemption. So, as Providence observes a kind of equal distribution of things it is not unlikely that the great spiritual birth of Christ, and the most glorious *application of redemption*, is to begin in this . . . The other continent hath slain Christ, and has from age to age shed the blood of the saints and martyrs of Jesus, and has often been as it were deluged with the church's blood. God has therefore probably reserved the honour of building the glorious temple to the daughter [America] that has not shed so much blood, when those times of the peace, prosperity and glory of the church, typified by the reign of Solomon, shall commence. There are several things that seem to me to argue . . . that the sun of righteousness, the sun of the new heavens and new earth, when he rises . . . shall rise in the West.

**Don't you have the feeling that America is still deeply imbued with these ideas? Take for example George Bush's words after the Gulf War about America as the guarantor of a new world order of peace and justice.**

I very much have that feeling, and there is good reason to believe that American millenarianism constituted one of the elements which went to make up the evolving identity of the new nation. In 1785, Timothy Dwight, who was Jonathan Edwards's grandson and also a millenarian, published a poem with the significant title, 'The Conquest of Canaan'. In it the soldiers who fell during the War of Independence were compared to the Hebrews led by Joshua towards the promised land. A new Eden, the fifth empire proclaimed by Daniel, was about to arise: 'an empire of peace, justice and liberty'. The new republic would be the agent and the motive force of the millennium. In 1795, a preacher claimed that the inhabitants of the United States would 'say to each other with happiness in their faces . . . the United States are now the vine of the Lord'. In the eyes of Daniel Austin, another millenarian of the beginning of the nineteenth century, the stone which, according to the prophecy of Daniel, broke free to fill the whole earth was obviously a presage of the Declaration of Independence in July 1776, the event from which the thousand years of happiness would be able to begin.

**Are millenarian theories the source of the different utopias which have been a feature of European literature ever since the work of that title published by Thomas More in 1516?**

I don't know whether millenarian theories generated these utopias. But there are certainly links between them. The literary genre of the utopia developed from the beginning of the sixteenth century and flourished particularly in the eighteenth century. At first authors created fictions of distant islands whose inhabitants lived happily under wise governments and just laws. Equality, or the communal ownership of goods, or both together, were most often given as the golden rules. But as imaginary descriptions of utopias came to be situated in a fictional place beyond this world, they came to suggest more and more a programme of change for a foreseeable future. The desire to promote radical improvements on earth was thus common to both millenarians and to the authors of utopias. The link between the two types of discourse can be very clearly seen in the work of the Italian Dominican Campanella. Yet the millenarian aspect of Campanella's writings has been little noticed up to now, perhaps because the works in which he expresses it were not published until the second half of this century. Now, in *La Profezia di Cristo*, which was composed in 1623, Campanella makes the following prediction, basing himself on both Lactantius and Joachim de Fiore:

> Then the righteous will be separated from the evil-doers, and there will be a new heaven and a new earth. The sun will shine seven times more brightly, and the moon will be like the sun as it now is; all this will go on for a thousand years ... The first restitution of creatures will not be the one which makes them immortal, as procreation will continue and people will draw nourishment from the fruits of the earth: this could not happen unless the elements continued to suffer corruption. In that time, the stars and the elements will undergo partial purification, and will have imposed on them the order and disposition consistent with those of the Golden Age, during which the saints will possess the world of men.

Like all millenarians, Campanella enjoyed engaging in complicated arithmetical speculations about the eschatological days of reckoning. For simplicity's sake, we may say that he thought them very close at hand.

**There is also a close relation between millenarian beliefs and the modern ideology of progress. Isn't the latter the lay, or rather secular, version of the former?**

In order to be consistent with the predictions of the Book of Revelation, for millenarians of all periods, the transition to a thousand years of happiness has to be accompanied by a period of catastrophes. However, when the notion of progress emerged in the West at the end of the seventeenth century in the writings of thinkers such as Fontenelle and Leibniz, this was more often than not linked to the notion of a gradual and relatively steady march of mankind towards moral and material improvement. However, I agree with you that there is one thing in common between millenarianism and the ideology of progress: the certainty that humanity is marching towards a better earthly existence and that a radiant future is just over the horizon. This is why one might think of looking for bridges which might have existed between the two outlooks. I'm sure that they do.

The case of Joseph Priestley, for instance, provides us with an object lesson on the links that united millenarianism and the belief in progress in the eighteenth century. As a man of science, he demonstrated that the law of interaction between electrical charges was the same as that which governed gravity. He discovered oxygen, and isolated a large number of gases. In another context, he was a unitarian theologian who rejected the doctrine of the Trinity. As far as the theme of our conversation is concerned, he was convinced that God desires man to be happy on this earth and saw science as the prime instrument of progress. It is through science that man was going to march forward towards the millennium. He wrote that thanks to science men would become happier day by day, in themselves, but also that together they would be more able to pass on their happiness to others, and, he was convinced, be more willing to do so. Thus, whatever the origins of this world might have been, its end will be glorious and paradisiacal, beyond anything that his contemporaries' imaginations could then conceive of. He was in favour of the French Revolution, and saw it as the earthquake which the Scriptures predicted would hasten the change to an Edenic situation. In 1799 he wrote an address to the Jews based, as in so many other millenarian writings, on the revelations of Daniel and the Book of Revelation, in which he predicted their imminent return to Palestine, the union of all religions, the abolition of the papacy and the defeat of the Turks, and of the kingdoms of Europe, and the establishment of the kingdom of God on earth.

**Isn't it the case that the great theorists of socialism, especially those of the nineteenth century, were inspired by millenarian ideas?**

The hope of bringing to pass a state of earthly happiness for mankind was indeed one of the guiding conceptions of the nineteenth century; it was expressed by very different sorts of people. Victor Hugo, for instance, proclaimed to young people in 1830: 'Oh, the future is magnificent! A pure and pacific age opens before you as you march forward with more confident steps . . . We shall see how like a sea sweeping up the beach irresistible liberty will rise higher and higher.' Belief in progress inspired both positivists and socialists. Pierre Leroux, who is thought to have invented the word 'socialism', declared that 'paradise will come down to earth'. So it's no exaggeration to claim, as you suggest, that a laicized version of millenarian hopes found its place in socialism. Marx declared that the action of the proletariat would bring to an end the exploitation of man by man, and that communism would resolve the 'enigma of history'. For Jaurès, 'mankind will for the first time obtain mastery over things' thanks to socialism, and art would be liberated. Even as late as 1921, the Marxist Ernst Bloch – he was later to become a Marxist dissident – wrote, with explicit reference to the whole millenarian tradition, 'It is inevitable that the time of the kingdom will come.'

**Isn't there a whiff of millenarianism even about Hitler, in his promise of a thousand-year Reich to the German people?**

As I assembled the material for my book, I naturally asked myself this question. I did some research on it with a colleague who is a German specialist. Now the promise of a Reich lasting a thousand years is not to be found in *Mein Kampf*, even though it's true to say that in a speech he made in Nuremberg in 1937 Hitler promised the German people 'a thousand years without a revolution'. But that's all we found. I believe that the idea of a 'thousand-year Reich' was spread about by Nazi doctrinaires. But it didn't come from the mouth of Hitler or from what he wrote.

**Be that as it may, we have seen since the Enlightenment millenarianism being changed into other forms and secularized. Does the traditional religious form of it still survive today?**

Indeed! Even while traditional millenarianism was inspiring utopian, positivistic or socialist currents of thought, it was continuing on its path, particularly in the United States, which is no coincidence. It constituted (and still constitutes) one of the important elements of doctrine for Mormons, Seventh Day Adventists and Jehovah's Witnesses. For instance, the following declaration is to be found in the Mormon creed: 'We believe that Sion will be built on the continent (of America); that Jesus will reign in person on earth; that the earth will be renewed and will receive the glory of paradise.' May I remind you that Jehovah's Witnesses constitute the fastest-expanding Christian sect in the world (there are 160,000 members in France alone); the belief in the millennium, which they have predicted several times over the last century, is at the heart of their teaching. One might also mention another type of religious millenarianism, largely divorced from Christianity, which manifests itself in the present-day expectation of the 'New Age'. In the eyes of those who live in this hope, the imminent paradisiacal era of 2,160 years will bring together under the zodiacal sign of Aquarius all the 'positive' aspirations of which mankind has been dreaming since time immemorial.

**Why the figure of a thousand years?**

This figure is an invention of the Book of Revelation. The division of history into periods of a thousand years was for long alien to the Old Testament, where one finds calculations of years by groups of seven (forty-nine years), after which came a jubilee. The origin of millennia is to be found in Babylon and Iran. To be precise, the first Jewish text to mention a period of a thousand years is the Book of Jubilees (4:29–31), written only a century or so before Christ, where it is said that 'Adam died seventy years before having reached the age of one thousand years, for a thousand years are like a day to heaven.' It's certainly through the Book of Revelation, however, because of its long-lasting success in Christian circles, that the period of a thousand years caught on.

## The Fear That the World Would End

**Didn't the thousand years of the Book of Revelation also create the idea that at the end of every millennium, something momentous would happen, provoking eschatological expectations or fears about the end of the world?**

Without doubt, especially if one takes into account Saint Augustine's interpretation of it. He rejected the literal sense of the twentieth chapter of the Book of Revelation and refused to believe that from a given point in time there would be a thousand successive years of happiness on earth. As I have said, he thought that the thousand years which are proclaimed by the Book of Revelation had begun with the birth of Christ. We do not have to wait for an intermediate period between our own times and the coming of eternity which would constitute a new version of the Golden Age. Since the Book of Revelation spoke of a thousand years, it wasn't absurd to think that around AD 1000 time had run out and that the last eschatological battle was close at hand. But it's important to state that the indubitable state of expectation found in monasteries and among the thinkers of the Church didn't provide what has been believed to be the 'panic terror of the year 1000', that is to say, a panic spreading throughout Europe; that is a legend. But I certainly believe that in monasteries in which the Book of Revelation was read, it was thought that the time had been fulfilled and that the last period of history had been reached.

**When did the legend of the panic terror of the year 1000 arise?**

It arose at two different moments. First, without a great deal of fuss, at the end of the fifteenth century when the German humanist Trithemius (that is the Latin version of his name) wanted to contrast the enlightenment of his own times with the darkness of the previous age (what we now call the Middle Ages). He represented this previous age as a time of fear; and among the fears, there was said to have been a fear of the year 1000. Second, much more importantly and quite independently of Trithemius, the period of Romantic historiography in the nineteenth century is the great age of this legend. This style of writing history had the same wish, to contrast the enlightenment of the present with the darkness of the past: a contrast which was common in Michelet's time.

**If there hadn't been any great fear in AD 1000, can you explain how and why eschatological fears recur from the end of the fifteenth century onwards?**

I believe this to be connected to the series of misfortunes which befell the West from the fifteenth century onwards. I shall list them. The first, and indubitably the most important, was the Black Death of 1348, which was a veritable demographic disaster. A quarter, perhaps even a third, of the population of Europe died in the space of three or four years – a truly vast number. Second, a little later, there occurred the great schism (1378–1417), with two, and at times even three, concurrent popes. The French theologian Jean Gerson was of the opinion that this could only be a punishment inflicted on sinning Christianity, and he even added that no one would enter paradise until the great schism was brought to an end. The schism was repaired at the beginning of the fifteenth century, but a century later, the Protestant reformation broke out. On this occasion, Christianity in the West was split in two and has remained thus divided to this day. To all this must be added the many famines, the Hundred Years War, the War of the Roses and the Turkish threat: the conquest of Constantinople in 1453, that of Asia Minor and a large part of the Balkans, the fall of Egypt at the beginning of the sixteenth century, the Ottoman protectorate extending over the whole of North Africa with protection being given to Barbary pirates who ravaged Christian shores, and so on. And on top of that, wars of religion broke out in the sixteenth century. It was in this dramatic context that the expectations and fears about the end of the world flourished again. It was in the spirit of the age to look for guilty parties, since all these misfortunes had occurred. And more rather than fewer were identified!

**Are you referring to the Inquisition and the witch hunts?**

Yes. Throughout the 250 years during which these misfortunes were befalling the West, there was a constant search for scapegoats: Turks,

Jews (it was the greatest age of anti-Semitism), heretics, witches. One has to realize that the great age of the persecution of witches was not the Middle Ages, as is often believed, but a period stretching from the end of the fifteenth century to the beginning of the seventeenth: in other words, the Renaissance. Think about Michelangelo's tragic *Last Judgement* on the wall of the Sistine Chapel, or Dürer's series of fifteen etchings of the Apocalypse, which made it famous at a stroke. People at this time did not have the notion of progress as part of their mental baggage. They did not think that humanity could have a long future ahead of it, or any future at all. They looked upon it as old and close to its end. Christopher Columbus wrote in 1500 that the end of the world would occur in the next 150 years at the very most. Nicholas of Cusa declared that the victory over the Antichrist would happen between 1700 and 1734. Luther stated that 'We have reached the age of the pale horse of the Apocalypse . . . the world will not last another hundred years.' I could give many other examples of quotations of this type. Millenarians were in the minority; for most people, the end of time was close at hand; the world was rushing headlong towards the Last Judgement.

**All the same, it is astonishing to note that the period we now call the Renaissance, which is marked by so many discoveries and new horizons, thought of itself as ageing and close to the end of history.**

It is indeed a paradox that needs to be explained. One might well ask oneself how the intellectuals of the time succeeded in reconciling eschatological hopes with the often expressed conviction that their age had seen the rebirth of arts and letters. The answer is to be found above all in the writings of Budé and Luther. The former declared in his book *On the Transition from Hellenism to Christianity (De transitu hellenismi ad Christianismum)* of 1535:

> O how unfortunate and catastrophic is the fate of our age, which has marvellously restored letters to their former glory, but which, through the crimes of a few and the sins of many, has become burdened by sinister and unforgivable impiety . . . as for me, I am inclined to think that the last day is coming to an end, that the world is in decline, and that it is old and lacking in sense, and that it indicates, presages and foretells its imminent fall and end.

Luther gives expression to a similar sentiment, while laying greater stress on the following: because mankind has reached a 'peak' not only of knowledge and of artistic production but also of sin and iniquity, the day of judgement cannot but be close at hand.

It can also be pointed out that the discovery of America gave new encouragement to eschatological hopes in two ways. First, for those who were expecting the world to end soon, the conquest of America would permit the conversion of as yet unheard of peoples; the whole world would become Christian, in accordance with the prophecies of the New Testament. Because all of humanity would soon be Christian, the end of time was from that time on imminent. If one now follows the millenarian current of thought – although there were naturally points of contact between the two forms of expectation – the Christian Golden Age was going to come back to earth again in America before the final age of the world. People tried to create ideal Christian communities, whether in Mexico, which was mainly evangelized by the Franciscans, or in North America, where the puritans, the majority of whom were millenarians, landed in the seventeenth century, or even in the Guarani republics founded by the Jesuits in Paraguay in the seventeenth and eighteenth centuries; they tried to reconstitute the Church of the first years of the Christian era, and their communities were supposed to be the models for the Church of the last age.

### When did these eschatological hopes and fears go away?

They started waning from the second half of the seventeenth century onwards, at the end of the Thirty Years War (1618–48). This was a disaster which decimated particularly the German population through the continual comings and goings of soldiers and outbreaks of the plague. From the reign of Louis XIV onwards, France also entered into a period of considerable internal peace that was to last almost until the French Revolution. The year 1660 also marks the end of the English revolution. So in spite of the wars of Louis XIV, the second half of the seventeenth century was incontestably a period of relative release from tension, during which people allowed their eschatological fears to subside somewhat. Added to which, the Catholic Church stifled anything which proclaimed the end of time.

**Why?**

Because Protestantism had used the Book of Revelation as a weapon against Catholicism by declaring that the Pope was the Beast of the Apocalypse and Rome was the new Babylon; and I don't think that this was just a piece of polemic for Luther and many other Protestants, but rather a deeply held belief. If one made this connection, you will understand that anything could be said against the Catholic Church. So it stifled all forms of discourse that were used against it. From the Council of Trent onwards, the Catholic Church, which had got a grip on itself, eliminated a good number of its internal abuses and placed greater emphasis on the judgement of the individual than on the Last Judgement, which was too closely linked to eschatological prophecies.

## The Regaining of Hope

**Let's turn now to the year 2000. Do you have the feeling that, as the end of the millennium draws near, there is a revival of eschatological fears or hopes?**

Certainly. The collective suicide committed by sects, such as the Order of the Solar Temple or Heaven's Gate, reveals the anguish that has taken hold of some fragile persons as we approach the day of reckoning which they take to be an apocalyptic one. Life on this planet, so their thinking goes, has become impossible and will become more and more so as a number of anticipated catastrophes draw near. Opinion polls show that such thoughts are widely held in the West: a recently published poll suggests that 59 per cent of the inhabitants of the United States expect there to be catastrophes in the near future. One might also remember the success enjoyed by such books as *Planet Earth: The Final Chapter** of which 28 million copies were sold. But to my mind, people have much less fear of the

* Hal Lindsey, *Planet Earth: The Final Chapter*, Western Front Ltd (1998).

year 2000 than of losing their jobs! What is more, the date has no significance for non-Christians. It marks no anniversary in the Jewish, Islamic, Hindu, Japanese or Chinese calendars. As a result, I believe that we must see it in relative terms for what it is.

**What led you personally to take an interest in fear in the West?**

Memories of childhood. When I published *Fear in the West*, I felt the need to give a brief explanation of my motives in the introduction. This ended in the following way:

> While I was planning this book and putting my material into order, I was surprised to discover that I was beginning again, forty years on, the psychological journey which I travelled in my youth and that under the cover of a historical investigation I was reliving the various stages of my fear of death. The way this two-volume work* develops will repeat in a transposed form my personal Odyssey, my early fears, my painful efforts to come to terms with fear, my adolescent meditations on the meaning of death and, finally, my patient search for serenity and joy in acceptance of it.

Generally, I don't have recourse to autobiography, but in that introduction I felt it necessary to do so.

**Do you think that people have to face their fears to be free of them?**

You have to confront them squarely. Climbers are advised to go down mountains facing into the void (except when abseiling, of course).

**Does today's world worry you?**

I have to admit that it does. And yet I am not by temperament a pessimist. I believe human creativity to be very great. There is more goodness in the world than people believe and say there is, because people pay too much attention to what is causing pain and

---

* I was led to give my investigation much broader dimensions than I initially intended. But the general trajectory is really what I said it would be then (in 1975): fear, the feeling of security, dreams of happiness.

what is going wrong. Having said that, I have just come back from a journey to Brazil, and there the situation has been getting worse for the last twenty years. Cities are getting bigger and bigger, there are more and more paupers, and it is obvious that the authorities have less and less control over the suburbs, which sprawl out as far as the eye can see. So from every point of view – social inequality, pollution, political corruption – things have got worse. We have to be very careful, very vigilant: humanity won't automatically win the battle.

**What in your eyes is the worst threat hanging over humanity at the dawn of the twenty-first century?**

It seems to me that the present movement towards ever-faster modernization that is affecting every nation and every individual, in so far as it is excessive, blind and overhasty, increases social inequality, gives rise to pollution of every sort and, as a consequence, constitutes a real danger for humanity. Yes, humanity is in danger. One must add to that diseases such as Aids, whose consequences are less grave than those to which plagues gave rise in the past, but are none the less disastrous for certain nations: I'm thinking particularly of African peoples. These threats cannot be underestimated. But that is no reason for giving up. The solutions to them – for there are solutions – are to be found in international dialogue and in a sort of planetary ethics.

**Do you think that our age is still an age of hope?**

It is true that the waning (in relative terms, at least) of religion and what has been called the 'death of ideology' (which has actually happened) have reduced the quotient of hope among us.

**Are you personally waiting for the end of time which will herald the Last Judgement?**

I shall set aside the question about the end of the world, because according to the scientists, the world still has several thousand million years ahead of it! Yet I have never disguised the fact that as a Christian I believe that I will have to give an account of what I have done with my life at the moment of my death. But I put my trust in God's mercy and I hope to know happiness in His presence and in the company of my fellow humans in the exercise of love.

*This conversation took place at Cesson-Sévigné*
*on 18 December 1997*

# Answering the Sphinx
*Jean-Claude Carrière*

## *Introduction*

The idea of reflecting on the end of time was just the thing to set
the fertile mind of Jean-Claude Carrière racing. As we shall see,
this versatile writer is haunted by the question of time's arrow,
with its paradoxes and dizzying perspectives, and it is a topic to
which his multi-faceted experience of the world of contemporary
thought and creative arts has made him particularly alive. In the
light of this great question nothing seems trivial to him: neither
the rhythm of our deeds and actions, nor the ticking of our
clocks, nor the learning of an 'art of slowness' like t'ai chi, nor
the humble task of planning a timetable. For him these
conversations were therefore an opportunity to bring together
reflections deriving from a wide range of different perspectives,
from a rich harvest of knowledge gleaned from the theatre, the
cinema, literature, philosophy, science and everyday life.

   As both playwright and actor, as well as being screenwriter to
the great directors of our time – Etaix, Buñuel, Oshima,
Schöndorff, Louis Malle, Godard, Milos Forman . . . –
Jean-Claude Carrière set the seal on a traditional combination of
roles by collaborating over many years with Peter Brook. But his
insatiable curiosity quickly led him to step beyond the footlights
and explore some rarely frequented areas of knowledge. And
almost all the adventures experienced by the author of *Le Cercle
des menteurs, contes philosophiques du monde entier [The
Liars' Circle: Philosophical Tales from around the World* (Plon,
1998)]* seem to have brought him closer to the distant *terra
incognita* to which his readers, in large numbers, have followed
him. There can be no question here of listing all the publications
which he has produced, nor even of hoping to give some idea of
the diversity which characterizes them. We shall content

ourselves simply with recalling his deep knowledge of Indian civilization, which has led him to offer the French reading public a new interpretation of the *Mahabharata*; his interest in Buddhism, as seen in *La Force du Bouddhisme [The Power of Buddhism]*, an account of his meetings with the Dalai Lama (Robert Laffont, 1994); and the quality of his exchanges with the astrophysicists Jean Audouze and Michel Cassé, which appeared in *Conversations sur l'invisible [Conversations on the Invisible]* and *Regards sur le visible [Perspectives on the Visible]* (Plon, 1988, 1996).

Being a free spirit with a passion for debate, he has always had a weakness for new issues, for the wisdom of far-off lands, for the marginals of this world, the awkward customers, the heretics, the seekers after truth, whether they be called Krishna, Hampate Ba, Proust or Einstein. Thus he has taken us, in the course of three unforgettable meetings with him, from the nanoseconds of particle accelerators to the thousandths of seconds in Olympic records, from Dali's limp watches to the artificial time needed to separate two night scenes in a film, from the incalculable duration of the Hindus' *Kali Yuga* to the universe and its 15,000 million years. Out of these discussions of sundry topics Jean-Claude Carrière has extracted the elements of a veritable metaphysics of time, complete with a series of questions to make our heads spin: How are we to manage our destiny as temporal beings? In what ways have human beings set about trying to tame time, to tame this dragon that is devouring them little by little? And how does language reflect humanity's ambiguous relationship with time? Is it true that for certain civilizations time doesn't exist? What is the significance, in Eastern cultures, of the notion of circular time? To what extent are these radically different conceptions of reality actually accessible to us? Is time's arrow something thought up by human beings or is it an objective reality coextensive with the universe? All food for some penetrating thought on the nature of time, raising still further questions: How can we persuade the members of various cults that time is not as they believe it to be and that nowadays the time of the Apocalypse is above all the time of commerce?

Although no longer a Buddhist, Jean-Claude Carrière seems to have borrowed from Buddhism the principle of wakefulness and made it his own: 'Keep the mind fresh,' like the mind of a novice. Hence the freshness of this conversation in which he gives of himself freely, without fear or favour. Not forgetting, of course, that for this man of the theatre the end of time is when the curtain falls, the lights come on and everybody goes home.

**Are we witnessing the end of time?**

The first thing that occurs to me, and which is indisputable, is that we are seeing the end of a number of grammatical tenses. Where has the future anterior gone? What's happened to the past historic? The imperfect subjunctive is only very rarely used nowadays. And what should we make of this simplification? What are grammatical tenses if not the painstaking attempt of our precise, meticulous minds to envisage all the possible shapes that time can take, all the ways in which we relate to time within the domain of our thoughts and actions? What is conjugation but an attempt to think and express the whole range of our various situations within time. It's a hopeless task, of course. We shall never be able to carve time up into a sufficient number of tenses to control it and be able to say, at each instant within its fleeting forward movement: That's the time it is.

**Well, this is a surprise! We begin our discussion of the end of time, and the first thing you do is lament the loss of the future anterior.**

We ought to be able to say: 'When I see you tomorrow, my work shall have been completed.' But people don't say that any more. The future anterior, which introduces a past into the future, displays an extraordinary degree of refinement. It shows how verbs have dared to attempt the impossible, to take on our great, immutable master. The capacity of our language to express the various changing or unchanging temporal rhythms of our lives had achieved a high degree of subtlety. The past historic is another miracle, but nowadays it's hardly used anywhere outside the Midi in France. My mother-in-law, who died three years ago, used to use it frequently: *'Lorsqu'il arriva, il me vit et me dit'* [When he arrived, he saw me and said]. That's quite different from saying: *'Quand il est arrivé, il m'a dit.'* The past historic doesn't exist in all languages. It's not to be found in English, which only has the past tense, called the imperfect, and the perfect tense: I came – *Je venais*; I have come – *Je suis venu*. But 'I came' in the sense of '*Je vins*' doesn't exist. The past historic seems to have merged with the imperfect. Where in French we use the imperfect to express duration or repetition, in English they have recourse to the present participle. Instead of saying 'He told me,' one says either 'He was telling me,' or 'He kept telling me.' To express the idea of duration or recurrence, you have to add an auxiliary to the present participle. It would be interesting to hear what a grammarian has to say about this disappearance of tenses. It's a phenomenon which isn't often remarked on.

**But what do you think about this new linguistic usage?**

I'm very careful not to attribute any particular significance to the disappearance of tenses. I merely note the fact. People might want to infer that this evolution of language is part of a more general simplification of language, an inevitable result of the fact that we're now living our lives – for reasons we don't understand – at an ever faster pace. Apparently we're now incapable of hearing certain tonalities in Couperin's music because our hearing has been damaged, and not only our hearing, I'm sure. Perhaps we've lost a certain element of sensitivity in our relationship with time. A new laziness has overtaken us. I don't know.

**Hebrew has no present tense.**

The relationship with time varies from language to language. In the sentence: '*Quand tu viendras, je t'offrirai un café,*' '*Quand tu viendras*' becomes in English, 'When you come'. In English the future is never used after 'when'. So one might investigate the various ways in which human beings have conjugated their tenses in different languages and at different periods in history. It would be very interesting to look at Sanskrit, for example, which is said to be the most refined, most scientific language there has ever been. You say that Hebrew has no present tense, but what does the absence of a tense mean? The present doesn't exist in Hebrew, and nor does it for scientists. They would like the infinitely brief to be the same as the infinitely small, but the fundamental building block of time is missing.

The infinitely brief, the very essence of the present, is not to be found, it can be neither fixed nor measured. It is therefore completely justifiable, grammatically speaking, to leave out the present. By its very act of omission, Hebrew has a lot to tell us.


## The Time of Kali

**You mention Sanskrit, so perhaps we might think about the Hindu concept of time. According to them, we've come to the end of a cycle, haven't we?**

Hindus believe we are now living in what they call the *Kali Yuga*, the age of destruction. It's an irremediable process. Shiva has, once more, prevailed . . . Which is no surprise: Shiva always prevails. At the end of the last of the *yugas*, which form a cycle, everything disappears. The world we know will disappear, but not for the first time. There is no use trying to resist this destruction, because the forces sweeping us away are infinitely more powerful than us. The main difficulty during the *Kali Yuga* is to maintain *dharma*, to maintain the order of the world and the integrity of our own actions, which are intimately connected in Indian thought, because we are in part responsible for the smooth running of the universe. If each of us observes his own personal *dharma*, if each of us accomplishes what he came into existence for the purpose of accomplishing, the universe will proceed along its course, and one day the world will be reborn. It's all a question, therefore, of knowing how – despite this prospect of inevitable destruction – to continue to strive for *dharma*.

**When did we enter the time of Kali?**

About 3200 BC, on the death of Krishna, the eighth avatar of the god Vishnu. But how long will the time of Kali last? I've never managed to find out, though I must have asked at least fifty people.

**The French comic Fernand Raynaud would have said: 'For some time . . .'**

If the time of Kali began around 3200 BC, it's already lasted more than 5,000 years. How much longer? Some talk of fifty years, others of 3 million. It is very difficult to know how long a *yuga* lasts. Probably because, for Indians, that's not exactly the point.

**It's the very idea of measuring time which is foreign to them.**

Yes, because you can't measure a circular phenomenon.

**What's going to happen at the end of the *Kali Yuga*?**

We shall see – are already seeing – an increasingly radical and increasingly evident decline in the whole idea of civilization. One can find very precise accounts of the *Kali Yuga* in the sacred texts of India, in the *Mahabharata*, for example. We shall experience a period in which all social ties disappear. The laws will be called into question, opposed and finally dispensed with. The texts speak of the 'laws of Manu', named after the Indian equivalent of Solon. These laws have provided the structure of Indian society for a very long time. When they cease to be in force, civil wars will follow, within states, within cities, within families, rifts of every kind. Wild animals will invade the cities. The texts are very precise on the matter. I remember Jean-Luc Godard saying fifteen years ago that the fact that the blackbirds had deserted the countryside to come and live in the towns and cities seemed to him one of the most important events of the last years of the century; within a short period of time the least tame of animals had become almost domesticated . . . One reads, too, in the *Mahabharata*: 'Crime walks abroad. Carnivorous animals lie sleeping in the streets . . . The vultures are gathering. Birds with iron beaks have been seen, crying: "It's ripe, it's ripe!"' And so on. Predictions of the end of the world share a number of common signs pretty well everywhere.

**Aren't these just metaphors?**

Absolutely not. It is presented quite clearly as a fact. The texts speak also of the human race degenerating: of people becoming shorter, of muscles weakening, of the hair of fifteen-year-olds turning white . . .

**If we look around us, the opposite seems to be true. The new generation is taller, healthier than any previous generation.**

The Indians argue that one does indeed see many people living to the age of eighty or ninety. But they belong to a generation born before the Second World War, when more than half the population still lived in the country and ate natural foods, produce that grew from the earth without the aid of pesticides and chemicals, and when they breathed clean air.

**Will the post-war generations face problems that we don't yet know about?**

It's quite possible. More often than not, what happens in the future is unexpected. But if everything is going from bad to worse, according to the traditional Indian view, one thing is nevertheless getting better and better: the quality of wine is improving, throughout the world. An exception to the rule which is not without its charm! There is absolutely no doubt that wine today – in the Hérault, for example, where I live – is better than it was thirty or forty years ago. And that's encouraging. But will wine survive the *Kali Yuga*?

**Perhaps it's our taste buds which have deteriorated?**

Absolutely not. Everybody agrees on the fact, the wine-growers especially. Consumption of plonk has fallen considerably, people are discovering quality wines all over the place. Individual wines, with their own personality, that refuse to be like the rest. The wine-growers have devoted considerable efforts to the choice of grape varieties. And to mention something I do know quite a lot about, Corbières wines are in the process of becoming very fine wines, on a par with the wines of Bordeaux. And even Bordeaux wine is getting better. So there's one good reason not to despair completely. There's some serious resistance going on . . .

**But according to your sacred texts, none the less, the human race is under threat.**

I remember talking to an Indian in 1985, in Avignon, on the banks of the Rhône. We'd both been giving talks on the *Mahabharata*. It was rather an amusing situation. France had just offered to send a group of scientists to India to help combat the pollution of the Ganges, and there we were, sitting on the banks of the Rhône, when we saw several shoals of dead fish floating past. Then, thinking of this country that was proposing to come to the rescue of the Indians while neglecting to protect the species to be found in its own territory, the Indian calmly and simply said to me: 'Watch out!' Throughout history, average life expectancy has varied. Historians contend that people in the West lived longer in Ancient Greece and Rome than they did in the fifteenth century. Great epidemics of the sort that decimated populations in the Middle Ages and the Renaissance were unknown throughout Antiquity. Since the introduction of chemicals on a grand scale into our agriculture from the 1960s onwards – into our air, our water, our soil – no one has been able to predict the long-term effects on the human species as a whole. It's equally possible, of course, that it will have no effect. I'm not trying to act the prophet of doom. I'm simply trying to caution against any unduly complacent assertions about the 'progress' made by our civilization.

**And how does the *Kali Yuga* end?**

The abandonment of the rule of law, followed by civil wars and the degeneration of the species, lead to wretched deprivation, everywhere. And there are disasters on a global scale, great rains, red vapours, yellow vapours, deadly clouds, which will all turn the earth into one enormous swamp.

**Richard Fleicher's film *Green Sun* seemed to be predicting a miserable end of that sort.**

Yes, it was a moving account. The age of Kali is terrifying. And there is no remedy. It's pointless to resist. There's only one thing left for us to do in these dramatic times: maintain our *dharma* in circumstances which will make it harder and harder for us to do so.

**But why maintain this *dharma* if the cause is definitively lost?**

Precisely because time is cyclical, and a certain number of values, of the elements that constitute the order of the world, cannot disappear for ever. When all that's left on our planet is a sort of grey mud, as the texts describe it, then at that moment Vishnu will admit defeat: Shiva will have triumphed, the world will be destroyed. There are two great divinities in India, Vishnu and Shiva, and one creative principle, Brahma, of whom it is said that he is the third divinity. In reality, Brahma intervenes very little. There are only one or two temples in India that are dedicated to him. Vishnu and Shiva, on the other hand, are constant rivals: one preserves the world and the other seeks to destroy it. The *Mahabharata* is a great Vishnuist poem in honour of Krishna, who is an avatar of Vishnu. In difficult times Vishnu comes down to fight Shiva and to delay the end by a few years. Indian statuary often depicts Shiva with four hands. The top two are at the same height; in the right hand, the god holds a small drum to signify that the world was created to the sound and rhythm of a drum. In the other he holds a flame, which reminds us that everything that has been created shall be destroyed. The gesture that Shiva makes with his third arm is also the gesture that the Buddha makes, the famous *abhaya*, meaning 'Be not afraid.' Fear is an illusion, it does not exist. Since everything that has been created must be destroyed, why be alarmed, why worry? The fourth hand is a finger pointing towards the god's feet. Shiva is standing on one leg and crushing a demon with his whole weight. He seems to be telling us: 'Be not afraid, for look! By the power of my thought, I have lifted one foot off the ground.' This is one of the most emblematic and meaningful figures in the whole Hindu pantheon, which has no shortage of them. Shiva has prevailed, but all hope is not lost. He demonstrates the fact himself. From his raised foot our eye travels back to the original drum: one day everything will begin again. We all have our own little *Kali Yuga* in us, our own sense of apocalyptic doom. There's even something strangely inviting about this sense that the end is nigh. If so many periods in history have experienced it, that's probably because the feeling is part of us, deep down, and surfaces on this or that occasion as evidence of our fear, of our sense of guilt. In India, too, they are familiar with this human sense of being haunted by an ending. They simply respond to it in their own way.

# Vishnu's Sleep

**And what does Vishnu do during this time?**

Vishnu sleeps. He sleeps for a very long time upon a limitless ocean. There are thousands of depictions of Vishnu sleeping. While asleep he must dream so as not to forget the beauties of the world that has disappeared. Which is why we must at all costs maintain our *dharma*, in order to help Vishnu not to forget. To help the god to dream. If all values, all beauty are destroyed at the end of the cycle, the world is in danger of never reappearing. If something of the equilibrium between the forces of destruction and the forces of conservation is preserved in the memory of the great 'maintainer' that we are, Vishnu and us together, then all hope is not lost. A new cycle will begin again . . .

**So dream has a function as memory.**

As non-oblivion, as the struggle against oblivion. Dream remains awake within the sleeping mind. Who decides when the world will be recreated? No one says. There is no text, I think, which talks about it. Indian thought is reluctant to give shape or words to what is not yet shape, to what belongs to the realm of the shapeless. *Tat tvam asi*, they say of the ultimate reality: 'You are that.'

**That's the essential message of the *Bhagavad Gita*.**

The *Bhagavad Gita* is a very dense text which cannot be reduced to an 'essential message'. We must stop thinking that we can summarize in a few sentences the great thoughts, the great texts, that come from outside our own tradition. In a sense, the *Bhagavad Gita* subsumes everything that went before and develops it in certain aspects. It's a complex text. People have even found Buddhist influences in it. I shall certainly not simplify it for you. I wouldn't be able to.

As far as the *dharma* of the Hindus is concerned (the word has a different sense in Buddhism), no one knows how it came to exist in the first place. It's simply a fact. That's how things are. There have been many people – Jorge Luis Borges, for example – who have been surprised at this obligation without explanation. As I said, it's almost impossible to assimilate Indian thought (or Chinese or Mayan thought) to our Western concepts. We are far from having a monopoly on ways of thinking. There's a certain intellectual racism to be found more or less everywhere in the West, and we should constantly be on our guard against it.

So it is with time. Indian time cannot be reduced to our own. It defies all human arithmetic. Taken to its limit, this way of thinking means that a civilization could disappear in a few seconds and then reappear. In a few seconds, in a few thousand million years; what's the difference in the eyes of an extinct cosmos? Brahma the creator acts in an instant. Shiva takes longer, being more tortuous about his destruction. But it all comes to the same. An age is an age. Often it all depends on us, on our feel for things, on our way of seeing, our attitude.

**For a thinker like René Guénon, manifestations belong to different orders, some of which take place in time and others of which take place in other dimensions.**

Yes, perhaps in those parallel universes that the scientists tell us about these days. But let me finish talking about . . . what am I saying! One's never finished with him, with Vishnu, our official protector. After a certain 'time', all at once and for reasons we don't understand, Brahma, the creative principle, suddenly emerges from the belly of Vishnu, seated on a lotus leaf, and recreates the world he was dreaming about. The job done, Brahma returns to sleep inside the stomach of the god, ready for the next occasion. Creation dwells in sleep.

**Krishna is the latest avatar of Vishnu. Will there be another before this world ends?**

Yes, we even know that it will have the head of a horse. Up till now there have been eight avatars of the god; *avatara* means 'descent' in Sanscrit. He may have manifested himself elsewhere, in other inhabited worlds, since the Indian universe is infinitely broader in time and space than our own. The capital of the world, moreover, is not on earth, it's a floating city called Amaravati. It's where Indra lives, the king of the gods. This city moves about in space, it never remains in one place. In the *Mahabharata* it's where Arjuna joins Indra, in a machine that is described like a rocket, more or less: there is mention of 'thrust' and 'vapour' and 'invisible horses'. To my mind that must be the first journey into space ever described. Before even that of Elijah.

**What purpose do the *avatara* serve?**

Vishnu is there to maintain the order of the world. From time to time, when things are going particularly badly in the world, he 'descends' and assumes some form or other, not only human but earthly. The series of Vishnu's *avatara* corresponds, in a slightly crude and approximate way, to what we believe we know about the evolution of species. He descends first in the shape of a fish, an aquatic animal. His second *avatara* is a tortoise, an amphibious animal which finds it as easy to live in water as it does on land. The third is a boar, i.e. a mammal that lives only on land. The fourth is a man with the head of a lion. This is the first appearance of man, in a hybrid form. Intuitively, long ago, the Indian texts already have us descending from animals, or at any rate from a common marine origin. The fifth is the first complete human being, but short and slightly hunchbacked. If one's determined to find equivalents, then that could be our Cro-Magnon man. Next comes Parashurama, an ascetic sort of exceptional strength, whose words have a magical power. Parashurama is the 'axeman'. He lives in the forest. He's a woodman. The last two *avatara* are the two great Indian heroes, Rama and Krishna. They are the heroes of the two great epics, the *Ramayana* and the *Mahabharata*.

**Who will be the ninth *avatara*?**

He will not be descending in the near future, some people say, because we have reached the irremediable stage. The *Kali Yuga* is now too far advanced for us to imagine any further chance of rescue. He will come even so, say others, because, while accepting the work of Shiva, Vishnu cannot do other than struggle one last time against him. That is his *dharma*. All that is known about this ninth *avatara* is that he will have the head of a horse. Why? Will we revert to an animal state? No one knows. Incidentally, there was a period, already long ago, when Hinduism tried to make the Buddha the ninth *avatara* of Vishnu: there was a real attempt to assimilate the other religion. Fortunately, the Buddha lived long enough to formulate his doctrine precisely and to defend himself stoutly against all attempts to turn him into a god (which he could sense was coming). Such time was not granted to Christ, who, it seems, preached for only two or two and a half years at most.

**'If you encounter the Buddha,' the masters of Zen tell their pupils, 'kill him.'**

Yes, exactly. Kill the man who calls himself the Buddha. Kill the self-styled god. You must find your own way for yourselves. By some miracle this fundamental attitude has survived throughout the whole history of Buddhism and allowed it to resist all attempts to turn him into a god, to make him divine, especially in the Ashoka period, in the third century AD, when Hinduism underwent a grave crisis, allowing Buddhism to become for a time the official religion of India.

## Getting Ready for the Night of Nights

**If the Buddhists have resisted the temptation to turn the Buddha into a god, there are still a number of them who are waiting for the last of the earthly Buddhas, the Buddha Maitreya, 'he who loves', the incarnation of universal love. The historical Buddha was only ever supposed to be the last-but-one Buddha. Don't most great traditions speak of the coming of some providential figure whose arrival, in the majority of cases, will precede the completion of the ages?**

That is clearly the case as far as Judaism and Christianity are concerned. The historians of Christianity take the view that if a specific threat that the world was going to end had not been hanging over the Jews at the time of the first prophecies, then Christianity would not have survived. In a way Christ benefited from favourable historical circumstances which precipitated the conversion of a number of

Jews amongst his followers. All the great religions invite you to hold yourself ready in the expectation of some imminent event. The danger said to be threatening is terrifying and powerful. And it's accompanied by repeated descriptions of what amounts to a Christian *Kali Yuga*. Time is up. This absurd and brutal world can last no longer.

During this often feverish period of waiting, which Jean Delumeau describes so well, it only takes news of one event of an extraordinary or supernatural kind to be spread on the wings of anxious rumour for this event to be considered the first stage of some doomsday scenario, as described in the sacred texts.

**Are you referring to the Book of Revelation?**

Imagine a time when people open the window each morning, look up at the sky, and say: Is today the day? The first Christians were deeply convinced in the matter, much more than they were in the year 1000. It was a period that seems to have been haunted by visions of parting clouds, of the Exterminating Angel appearing with a cosmic roll of thunder, of a bolt of lightning destroying the world the same way it reduced Sodom and Gomorrah to ashes. One must be ready to depart . . .

**The Gospels are full of such Cassandra-like pronouncements: 'Within a generation there shall be . . .' The Book of Revelation belongs to a Jewish literary genre that was particularly rich. Saint John borrowed some of its formulas. It was he who brought the genre to its peak of supreme achievement, thanks to the two centuries of apocalyptic literature that preceded and foreshadowed him.**

We don't know if the John who wrote the Book of Revelation is the same as the person to whom the Fourth Gospel is attributed. They are probably two different people. The Gospel of Saint John is later than the Gospels of Matthew, Mark and Luke. Oddly, it is the only one to report certain major events like the resurrection of Lazarus. It's surprising that Matthew, who was one of the earliest disciples, doesn't mention it. Would this man who never left Christ's side have passed over it in silence? For what reasons? Would he have regarded it as negligible?

In other traditions this providential person you were mentioning suddenly disappears. He becomes the hidden hope. You find this in Portugal with the 'hidden king', and in Shi'ite Iran with the 'hidden imam'. Giving the state of the world as their justification, these all-powerful figures have decided to leave it. They are somewhere else now, biding their time – rather like Vishnu, in fact. In the case of the hidden imam, the metaphor tells us clearly that true power, power that is just and justified, is not visible. Whence the evident heresy which consists, in modern-day Iran, of giving this power to religious leaders.

**Do you think that the dramatic ordeals undergone by humanity in the course of the twentieth century have been seen as signs of foretelling an end of time?**

It seems to me very difficult to say why a whole people, at a given moment in its history, should feel threatened with extinction. Where does it come from, this sense of a human adventure on the point of coming to an end? From some collective sense of guilt? From an accumulation of misfortunes and fears? From some acute awareness of the scandalous imperfection of the world?

We don't really know at all. But I doubt if today's inhabitants of the earth, with one or two exceptions, are convinced that the end of the world is nigh, at least not in the sense in which that used to be understood, i.e. some brutal and definitive end. We would all four of us agree about that. Despite the nuclear threat, and the possibility of collective suicide we've provided ourselves with, we're more likely in our blacker moments to envisage some kind of slow death.

And what I find interesting also, as Gould does, are the different ways people have imagined of continuing to live on after the predicted disaster, when it's quite clear that it hasn't actually happened. So today was not the day? Oh well, it'll be tomorrow then. Tomorrow comes, and still no disaster. It'll probably be the day after then. Or next month. Who knows? Gradually, as the months go by, and the years, and the decades, we get used to the idea that maybe time has not been measured out quite as stingily as we thought. So we have to go on living, until the sky falls in on us. But how do we transform an emergency situation into a permanent state? This is a very rich theme in the history of religions: to prolong the ephemeral but without losing it completely.

In a sense, yes. Disappointment at still being alive. The sky hasn't fallen on our heads, so now we've got to go on living here on earth. To live, we have to organize ourselves, to establish a church, with people to run it, and rules, and hierarchies. Which leads on quite quickly to the problems connected with the Churches' exercise of temporal power. The emergency situation has gone. We have to live on. We have to accept time, which has decided not to end just yet.

This attitude can be seen throughout the fifteenth and sixteenth centuries. Then it disappears, only to return in attenuated forms. On several occasions during the nineteenth century, local prophets predicted that the world would end on a particular date: it's a *locus classicus* of prophecy. The seer fixes the night of 15 May, for example. The followers, the members of the sect, arrange their affairs on the evening of the fourteenth. Then they climb a hill, take all their clothes off and wait, shivering, for the heavens to be rent. There are maybe 200 or 300 of them, all huddled together. Fervently they pray. The end of the world is due at dawn. The sun rises, and these poor people gaze in astonishment. Nothing happens. The light of day floods the world just like every morning. Then they begin to look at each other. The babies are hungry. They'll have to go back down, put their clothes on again. The prophet, who has kept a prudent distance from the proceedings, is nowhere to be found. They go looking for him and finally, when they find him, they hang him. If he gets the chance to explain himself, he plays his final card: 'I made a mistake, it wasn't 15 May this year, it's next year.' And life has to be resumed, a life they had thought was lost. It is perhaps at such a moment that people become truly human. One stops looking up at the sky and starts thinking about the problems of everyday existence. And what happened like this to a group of fanatics in the space of a single morning has been spread out over several centuries in the case of the Christian Church. It's always fascinated me, this. We stripped naked to follow Christ, because Christ had told us that he would return. But he has not come. So we've created a situation, a comfortable situation, in which to wait for him. We've placed stone upon stone and built a church to shelter us. We've learnt to live on. We've become patient. We have to organize ourselves to make our faith last, the faith formerly born of an emergency.

**Whether it's this promise that's been made to us or the threat of ultimate disaster, don't we feel in both cases as though we're being offered a form of release, a means of escape from the prison-house of time?**

Everything turns on whether one believes or doesn't believe in another life. If you're a monstrous criminal, or simply being pursued by a horde of angry creditors, or else suffering from an incurable illness, then death followed by eternal life is an admirable solution. That's one of the reasons why sects find it so easy to recruit. Everything that's gone wrong for us in this life will go right for us in the next. And, unlike Vishnu, you won't even remember a thing about the suffering and failures of this life. Your existence is like a chrysalis from which tomorrow a butterfly will fly away to skies more wonderful, skies that never change. But if instead you believe in nothingness, then you can feel a similar sense of relief as your story ends. Why fear what does not exist? By which stage you may not be far from hastening this end, since this kind of end is also perceived as a form of release. There's always some way of giving one's destiny a little nudge in the right direction. These two attitudes – hope for eternal life, or else the open-eyed anticipation of the end of living – persist to this day. At opposite poles, but inextricably linked.

**Have you met any of these groups that are preparing for the world to end?**

I've met members of the Order of the Solar Temple cult. It's rather surprising to observe the ones who have remained behind but who participated – quite how, we shall never know – in the 'departure' of their comrades. Those I met were calm, genial people, who had settled down to life again. When they talk about those tragic events, they sound like people who have returned from another shore. All the same, their experience was one in which credulity was pushed to its absolute limit, to the point of hating the world and one's own condition.

**Perhaps the most extraordinary case is that of the Heaven's Gate cult in San Diego. Particularly because the members of that group were the sort of people who move about in cyberspace the way**

other people go for a walk in the forest. One journalist wrote of them that 'they all belonged to that tribe of anoraks who surf the Net as a way of escaping the void of their own maladjustment [ . . . ] All experts in computing and remarkably competent on a technical level, they drew on biblical, astrological and ufological myths to concoct a morbid theory, whose only possible outcome was suicide.'

I read that they never engaged in sex and that they wore black clothes and had short hair. One or two had even had themselves castrated. Then, on a date fixed in their calendar (this chronological precision is a constant feature), they took poison and lay down on their beds – each of them, apparently (and what a curious, awful detail this is), carrying a passport. The words of Luc Jouret, one of the gurus of the Solar Temple cult, were just as confident: 'You'll see,' he told one of his relatives on the telephone, 'it's gonna be fabulous over there . . .'

One could find encouraging words of this kind about 'departing the world' in the gnostic literature of the early Christian period and, no doubt, elsewhere.

Whatever 'progress' civilization makes, however much our awareness and our laws evolve, whatever use we make of cyberspace, something in us remains wedded to the certain conviction that time is going to end. Where does this conviction come from?

This approach to time as being linear, irreversible, has generated particular ways of thinking in the West, a philosophy, a way of seeing the world. In every story that has a beginning we unconsciously anticipate some form of downfall. If God as creator begins with 'Once upon a time, there was a world ready to welcome the first man and the first woman,' one can expect this God to end his narrative one day with a final full stop. No doubt so that he can start on something else.

I've already talked about what follows,* but it seems to me that it bears repeating. On the basis of Oliver Sacks's book *The Man Who*

---

* In *Raconter une histoire*, Paris, Editions de la FEMIS (1993).

*Mistook His Wife for a Hat,*\* we were working with Peter Brook on the mental disturbances caused by certain lesions of the brain. One day I asked Sacks: 'What constitutes a normal human being?' an old chestnut of the kind regularly set as an easy question for the *baccalauréat*, and not very interesting. But I added: 'I mean, from your point of view as a neurologist.' He replied: 'For us, a normal human being is someone who can tell his own story.' Odd that he should say that to a screenwriter. 'That is to say,' he added,

> someone who knows where he's come from, who has a past, who is situated within time. He remembers his life and everything he has learnt. He has a present, too, not just in the sense that he lives at a particular time, but in that he has an identity. The moment he speaks to you, he is capable of telling you correctly his name, address, profession, etc. And finally he has a future, i.e. things he plans to do, and he hopes he won't die before he's done them. For he also knows that he is going to die.

A normal human being is therefore someone capable of telling his own story and consequently of situating himself in time.

**That definition also works for a society.**

But a society would have much more difficulty than an individual in admitting that it is mortal. I would change one word in Valéry's comment, I'd have him saying: 'The rest of us civilizations now know that *other* civilizations are mortal.' No society can accept such an assertion about itself.

**Societies also fail to understand the circumstances in which they themselves came into being. The future is no more transparent than the past. If a normal human being is someone who can tell his own story, can one consider as normal a society which knows almost nothing about its own past and which conceals from itself the risks that threaten its future?**

Take *Montaillou*, the book by Leroy-Ladurie,† which is set in a small village in the Pyrenees at the beginning of the fourteenth century.

\* Touchstone Books (1998).
† Translated by Barbara Bray, Random House (1979).

When the judges, from Toulouse or Pamiers, asked the mountain-folk: 'When did our Lord Jesus Christ live?' they replied that he'd lived at roughly the same time as their great-grandfathers. The time that had elapsed since Christ seemed very short to them. And what's more, if they ever came across any pictures or pious images of Christ, they would have seen him depicted in the clothes of the Middle Ages. The notion of historical perspective didn't yet exist. In medieval miniatures Roman soldiers are shown with contemporary weapons.

**When did people start to measure the real length of time?**

In the sixteenth century, it seems to me. Two parallel phenomena occurred, within a few years of each other, which indicate that horizons were broadening. For the first time in illustrated books one sees Caiphas, for example, the great priest who pronounced sentence on Jesus, depicted in the Jewish dress of the period. That constitutes an as yet crude attempt at historical reconstruction. Knights' armour is dispensed with in favour of Roman military uniform. Time enters history. At about the same period Thomas More published his *Utopia* in Latin. All at once time became like a piece of elastic being stretched into both the past and the future. Science fiction makes its appearance, all of a sudden the future is an object worthy of interest and reflection. It will exist and it will last, there is no longer any doubt about it. The 'end of time' is indefinitely postponed. This is also the period which saw the myth of the Golden Age disappear; that idyllic, original time which we would later try to reinvent. We haven't stopped stretching that piece of elastic, in one direction towards the Big Bang, in the other towards the death of the sun, predicted to occur in 4,500 million years' time. When I was a history student, I was told that man, or the humanoid, had existed for 300,000 years. That's now increased to 3.5 million. As for the end of the universe, scientific minds have not yet been able to reach agreement on the subject. But they reckon that it will indeed end.

**Is science today better able than syntax to define time as a phenomenon?**

You'd have to ask the chemist and Nobel-prize winner Ilya Prigogine, who – like Marcel Proust – has devoted his life to searching for a time that is lost and, by its very nature, ungraspable. I have met Prigogine on two or three occasions. Bernard Pivot invited us both on to his programme, along with Jean d'Ormesson and the astrophysicist Jean Audouze, especially to talk about time. A fairly lively discussion arose between Audouze and Prigogine, the two scientists, while d'Ormesson and I looked on in blissful ignorance. The discussion centred on what preceded the Big Bang, before the moment when matter is known to have existed. The Big Bang may not be the beginning of the universe, but it is the beginning of our being able to talk about the universe. At present there is nothing we can say about what was before this 'beginning', which itself may not even be a beginning. The Big Bang means the birth of time and space, an old couple whom we shall certainly have cause to mention again in the course of these conversations. Prigogine was trying to imagine something before the beginning of time. Audouze said it was inconceivable, that one couldn't talk about time before there was a basis in time, some matter for time to leave its mark on. Time does not exist if nothing is subject to it, he said.

You have to realize that Prigogine is a chemist and Audouze a physicist who studies particle physics. Both of them find themselves faced with a disconcerting fact: everything is subject to time, all the things we can talk about are swept away on the river of time, which flows in a single direction. Hence the phrase 'time's arrow', which physicists use to describe this inexorable process. The first question they ask themselves is: Why does it always go in the same direction, why does nothing come back in the opposite direction, towards birth, towards the source? Why do all things age? Scientists then note the following: for all that there exist at least ten or eleven dimensions of space, and maybe even more, time still has only the one. Everything is swept away by time, with one single exception: elementary particles.

To be subject to time involves transformation, evolution. Everything that time touches wears out and is destroyed. But, as things stand, particles don't evolve. They do not undergo a transformation. No one has ever seen an electron or a neutron die. As soon as a form is obsolete, as soon as a body has 'served its time', the particles of which it was constituted are set free and hold themselves ready for some new adventure, for some new form . . . It is this imperturbable matter, too slippery for time to gain purchase on it, that the physicist observes with fascination, or rather tries to observe, for at that level 'reality' is ungraspable.

**You mean that no one has yet been able to see these elementary particles?**

Only traces of them can be detected at present. From the observation of these traces one can deduce that time is an attribute not of elementary matter but of form. When the particles begin to form themselves into atoms and the atoms into molecules, at that moment, implacably, time appears and sweeps the forms away. That's the price to be paid – and especially when the forms in question are complex, like our own. Whatever the forms that the universe and the bodies that go to make it up may be, they are swept away by time in one single direction, while the essential matter of which they are made up remains indifferent. A paradox on which Prigogine is working, with profit and imagination.

If you ask me what I think I understand – the texts are often difficult – I shall say that it seems to be that the irreversibility of time, which applies uniquely to forms, to systems, and not to elementary matter, can be interpreted in two ways. The first consists in saying that time is simply an illusion. As Einstein said in a letter quoted by Etienne Klein in a collection of articles by different writers:* '. . . for us, as hardened physicists, the distinction between past, present and future is simply an illusion, albeit a deep-rooted one.' Prigogine, in contrast, displaces the illusion. Time's arrow exists, even if the apparent indifference of particles would seem to lead us to believe the opposite. Time 'existed' even before the beginning of the universe. And that beginning was itself complex, with infinite ramifications. That's all I can tell you at the moment, without consulting a few fat tomes.

* *Dictionnaire de l'ignorance*, ed. Michel Cazenave, Paris, Albin Michel (1998).

**Is there not a parallel to be drawn here with myths about origins? Cosmogonies don't really describe the origin of the world as such. They represent a divine will to set order above chaos. Ritual, on the part of the priest, would thus be the daily repetition of this will to ensure that order prevails over chaos. But whether order prevails over disorder or disorder over order, these two realities continue to coexist, just as particles indifferent to time (at the microscopic level) coexist with bodies (at the macroscopic level) that are being gobbled up by time.**

With the creation of the world, form prevails over formlessness. But the price to be paid for this 'forming', this ordering, is time, is death. All form is mortal, and death is born with life. Actually, not all peoples have had need of a creation. There are certain quite rare traditions – the Aboriginals in Australia, for example – in which the world is presented as existing for all eternity. But the majority of traditions present a founding myth, an original scenario that is sometimes quite elaborate. Even in the Indians' cyclical way of thinking about it, there was, inevitably, a beginning. In India the question of beginnings is approached in several ways through different myths. In one of the commonest traditions, the story is told that in the beginning was music, or more especially a series of harmonious vibrations, like waves, which, over immeasurable periods of time, spread through the cosmos. These waves began to form sounds. These sounds formed musical modulations. Gradually, out of these musical modulations, came voices which formulated the 'Aum', the fundamental sound. And little by little the cosmos, thanks to these modulations, expressed the Vedas. The Vedas have no author. It is a text whose authenticity cannot be questioned, a text given to us by the cosmos. At the same time, or a little before, an egg appeared in the cosmos, called variously 'Hirynia Garba' or 'Brahmanda' – Brahma's egg. This egg exploded and from it sprang an indefinable being called 'Prajapati', the creative principle. Prajapati then broke into pieces, and its limbs formed the different parts of the universe. This universe, as in the Aztec tradition, has a tendency to re-form. Its scattered members have a tendency to reunite, and the power which works towards this reunion is called 'love'.

**One could find similar founding myths in a large number of traditions.**

What is particular to this Hindu account is the attempt to justify an origin for time, which Indians nevertheless envisage as an eternal process of new beginnings.

**You have worked on the great mythologies of India. How do the Indians perceive what we call time?**

One of the only scientists to argue against the Big Bang theory today is an Indian: he is the astrophysicist Narlicar, who is always being called by Western or American astrophysicists – who admire him a lot (he's a great scientist) – a closet metaphysician. He rejects the Big Bang – in a rather literary and indeed quite amusing way, for he has a well-developed sense of humour – because his culture prevents him perhaps from conceiving the idea of a single time with a single origin.

**Our scientific attitude is dictated by our tradition.**

Obviously.

**Whether or not one agrees with the theory itself, the Big Bang theory has made us perceive the real dimension of time. Newton still believed that the universe was 6,000 years old, while nowadays astrophysicists talk of 15,000 million years . . . Time has a tendency to make our heads spin, doesn't it?**

We just can't conceive of time on such a scale. Our brain is equipped to cope with a certain historical unfolding, a certain 'time span'. Is that perhaps why some people still reject the principle of the evolution of the species? We live for between fifty and a hundred years. At best we can hope to know our great-grandparents and our great-grandchildren. So from our own individual perspective we can contemplate up to 200 years of life either side of us, of visible, palpable life. An old uncle passes away, a baby is born. Our study of history allows us to broaden this perspective, to go back in time some 2,000, 3,000, 5,000, 10,000 years. By a great effort of imagination we can go back as far as the Combe d'Arc, or as far as the Grotte Chauvet that was discovered three years ago in the Ardèche: 32,000 years; that's not bad at all. And yet between the Combe d'Arc and the Lascaux cave, which we see as both belonging to the same period, 160 centuries passed. People ask me how it is possible. Sixteen thousand years between the cave paintings in the Grotte Chauvet and those at Lascaux! But it can't be true! And yet it is.

**About the same amount of time elapsed between the Combe d'Arc and Lascaux as between Lascaux and ourselves.**

Roughly speaking. Which is food for thought, wouldn't you say? The Combe d'Arc is not the vestige of some primitive world. On the contrary, it is already a very elaborate, almost sophisticated work, created by great artists. No one disputes the fact. And so now we are beginning to wonder about the extraordinary thickness of the ancient base upon which our lives are founded. If then we pass from the Combe d'Arc to Lucy, it is quite clear that we run the risk of getting completely lost. How shall we conceive of the time in which that young woman lived, our distant cousin, discovered in Africa by Coppens and Johanson, who is 3.5 million years old? How are we to understand the evolution of a species that stretches from *Australopithecus Afarensis*, discovered in Ethiopia, to modern man? And the history of man is so short compared with certain other species. Ants, for example, are 100 million years old, and termites 300 million. In China they have discovered the vestiges of living organisms dating back 570 million years. How are we to conceive of or apprehend a time span like that, given the organic limitations on our own 'brain time'? That's why, for all its extreme simplification, for all its manifest falsity, we're still gripped by the idea of the creation, not because we suffer from mental laziness, but because of our real inability to understand how old time is.

**Whereas astronomers, on the contrary, merrily journey across temporal distances which to us are inconceivable. And the closer they get to 15,000 million years ago, to the famous Big Bang, the more they have to slow down, the more the problems become intractable, and the more one senses their jubilation whenever they manage to advance 1,000 millionth of 1,000 millionth of a second towards time zero.**

There is a moment in time from which we can begin to think and talk of the universe. Scientists speak of nanoseconds.

### Did time exist before that moment?

I agree, the question just won't go away. Scientific research has undertaken to lift the veil and tell us tomorrow, perhaps, if time extends beyond the 15,000 million years. No one can possibly keep up in this race to discover lost time. Even the numbers are like an impassable Great Wall of China, numbers so huge that one can only plot them by using mathematical powers. The 'Planck era', named after the German physicist responsible for the quantum theory from which all quantum physics derives, designates the evolution of the universe between the time zero and the time estimated at $10^{-43}$ seconds after the Big Bang. During this short, this very short period of time, the temperature rose to $10^{32}$ degrees centigrade. The following era goes from $10^{-43}$ to $10^{-32}$ seconds and is called the 'quark era'. Who can keep up with that kind of mathematics?

### Isn't the prediction of a possible end of time, or end of the world, lent extra weight by the fact that today our past is getting away from us, that we can no longer conceive of it?

This is probably true. That which made us, that of which we are the effect, is not physically perceptible by us. We haven't the time to feel time, not least because we have taken the gamble (which is perhaps the only one we have taken in the modern age) of trying to overtake time.

### Of trying to travel at the speed of light . . .

That would be the only way of reaching other planets, coiled into other solar or stellar systems, which are several thousand light-years away. We have positively worshipped speed in this century. Our means of transport – the train, the aeroplane, the car – break banally terrestrial speed records, and it's a scandal nowadays if the TGV from Paris to Lyon, which can cover half of France in two hours, is so much as five minutes late. Today's heroes are the athletes that beat world records by a few hundredths of a second. You can be a hero of the planet for a few dust particles of time. If you break the 9.93 second barrier by one hundredth of a second, they hang gold round your neck.

## The End of Time, or the End of Times?

Let us be a little more precise. The end of times is clearly not the same as the end of time. When we talk about the 'end of times', we're talking about the end of human times, of times as defined by man. In one sense, the end of times, of particular stretches of time, represents the triumph of time. On the one hand, we have unassailable time, our sovereign ruler, and on the other, we have the times on which we wreak our vengeance in oh-so-ridiculous a manner. I reread the famous passage in Chapter Three of Ecclesiastes, where it talks about a time for this and a time for that. Within time we have created many different times. These times are our doing.

There is a time to love, a time to die, which are inscribed within us. It would be very interesting to ask oneself if the time to love is over or if the time to love can ever be over. Is there a time to love? Is the time to love limited to one single period in one's life? When does it begin? When does it end? Who decides? We also defer the time to die. Death, which was once unanimously accepted, has been blotted out in the most advanced societies and almost abolished. Equally, does the expression 'in time of war' mean anything any more? Are wars as precisely dated as they used to be? Are they declared or ended as precisely as they used to be? Are we not now surrounded by a whole proliferation of little wars that dare not speak their name? Are we not living in an age when these times, which we ourselves invented, are themselves also in the process of disappearing? Is that a good thing or a bad thing? I don't know. Previously our lives were divided into periods or seasons that were variously shorter or longer. We have done our best to abolish these differences by heating ourselves in winter, by eating strawberries in January, etc. Similarly, by doing away with the seasons, haven't we in fact deprived ourselves of this diversity, this wealth of multiple and various times?

Of cherry time and chestnut time? What do we gain by homogenizing the minor times of our life?

I found this striking remark in Cioran's *Notebooks*,* which were published after his death:

> The angel of the Apocalypse doesn't say: 'there is no more time' but 'there is no time to lose'. Throughout my life I've always felt as though time were being eaten away on the inside, as though it were on the point of using up all its possibilities, as though it lacked *duration*. And this lack on its part has always filled me with both satisfaction and terror.

It is satisfying, in fact, to imagine something missing from the omnipotence of the master. Satisfying, but also terrifying. For this master is perhaps more fragile than we realized. When we've abolished our own time, will Time with a capital 'T' still exist? One can ask the same question about what follows the end of time as one can about what preceded its beginning. Some people will say that there will still be God, who is outside time. Believers will say that. But what exactly could God do in a world from which time had disappeared? I can perfectly well understand God wanting to destroy the human race, and I'd even say that I see his point sometimes. But I find it difficult to understand why he would want to destroy time. True, I don't believe in him, which is maybe why I find it difficult. For those who believe in him, God is as indifferent to time as he is to an elementary particle.

**God is so far removed from time that he has been able to act within time throughout eternity. Theology tries to resolve this series of paradoxes which are linked, on the one hand, to human times and, on the other, to the time, or non-time, of God.**

Yes, how about a bit of theology? What a treat! We might even try a touch of patristic hermeneutics – just a little, don't worry! Let's look at how the early Church Fathers approached this question.

The major difficulty – and one that we still face – was to introduce, as it were, divine time into human time so that they interpenetrate. The Fathers of the School of Alexandria, like Origen, or of the School

---

* *Cahiers*, Paris, Gallimard (1998).

of Antioch (Theodorus of Mopsuestes, Diodorus of Tarsus), who were no doubt the quickest, sharpest minds of their day, tried to establish correspondences between the various revealed texts, either vertically, proceeding from type to archetype, which is the usual way (the new Jerusalem is an image of heavenly fulfilment), or horizontally, which is less common.

**For example?**

How was Christ, who is God, able to submit to human time in becoming man? How was he able to be born and to die, when he *is* for all eternity? This difficult question has stirred no end of stormy debate. Certain Fathers went so far as to say that just as Solomon's temple is already an image of the Church, so Christ *was* already the manna that fell from heaven when the Israelites were in the desert, that he *was* the rock from which Moses drew water after striking it with his rod, and that this beneficent rock even followed the Hebrew people throughout their long wanderings. Even if he hadn't yet manifested himself in human form, the Christ–God was already walking among the chosen people. For the same reasons, after his human death, he has not ceased to be. He is here, still, among those who believe.

One would have to make divine (supreme, absolute) time coincide with the human (limited, relative) time which constitutes the ages of mankind. This is an impossible task or, at the very least, a difficult balancing act, beset on all sides as much by ineffable divine abstraction as by our incorrigible anthropomorphism. In this sense, we could envisage the end of times as the end of this intolerable contradiction, of this cursed divide between time and times, which we keep coming back to. The end of times would be the definitive fusion into one unity, the end of the mortal arrow, the desire for a rising up to God, for a *loss of time*, without us thereby forfeiting life, the true life.

Quite obviously, alas, it is the opposite which is true. Time – absolute time, whether we call it divine or cosmic time – pays no attention to us, it treats us with disdain. It is our cold and distant lover, remaining studiously indifferent to our ardour, our prayers; to us who wish only to be able to disappear into it without necessarily having to die. We want to have done with counted times, measured times, and to accede to a time that has ceased to measure itself – an ever-repeated revolt against the time that is sweeping us away, a revolt which, desperate as it may be, nevertheless constitutes the most ambitious, the highest form of revolt. For the end of times, the end of counting and measuring, the end of terrors and hopes ('Abandon all hope,' the *Bhagavad Gita* tells us) can only mean one thing: eternity.

> Elle est retrouvée.
> Quoi? L'éternité.
> C'est la mer allée
> Avec le soleil.*

Rimbaud sensed it: yes, one day the sun will swallow up the sea, all seas. The astrophysicists are agreed on it. Matter in fusion, on the point of extinction, and dried-up seas, all will be one. Matter will be abolished; perhaps then we'll see particles die. Perhaps then, for lack of a universe, time will abolish itself of its own accord. And us – oh, the power of our imagination – we *shall* finally be in nothingness, we shall have been reunited with real being, delivered from times and from time itself.

**And this is what is called 'nirvana'?**

Perhaps. Nobody quite knows what nirvana is. The notion is more complex than our notion of paradise. In nirvana, at any rate, there is no consciousness. Nothing more exists. Time has submitted in the face of the accomplished *dharma*. And since we've now returned to India for a moment, let me quote the Vedas: 'I am time that grows not old.' But in the *Bhagavad Gita* Krishna himself declares: 'I am time that has grown old.' What has taken place between the two if not the creation of forms, of life and the immediate fall into times, into History? For Vishnu, as for the God of the Bible, descending to earth – and in human form – can only be fatal. Before Christ, Krishna had already died of his humanity.

---

* It is found.
  What? Eternity.
  It is the sea, gone
  With the sun.

We are here at the very heart of our subject: objective time and subjective time, the world's time and the soul's time. As Jean Audouze said, nothing allows us to assert that there is an absolute time which precedes the world and all forms. Absolute time and absolute space have ceased to be the natural, immutable framework of phenomena. They are, at least in part, determined by the phenomena that occur within space-time. If there is an absolute time – and it is I, the miscreant, who acknowledges the fact – it can only be subjective time, the soul's time, of the soul that is unable to resign itself to the idea of ephemerality. The scientist's question (Is there an absolute time, outside the world?) is quite similar to the theologian's: If God destroys time, will there still be a time for the soul?

**Hasn't the death of God in the nineteenth century in fact resulted, one century later, in time losing all differentiation, its relief?**

But it's not certain that God *is* dead. In fact, life is entirely organized round the alternation of day and night. We disrupt our relationship with time at our peril. Now, our lives are based on solar times. Being solar, they are false. First we were told that this was the time it took the sun to go once round the earth. Later we were told that it's the earth that goes round the sun. Then they told us that the earth also turns on its own axis. Now we learn that the solar system itself is shifting about within the galaxy, and finally – horror of horrors – that the entire galaxy is on the move. We're caught up in a whole series of movements which remain imperceptible to us. Time is the synthesis of all these shifts of which we have no knowledge, but which are altering our position in space with each fraction of a second. Which of all these rhythms has the most effect on us? In all likelihood, the rhythm of day and night.

In films, you know – and this rule of thumb is rather obscure and not very well understood – night scenes have to be spaced out at regular intervals. If in a Western two so-called 'campfire scenes' come too close together, something does not seem quite right. The day between them is too short. Similarly, while you can switch from one day to the next without any problem, you can't switch from one night to the next in the same way. Why so? I have no idea. Nobody has ever been able to explain it to me. If you switch from one night to the next, it is still the same night. I have talked in the past about the example of duels in Westerns.* The first to draw is always the first to die. He stands there, revolver in hand, as we switch to the other man, the one who is going to win. He draws, pulls the trigger and wins. What has the first man been doing during those two fateful seconds? He has remained paralysed, not pulling the trigger, waiting for death. Two simultaneous actions are in fact shown one after the other. If it's well done, we don't notice anything wrong with it. It's the same with meals in films which, thanks to clever editing, often take no more than four or five minutes from the soup course to coffee. And it's the same with people getting dressed, and hundreds of other actions. Time has become no more than a backdrop with holes in it. Almost a toy.

**But this plurality of times still persists at the level of the planet as a whole. A businessman in Paris doesn't experience time in the same way as an artisan in Bombay or a Touareg somewhere in the vast reaches of the Algerian desert.**

Human beings relate to time in complex and tremendously diverse ways. I was once present, for example, at a slave market in Nepal. There were representatives there from the Arab Emirates who had come to find workers to work in oil production. Every boy old enough to work had been brought there. They stood to attention when the people from the Emirates approached them; their mothers then started brushing their clothes for them, and the merchants would inspect their teeth and test their arms for strength. What time were we living in at that particular moment, I wonder?

**It would seem as though the twentieth century has dug a very large trench between these human times.**

Liv Ullman tells the story of how she was once accompanying a Unesco delegation that had gone to visit a community somewhere in Sudan or Ethiopia, in a very remote place. These people had been warned that the Unesco envoys would arrive in a great metal bird, but that the chances of this great bird being able to land depended on their having previously prepared a place for it to do so. So,

* In *Le Film qu'on ne voit pas*, Paris, Plon (1996).

equipped with stones and bits of wood, all the men set about clearing such a place and creating a landing strip. The work took almost six months. Once the landing strip was ready, they sat down all round the edge and waited for the great metal bird from Unesco.

The bird eventually appeared in the sky and landed. It taxied up to the end of the strip, over the stones and the wood, and then finally turned and came back towards the welcoming committee, who were terrified by this supernatural spectacle. The bird came to a halt and the door opened. They then saw a blond, blue-eyed angel come down the steps, laden with chocolates and all sorts of presents. This angel, followed by the representatives of Unesco, had come from another world, and they had never seen anything like it. The custom of these people was to offer a gift to passing travellers. But what can you give when you have nothing?

A woman then walked up to the blond angel – i.e. Liv Ullman – and asked her if she was married. The angel turned her head to right and left, a sign that no man had yet taken her as his wife. So they asked her to choose a husband for herself among the handsomest young men in the village. Here we have a scene that shows us the extent to which human beings today think on radically different wavelengths. Each age of humanity has left its mark. We live on top of an enormous palimpsest. Incidentally, I have no idea how Liv Ullman managed to get away without a husband.

## Oedipus at the Gates of Thebes

**Do you think there is anything unique about our age compared with all the others?**

Every age is unique. And anyway what is an age? When does it begin? When does it end? At the moment I am living on this earth at the same time as my grandson who is eleven months old. Can one say that we belong to the same age? What is an age but a tangle of generations, each one woven into the next, with no clear dividing line between them. One must be careful about ages: at best they're no more than a historical framework devised by historians for their own convenience – the *Ancien Régime*, the Restoration, the Second Empire . . . But for the people who lived together at those particular moments, such terms would have meant little. For example, what age are we living in? The age of the population explosion, of a united Europe, of the end of history? How should we define the period we live in? It's very difficult. After the battle of Valmy, which marked the defeat of the Prussians, Goethe proclaimed: 'A new age has begun in the history of the world.' It's just a formula. He didn't say when the new age would end. He hadn't a clue. And, in any case, we always get it wrong when we try to judge our own age. We can't be both the judges and the judged. We can't withdraw on to the summit of a mountain or the top of a column, like Simon Stylites, and calmly evaluate our own age. Indeed any honest journalist accepts the fact: an editorial is, at any given moment, no more than a kind of gut reaction. In other words, an editorial isn't a piece of re-flection or an overview, but a kind of automatic twitch at one particular instant in time. The 'age we live in' is something that we are far from able to comprehend in all its diversity. Several narratives have become interconnected, but without necessarily borrowing from each other. Each has proceeded in ignorance of the rest. Subterranean currents flow through the base of history, and these are currents which the historian, like the writer of editorials, finds very difficult to detect.

However, while our responses may be difficult to isolate, a certain number of facts are indisputable. Overpopulation will be an enor-mous problem for future generations. The overconsumption thereby caused in turn leads to overpollution, which poses a potential threat to the survival of the species in its present form. From the point of view of Buddhism, the word 'environment' is inappropriate because it supposes that things are around us, whereas we are part of them, we are at one with the world. All these problems will probably become very acute over the next thirty years. On the other hand, there are many positive things to mention. People even write books about the end of poverty. There are banks for the poor, as in Bangla-desh, and they work well. There is evidence in a number of countries of a rise in the standard of living, however modest. Latin America is in a better state than it was thirty years ago.

**So you differ from Jean Delumeau on this . . .**

Perhaps we're not using the same sources. It's commonplace to say that the great illusions of the eighteenth century, of the Age of Enlightenment, are dead. Nobody believes any more, for example, that by changing institutions, by changing society, you can change human nature. No alternative model has changed us. Yet society functions in a more satisfactory manner. We have improved justice, economic relations, solidarity, perhaps even the sharing of knowledge and, hence, of opportunity. The human being remains just that, a human being: as disappointing and as wonderful as ever. We have to admit that the progress of man through culture is simply an illusion, but that is not true for societies. And it is very difficult to distinguish the one from the other.

We feel a sense of disappointment because we are well aware that we have not changed, and a sense of hope because we observe that society is working much better than it did. Nothing is either grey or black or white. Everyone's entitled to their own opinion in the matter. As far as I'm concerned, I come from a tiny village in the countryside, where I spent my childhood, and I tend therefore – though I'm aware of the fact – to be somewhat pessimistic, because the paradisiacal world that I knew up to the age of fifteen has been destroyed. This destruction of my childhood makes me think that everything has been destroyed, which is not true, because, for a start, I still find traces of this childhood when I return home. Nature is more resistant than one thinks, and not only human nature. Has this lost paradise been replaced by others? As I am no longer a child, I cannot say.

**The twentieth century is, above all, the century of paradoxes, as you said in *Regards sur le visible*, your book of conversations with Jean Audouze.**

There are two words which I would put forward for the description of 'our age'. The word 'paradox' and the word 'enigma'. They are quite closely related. In that book we identified six paradoxes to be observed in our present *fin de siècle*, and perhaps we shall be coming back to them. As for the word 'enigma', it refers to a certain number of questions which science has not been able to tackle satisfactorily and which still keep us awake at night.

**Enthusiastic, all-conquering scientism, once confident of discovering the universe's ultimate equation, has had the wind taken out of its sails.**

At the time of the inauguration of the Academy of Sciences in 1893, Marcelin Berthelot maintained in his inaugural address that the universe held no further mystery. That's what scientism is. Official science approached the turn of the century with the assertion that it knew everything. When you ask scientists today, they tell you that the twenty-first century offers a vista of enigmas. They say they don't even know what they don't know. We are rather like Oedipus at the gates of Thebes. At the dawn of the new century, there are several sphinxes waiting for us. They're going to interrogate us, to put strange questions to us. One will be about the problem of overpopulation, and with it the problem of desertification. Another will raise the issue of loneliness and communication. Another will concern the growth of knowledge and the growth of ignorance – the level of illiteracy in France, for example, is probably higher at the end of the twentieth century than it was at the beginning. Will we have the answers?

## The Blind Man and His Daughter

**To continue the metaphor, we could say that Oedipus triumphed over the sphinx and became king of Thebes in the same way that science seemed to be on the verge of victory at the end of the nineteenth century. But it is with eyes gouged out that Oedipus is leaving Thebes accompanied by his daughter Antigone, who now shows him the way.**

Oedipus' ordeal is ultimately beneficial: while briefly king of Thebes he had the time to measure the extent of his own ignorance. We are now entering the new century as blind men, guided by what little reason, what little wisdom, we still have left. And leaning on electronic crutches, whose fragility we are well aware of.

**It is impossible to judge an age as long as we lack the necessary distance from it. Yet with Jean Audouze you nevertheless drew up a list of the great paradoxes that seem to characterize our modern societies, as you were just saying. Could you remind us what they were?**

The twentieth century is above all the century of the population explosion, or so it seems to me, at any rate. The world population curve climbs very gently for fifty centuries, and even dips occasionally, and then suddenly, from 1929–30 onwards, there has been a meteoric rise. In one century the world's population has increased by a factor of seven. Now, at the same time as the birth rate has shot up – and this is the first of our paradoxes – deserts have grown in size. Desertification has proceeded at the same rate as overpopulation. The more laden the planet becomes with human lives, the more we see populations crowding into particular zones and abandoning previously cultivated areas to the mercy of the elements. Accepting the challenge of desertification would have been just our thing. Why haven't we done so? It's worrying how we've simply given up.

**You also pointed out that the communications era is also the age of loneliness.**

One can best express it by borrowing a fine expression of Valéry's, who talks of '*la multiplication des seuls*' [the proliferation of singles]. The more we invent ways of communicating, the more people experience loneliness. This sense of solitude was never expressed by poets of ancient times to the extent that it is by the artists of our own time. Whereas we can well imagine the isolation in which the individual lived in previous centuries, without a postal service or a fax machine or a telephone, and travelling from town to town at the speed of the horse. The sense of solitude appears with the Romantics. But the real champions of spleen and anguish are the poets, playwrights and film-makers of the twentieth century.

**Is this feeling linked to a certain loosening in family and social ties, to social reform programmes losing some of their legitimacy or else to the absence of God?**

The 'absent God' is certainly not without relevance to the disintegration of social ties. The fact of going to Mass together and praying together most certainly constituted that sort of bonding between human beings. It helped people struggle against anguish, helped them sleep better. No doubt about it.

But in the West, at any rate, we have separated from God, cut ourselves off from other worlds. And you can't blame anyone; it's all perfectly justifiable. But, of course, in renouncing our illusions, which bound us to an imaginary world that had the power to reassure, we found ourselves alone. Alone in space – at least in immediate space – and alone in time: nothing before, nothing after. Just passing through, from one void to another.

**Perhaps there is a parallel to be drawn between the crisis of the modern world and what we call the 'crisis of adolescence'. Could it be that humanity, bombarded by disturbing items of news that occasionally cause it to question its normal view of existence, is now entering its adolescence, rather as the individual finds his world turned upside down at the age of twelve or thirteen when he discovers things about himself or those around him which his powers of understanding had not previously allowed him to grasp? In this way humanity would be going through a 'stage', going through periods of turbulence that are the guarantee of its future maturity. At stake in this crisis of adolescence, whatever its price, would be a certain 'growing up' on the part of human beings and nations.**

The optimist's vision of the future runs parallel to the pessimist's. As we said, we don't have reasons only to despair. Nor indeed only to hope. It's clear, for example, if we look around us, that we have entered the *Kali Yuga*. The lesson of present-day Algeria is that people have begun to carry out massacres for massacres' sake. Think of Rwanda, think of the Hutus and the Tutsis, of the end of Bosnia-Hercegovina, of Algeria and Colombia and now Mexico. I don't kill you for a particular reason any more, I kill for the sake of killing you. *Kali Yuga*: assassinations both inexplicable and without expiation. Sociologists also talk about the 'Ratopolis syndrome'. You know the principle: put rats in a certain environment, increase the number, but increase their ration of food at the same time. Once the numbers reach a certain level, they start killing each other savagely even if they have enough to eat and drink. It would be interesting to relate the question of the end of times to the end of spaces, and to consider the notion of living space which, in the case of what we've just been talking about, is perhaps absolutely relevant. The idea has been marked politically by Nazism in such a despicable way that we don't dare talk about it any more. But perhaps it's a much more fundamental idea than we think. It is for rats, at any rate.

**So these massacres carried out for no apparent reason might be connected with some obscure sense of a lack or loss of space?**

It's a difficult notion to be precise about. It isn't objective. Take a crowd in India. It's perfectly tolerable when, as I have done, you're taking part in one of those great pilgrimages they have there from time to time. I found myself stuck fast in a sea of several million people, reduced to moving with the flow of the crowd, i.e. deprived of all means of personal initiative. And it felt rather good. Who knows if we could tolerate this level of crowd density in the West?

**And when one comes back to France, the streets seem empty. But let's go back to the paradoxes you began to discuss.**

Next paradox. No other period in history has invented and produced so many consumable goods, starting with money itself. Consumer goods have never been as plentiful, as desirable, as accessible, while at the same time the gap in living standards continues to grow, making the poor even poorer and leaving them feeling even more deprived. Every society, even the richest, now has its pariahs, and you even see entire nations reduced to beggary! Thus the experts are predicting imminent famine in the Niger, while we disappear under mountains of surplus food.

**In *Violence and Compassion: Dialogues on Life Today*\* you wrote that the disparity in wealth between rich and poor countries was of the order of 1 to 5 at the end of the seventeenth century and is now, at the end of the twentieth century, 1 to 4,000.**

\* Doubleday Books (1996).

The ratio of 1 to 5 holds, I think, for the end of the reign of Louis XIV. The ratio had increased by the 1970s to 1 to 800. One can bet that the disparity is even greater now, and indeed probably about 1 to 4,000. And the economic hegemony of the United States, where money has ruled supreme for so long, doesn't help.

A further paradox consists in the present mania for making more and more copies and reproductions and imitations of things – Eco is very good on this subject* – even to the extent of inventing and distributing the virtual image, composed outside all reality, whereas at the same time we are witnessing an extraordinary renewal in the theatre. Exhibitions of paintings by the great masters attract large crowds, and in each case the viewing public manifests a real, almost maniacal passion for the original work. In a different area, no period in history has allowed atheism to speak out so powerfully, with so much freedom and clarity – we have even seen a huge empire rise up on the basis of materialism alone – while at the same time new forms of religion are appearing all over the place which, while proclaiming their own spirituality, do not shrink from having recourse to the most cruel violence in order to establish their power on earth. The irrational is flourishing everywhere. Mediums have an annual fair which one can go and visit. Newspapers contain ridiculous astrology sections, but which are no doubt much appreciated by their readers. A never-ending series of cranks are blithely invited on to the television to tell of their encounters with strange visitors from Venus, their out-of-(astral) body experiences, who they were in their previous reincarnation (always someone flattering), their various experiences of second sight, and I don't know what else.

**Isn't it inherently a bit high-handed to proclaim the death of God?**

In 1968 Buñuel and I wrote La Voie lactée [The Milky Way], a film which is set in the world of heresies specific to the Christian Church. Two latter-day pilgrims set off for Santiago de Compostela, and the point of the film is to have each conversation bear on the question of heresy. At the time everybody thought we were mad: what could they be thinking of, making a film about heresies? In 1968 God was dead. Everything had become politicized – at work, in the family, at

* In La Guerre du Faux, Paris, Grasset (1985).

school – the only way was the political way. The film came out in 1969, but if you see it today, it will perhaps seem to you to be an exploration of fanaticism with sadly topical echoes.

**And now it is the politicians' turn to go through a bad patch.**

Another paradox Jean Audouze and I drew attention to was one we've already touched on: the discoveries and achievements of science are so remarkable that most of the time they remain unintelligible to us, hermetically sealed, and the main beneficiary would seem, in the end, to be ignorance. It may even be the case that this ignorance is systematically appealed to, and error systematically taught: I'm referring, of course, to the fanatical and intolerant discourse which can be heard all over the world and which, needless to say, is just the noise people make when they've lost the argument.

**You talked about the gulf which separates the small group of people who keep up-to-date with scientific progress and the great mass of people who are absent from the debate and haven't the slightest interest in it. So the twentieth century hasn't bridged this gulf as it claimed to be doing?**

There has always been this wide and persistent gulf between a handful of people who possess knowledge and the great mass of people. For example, when the Venetians began to engage in world trade, it was very advantageous to them to know distances and how long it took to get from one place to another. The secrets of construction on cathedral building sites, the secrets of navigation, were rarely divulged. From the end of the seventeenth century, with the renewal of pedagogy, the gradual introduction of education for all during the nineteenth century, and free, obligatory school attendance, it was hoped that the gulf would be bridged. But it never is bridged. One of our last illusions – of my generation, I mean – was television. We imagined that television would be a means of diffusing knowledge, over the heads of all authority, across all barriers, and reaching people directly in their homes: in short, thanks to television, we were going to achieve a real increase in the average level of education. What a delusion! The only country in the world that has tried to use television as a pedagogical instrument is India. Indira Gandhi and her ministers imposed educational programmes for twenty years. The Indian people have made considerable progress in the acquisition of knowledge, which has allowed them to reach a very respectable level in the domain of international science. With us the opposite has occurred. The crudest of commercial criteria have prevailed.

**Perhaps where we failed with television, we will succeed with the Internet.**

Are we really worthy to communicate? That's the great objection that can be raised against communication. Given what we are, that we are likely to transmit much more evil than good, wouldn't it be better if we were forbidden to communicate? Isn't our vast 'communications network' in fact, contrary to appearances, a pernicious instrument, one of the last inventions of the *Kali Yuga*?

**How would you distinguish between knowledge and experience?**

Marguerite Duras used to say that knowledge is what we learn at school, whereas experience is the knowledge we acquire by ourselves. Experience can only supplement knowledge. It allows us to use knowledge and not be its slave. What we realize today is that knowledge necessarily entails ignorance. The reason being that if you really want to know about something, if you want to possess a precise knowledge of some particular field, you have no time left over to explore everything else. You have to condemn yourself to being ignorant. But what matters is not how much knowledge or wisdom of experience you have, but *prajna* – your aptitude for acquiring them, the ability to get to the bottom of things.

**The so-called 'hard' sciences we've been talking about put me in mind of Dali's limp watches. Didn't he have a premonition of this 'end of time' that we're discussing? What's the point in having limp watches?**

It must be said that certain expressions that have passed into popular usage are, strictly speaking, meaningless. What is a curved space, for example?

**The answer is in René Daumal's *Le Mont analogue*.**

And in Dali's limp watches. Dali is using them to suggest the possibility of time melting. Of time being like soft caramel. And why not? Eluard called Dali 'the thought machine'. He was a very strange man, with a great mind, yet very blinkered about certain things: about money, for example. Contrary to what people think, it was Gala who took care of that side of things. But his failings apart, he was capable of the most extraordinary intuitive insights. We were talking about the limp watches, but his figures of people with drawers in them probably rank among the images of the century.

**His Christ seen from above is also reminiscent of those synthetic images you were talking about earlier, when the camera can move around its subject . . . and even of Dali himself, who seemed to be an integral part of his work and its message.**

In a certain sense he was also a product of the media, which indeed he manipulated with unrivalled genius. He is a striking caricature of man in the twentieth century. The question remains whether his extravagant posturings were a smokescreen to conceal the vacuity of his art or whether in fact they provided a cover under which he could work towards a coherent and highly organized body of work. As usual, only posterity will be able to answer that question. That's what posterity's for: to make adjustments to our knowledge, and even to our tastes. It's the old story: 'Tomorrow we shall know.'

## The Watchmakers' Secret

Peter Brook once recounted this story to me of how an old watchmaker had told him that at the end of the seventeenth century all the watchmakers decided to get together to regulate the speed of ticking and to make it go progressively faster from century to century.

**Sounds like the opening lines of a chapter in Umberto Eco's**
***Foucault's Pendulum.***

The length of a second doesn't change. But the way we measure time does. And it's true. When I was a child we had an old clock at our house in the country which used to give a slow 'bong, bong'. Now it's all tick-tock-tick-tock-tick-tock, as if the movement itself were trying to keep up with the rhythm of modern life. Did you know that you must be careful not to have an alarm clock on your bedside table, next to your ear when you're asleep, because apparently our heart tends to match its beat to the ticking of the clock? If the ticking gets faster and faster, just think what that's going to do to our pulse!

**Why did the watchmakers want to speed up ticking?**

To bring it into line with the pace at which people live, I suppose. One can just imagine these old watchmakers turning up to their meeting and saying: 'It's true, you know, history's moving faster and faster. We really ought to speed up the movements in our clocks a bit.' A secret society of watchmakers secretly deciding how fast the world's clocks and watches should tick . . . *Si non e vero* . . .

**We've been led to believe that we live longer now, but perhaps it
isn't true at all. Perhaps we're not as old as we think. In fact you
may be no more than thirty . . .**

No, no. As I said, time itself doesn't change. It's the rhythm, our way of reading time, that changes. Since everything is arbitrary, this ticking – whether it be fast or slow – makes no difference to the length of a second, nor to the ageing process. Contrary to what many people believe, the ticking of an alarm clock doesn't mark out the seconds. It has been arbitrarily regulated by the watchmakers. By the watchmakers' sect! In the past you could count a good second between the tick and the tock, whereas now our tick and tock follow at what would seem a quite vertiginous rate to our great-grandparents'!

**So the ticking doesn't depend on the way clocks have to be made?**

Absolutely not. It's simply a way of perceiving time through sound. One more illusion to add to the list. The impression has to be given that time is going faster, because society is moving faster. After that conversation with Peter Brook about watchmakers, I met an Indian friend, Moshe Agashi, a fascinating person who is simultaneously a child psychiatrist, a famous film actor and the director of the film school at Poona where I was working. We've known each other for ten or fifteen years. He came to see me a fortnight ago and spent two hours here. A very shrewd, subtle man. Naturally, we began to talk about time. I told him my story about the watchmakers, which he loved, and he said: 'Have you noticed how our watches – the numerical, digital ones – simply display a number on the face of the watch?' I said that indeed I had noticed this small fact. Then he said: 'Have you noticed anything else?' I said nothing, waiting for all to be revealed.

**So are we!**

'On digital watches,' he said, 'a small rectangle gives the time, but the face of the watch is mute. You see a number, a point in time, but that's all. We have watches that tell us what time it is, but not what time it isn't.' That seemed to me truly luminous! He continued:

> When you look at a watch dial for the time, that time is situated within the circle of time. You immediately recall what you have done in the course of the day, where you were this morning, what time it was when you bumped into your friend, you remember when dusk is going to fall, and you see the time that's left before bedtime, when you'll go to bed sure in the knowledge of another day well spent, and with the certainty also that on the following day time will resume its daily course around your watch. If all you've got is a little rectangle, you have to live life as a series of moments, and you lose all true measure of time.

It seems to me that this loss of time is what our book is all about.

**Talking of which, there are also those big clocks at the Beaubourg and the Eiffel Tower which will stop in the year 2000.**

It's the same thing: no bearings, no context.

**Sociologists claim that young people nowadays have lost all sense of the past, that they've lost all knowledge of what used to constitute the memory of previous generations. They are the apostles of the Immediate . . . which just happens to contain the word 'media'.**

It's the watches that have done it!

**Living without a past is rather like walking along a tight-rope over the abyss, and without a safety net. If the present doesn't suit you, you've nowhere else to go.**

There have been other stories to savour. In 1582, as Gould recalls, Pope Gregory decided to reform the calendar. So we went over to the so-called Gregorian calendar. In the process they suddenly abolished ten days, and we went straight from Thursday, 4 October to Friday, 15 October. Yet another hole in time, another piece of time that has been well and truly *lost*.

## The Age of Lawyers

**Isn't it true that people in the West find it difficult or even impossible to talk about time?**

In Hong Kong last year I heard another story about chronology, which I will pass on, for what it's worth. It's about an old Chinaman who realized recently that in conventional dating we've left out a whole year. It's quite simple: you open your dictionary and look under the name of the Emperor Augustus, for example. Born in 63 BC, he died in AD 14. We add 14 to 63, which means he lived for seventy-seven years. But within these seventy-seven years, the old Chinaman pointed out, the year zero, the supposed year of Christ's birth, has been forgotten. So Augustus in fact lived for seventy-eight years. All the people in Antiquity whose lives spanned this arbitrary break in time therefore lived one year longer than we thought. Gould explains this phenomenon by the fact that, at the time the calculations were made, people didn't know about the number zero. Our time depends very much on us.

**One only has to think of the impossibility we face, twice a year, when we put our watches backwards or forwards, of situating ourselves in time. For some people it represents a brief moment of distress.**

We're about to celebrate the year 2000, when the whole thing is completely meaningless. It's not the end of the twentieth century, nor the beginning of the twenty-first century. It's simply a passing from one to two. An arithmetical feast.

**But even if this figure of 2000 isn't based on any reality, it nevertheless represents a cultural reality that is undeniably powerful. One has only to think of all the problems that this transition to the number two is going to create, notably in areas where the computer rules.**

This problem of the millennium bug seems to me, quite literally, marvellous. Eco is good at showing how revealing the problem is. An apparent catastrophe is foretold. Another end of time.

**In a very hard-hitting issue of the *Courrier International* we are told that the professional category which stands to profit the most from this transition from one century to another is lawyers, because every company is going to turn on the people who equipped them with the computing systems that will suddenly be rendered obsolete by the arrival of the year 2000.**

It is plain that if there is one profession which need have no worries in the coming centuries and which will not be adding to the ranks of the unemployed, it is indeed the legal profession. Our descendants will inherit an unimaginable number of problems in every domain. In the area of copyright, which I know a bit about, some of these problems will be totally insoluble.

**What do you think about these delayed-action ends of time? Men who are judged several years after the crimes they have committed? People are saying it may take 300 years to locate all the anti-personnel mines buried beneath African soil . . .**

And fifty years to clear the mines from Papon! Your question immediately made me think of nuclear waste as well. We're taking mad gambles with our future. Our attitude is a bit like that of those optimistic people who have themselves sealed in cryogenic cylinders. They've died of an illness which they reckoned, while they were still alive, that science would be able to cure them of in the near future. So they have their bodies preserved in that expectation. We're taking the same sort of gamble. We're betting that in a hundred years' time we'll know how to repair the damage which, two or three generations earlier, we deliberately incurred. Why not imagine, for example, that tomorrow's satellites will be able to clear any given area of mines? The same applies to nuclear waste.

**Hölderlin wrote, 'Where danger grows, there grows also the means of our protection.'**

In other words, it's at times of great physical and moral anguish that the great saints appear. Perhaps so. But the fact remains that we're taking some outrageous gambles. We're banking on something becoming possible that for us still remains impossible.

**What attitude should we take towards those who have placed the beauty of the world in danger? One of indulgence?**

It is sometimes impossible, within the space of a single generation, to pardon a man for the things he has done wrong in his youth: as in the example of Papon. We have sentenced him for what he did fifty years ago. But the point is: is he the same man? We are wagering that he is. And yet there is a whole body of writing which says that he isn't. For Restif de la Bretonne, for example, a man who has spent thirty years in prison is no longer the same man when he gets out. Yes, a certain idea of justice can lead us to punish a man for the wrongs he has committed several decades earlier, and no doubt you are going to point out that Papon has not spent thirty years in prison.

Which is perfectly true. But this idea of justice becomes crazy if we try and apply it over several generations. We cannot make a people or a family or a group pay for crimes committed several centuries earlier. I remember the example of a respectable family being deemed a family of thieves just because in the sixteenth century a member of this family was caught stealing a sheaf of corn. It makes a mockery of our system of justice.

**But aren't we, more or less, held responsible for the misbehaviour of Adam and Eve?**

Mind you, if you believe that old tale, men are ever so slightly less guilty than women! But seriously. We cannot reasonably believe in this notion of some original sin that we have a duty to expiate – except at the cost of an almost unforgivable effort of naivety. Jean Delumeau puts it very well. On the other hand, reading this myth leads us to ask ourselves questions about the human race and to wonder if in fact it may not indeed be guilty. It offers us a quite astonishing perspective on ourselves: we are born guilty. How would you describe the human race? The human race is guilty. Guilty of what? Just guilty.

## Withdrawing from the World

**The millennium bug is one thing, but the ecological dangers facing the planet are much more threatening clouds on the third millennium's horizon. Humanity is in a position to self-destruct, and that must be what is unambiguously different about the age we live in.**

Does it really want to? It does not appear to have gone very far down that particular road. No one has ever seriously thought of blowing up the world.

**It's the monsters we ourselves have created that tomorrow will
devour us.**

The difficulty, of course – no matter what the means of communication at our disposal – is the degree of ignorance in which the great
majority of people live, even today. How can we instigate a common
programme of action to repair the damage, if most people don't
understand the need for urgency? Julius Caesar knew the earth was
round. He even knew its circumference – give or take a hundred
kilometres – thanks to Eratosthenes, who had calculated the distance
in the third century BC. A small group of people round Caesar
probably shared this knowledge, educated people who had heard of
these celebrated calculations. But how many Romans or Greeks or
Barbarians were in the know? A tiny number. It was a piece of
knowledge reserved for a small number of people. Forty per cent of
French people still think that the sun goes round the earth.

**The globalization of the problems, however, will necessarily require
solutions at a planetary level. And yet it is precisely at this time
of globalization that we feel the need to fence off our own sphere
of action, the need to narrow our focus, the temptation to cut
ourselves off.**

You have put your finger on a problem that, personally, I find very
troublesome. The problem of non-engagement. What should one
refuse? In the name of what? Why? And to what degree? We cannot
accept everything. We cannot, despite our best efforts, be well-
informed about everything. Among all the technical advances on
offer, there isn't one that stretches time, or gives us more than two
eyes or more synapses in our brain. We remain physically the same,
and yet we are confronted by a range of possibilities, distractions
and knowledge that is practically limitless. Thus I am obliged to
refuse something. Necessarily. Otherwise I shall be lost, I shall despair.
I shall lose my mind and go mad. The temptation of certain cults is
to refuse everything, to say: This world is not my world, I shall chuck
my television out of the window, I shall get rid of my computer, and
I shall go off and live with a small group of friends. We shall think
up our own little stories, perhaps even create one or two myths, some
values and a pecking order among us, naturally. We will manage to

sort something out. If we find we need a leader, which we probably will, then here I am. We shall not cut ourselves off economically from the rest of the world, we are just going to refuse the information we are being bombarded with. This is a temptation we all feel, to varying degrees, and I'm not sure one should condemn it entirely. The desire to get away from it all, from the noise and the bustle, is an age-old monastic instinct. One is not necessarily cutting oneself off from the world, and one does not stop having a view about the world. The Byzantine emperors used to go off into the desert to consult the anchorites about the affairs of the empire, thinking that these ascetics would have a more profound insight into public matters than the ministers bogged down in the minutiae of temporal administration. This total non-engagement is not to be rejected out of hand. There is a certain beauty in it.

**But isn't it also rather dangerous to set oneself culturally and intellectually apart in this way?**

There are two things I find suspect. The first is choosing to be ignorant. What can cover the earth, asks the *Mahabharata*? Darkness, much more readily than light. Choosing ignorance is a dead end. When I see rabbinical schools in Paris, for example, teaching Jewish children that the world was created 6,322 years ago, that all the fossils we find lying about the place have been put there by the devil just to confuse us, my first reaction is to think to myself: poor children who will have to unlearn so much nonsense! And then, of course, I wonder about freedom of education. The second thing that strikes me as dangerous is this. A family I know refuses to have a television: the children do not watch television, but they hear about it all day long at school and are thoroughly perturbed. They have the impression that there exists alongside their own world another world to which they have no access. One cannot not know anything and one cannot know everything. Each of us has got to find a balance. So here we are again on the road to Thebes. Which path should tomorrow's sixteen- or eighteen-year-olds follow? In front of which sphinx should they stop? The range of possibilities has become unbelievably diverse, but so much so that you have every chance of missing the turning to *your* path, of losing your way.

**But wherever one withdraws to and however far away one goes, one still remains more or less in the same world, suspended between day and night, summer and winter, birth and death. Where do we get this idea of cutting ourselves off culturally and economically from the rest of the world and ceasing to have any further contact with it?**

It may be based on the conception people once used to have of the earth's dimensions. It used to appear huge, almost limitless, with room for every sort of experience. Right up to the end of the nineteenth century, all human action seemed to retain an element of harmlessness. If some breakaway group made a mess of things, that didn't necessarily entail a particular form of damage that would put the lives of the remainder in jeopardy. Even more than that: there weren't enough people on the planet. All the ancient texts insist on the fact that the earth is bare. I remember a hymn people used to sing when I was a child:

> Guide me on my way, O gentle Lord,
> Across this earth so bare.

If we were to help ourselves to a piece of land in all this immensity, we would not be taking anything away from other people, we would not be monopolizing anything. One hectare deducted from infinity would make no difference to infinity. When Charles Fourier described his phalanstery, he talked about establishing an ideal society within a place that would be protected from the outside, safe from its damaging effects, but doing it no harm.

**What distinguishes twentieth-century utopias from those of previous centuries is that they have been open-air laboratories in which the whole of humanity has been the guinea-pig.**

All utopias – including those attempted in the twentieth century – entail two problems that have never been solved. The first concerns the way in which the artificially created society is to be defended against the outside world. While some utopian communities develop determinedly pacific lifestyles, as in the case of one or two present-day cults, none can neglect the possibility of being attacked by a neighbouring country or group. If we can be attacked, then we have to defend ourselves. If we have to defend ourselves, then we need a military caste. We will need armaments and munitions. So we get caught up in a logic which is precisely the one we had wanted to condemn.

The second problem concerns menial tasks. They exist. Who's going to do them? Up until the French Revolution the problem did not arise. One class of men and women was born to serve the other. The menial tasks fell to them. But after the Revolution the issue became one of the rights of the individual, justice for all, equality of life, and the problem became acute. The lower classes might rise up in revolt at any moment. The nineteenth century was haunted by that prospect. Fourier imagined rota systems: each person would take it in turn, from district to district, to see to the emptying of night soil, or the chore of digging potatoes, etc. But the moment this rota system is put in place, there have to be *exceptions*, because there are always people who are ill, or not strong enough, or allergic, people who are richer than others and can afford to pay someone to replace them, which is what happened in the case of military service during the nineteenth century. The problem of menial tasks remained. It was going to be solved by Nazism and Communism. Nazism, for example, borrowed the ancient theory of helot classes. So the Germans imported workers from the countries they were occupying. Which meant, to cut a long story short, that the forced labour camps were merely the application of an Aristotelian principle.

**And these menial tasks now fall to immigrants?**

In our own utopian societies – for our societies are nothing if not technical utopias in action – during the 1950s and 1960s, we did indeed think we could solve the problem by turning to immigrant workers. Since we can't have slaves any more, then let's call on the populations of poor countries! And they were to experience working conditions in France that no French person would accept. This dangerous idea, which deep down was a form of racism, has brought us today to a situation that seems insoluble and that has led to the emergence of some nauseating political ideologies that are now gaining ground. It wasn't the appeal to foreign workers that was reprehensible, but the living conditions they were offered. Any society today that claims to be ideal, or tries to be so, always comes up against the same obstacle: how, in a world where nothing, or nearly nothing, remains secret for very long, can one arrange for such dramatically unequal sets of living conditions to coexist on the same soil?

Hence the absurd accusation that 'these foreigners have come to steal our jobs from us', hence this turning-in on ourselves, this desperate nationalism, which is no solution. For the time of isolation is past. Yes, there's another 'time' that's past. No population in the world can exist without exchanging with others. Numerous anthropologists have said as much. Cultural and racial autarchy is a road to the grave. It is every bit as unrealizable as its opposite – a single, uniform world culture.

The United States have quite clearly derived a great part of their strength from the extraordinary mix of peoples that have gone to make up their country. There is no other such example in history of a new nation being formed out of the inhabitants of all other nations. But in the end this federation of people has become so powerful that American culture is tempted to believe that it's the only culture in the whole world, and it is now experiencing a real sense of isolation. This feeling is quite widespread in the United States among, what are called, the 'educated classes'. Every time I go to teach at Columbia University or elsewhere, I hear my friends complaining that they don't seem to receive anything in return any more, from Japan or Europe, let alone from the rest of the world. Where can you see an African film in New York? The Americans themselves talk of their 'loneliness'. And they're aware of a danger here. Is it possible to conceive of a culture being self-sufficient, no matter how powerful it may be?

This dangerous feeling is becoming evident in the country which is today (but for how long will it remain?) the most powerful in the world. It's particularly typical that this economic and technical dominance is accompanied by a new kind of cultural arrogance. Since we're the richest, we're also the most sensitive, the most gifted, the most artistic, etc. The old saying – from Cicero, I think – 'Greece, having been conquered, conquered its savage conqueror,' is no longer relevant in this case. The United States is in the process of reducing artistic creation to a pure exercise in commercial exchange, or rather of trying in vain to invent a money culture. It won't last, of course. We can rely on time. It will sweep this empire away, like all the others.

**Isn't it possible to envisage that menial tasks will soon be carried out by robots?**

Yes, but who's going to make the robots? My wife spends less time in the kitchen than my mother used to. But while the dishwasher may have made women's work easier, you still have to ask the question: who makes our domestic robots and in what conditions?

**Slaves in Asia. But can one imagine humanity one day ceasing to live at the expense of a population of slaves?**

Yes, because utopias evolve, like everything else. Shall we be able, one day, to live without Peter exploiting Paul, without Peter and Paul being two peoples, two classes, two generations, two people, a man and a woman? A utopia of that kind is always there in front of us, like a carrot at the end of a stick. It's what impels us to act: the search for a better world.

**It's still the old story of 'tomorrow is another day'. Shouldn't we view this rhetoric of hope with some suspicion?**

If we get rid of this hope, if we give in to cynicism, to 'blaséism' if I may call it such then we're lost. We'll just go back into our little shell and live to a miserable old age, as De Gaulle used to say. I did feel like that at one point in my life, when I was approaching fifty. I'd achieved more or less what I'd wanted to achieve in my professional life. I had enough money to retire on and go and spend the rest of my days living quietly in the country. I could have been happy raising a little statue to myself and, possibly, cultivating my bank account. But a certain sense of gratitude saved me from that wrong road. Coming from humble origins, I felt the moment had come to give back a bit of what I had received. I undertook a number of commitments, convinced I could do some good. A society without utopian thought is inconceivable. Utopia, in the sense of wanting something better. We all know that lazy, sleepy feeling that persuades us that the society we live in is generally OK, that we can hardly hope for anything much better, that we ought to leave things as they are and avoid risky undertakings. That's somewhat the traditional attitude of mind shared by a large section of what we call the 'Right'. But there exists

– in a different relationship with time – another way of envisaging things, another attitude of mind, which strikes me as quite Buddhist; and in this sense, it seems to me, the Left is Buddhist by definition.

**Well, that should hit the headlines!**

Why is Buddhism left-wing? Quite simply because it admits, as perhaps the most fundamental of innermost components, the notion of impermanence. There can be no abiding fixity. We live in time. Everything eludes us, including our self. Heraclitus says: 'We never bathe in the same river twice,' but Buddhism would add: 'And it's never the same person bathing twice.' Given this essential component, how can we allow a political regime to exist, whether utopian or realist, that wants to determine things once and for all?

**In any case impermanence cannot be conceived of without the notion of interdependence.**

Among the hundred concepts most commented on by different schools of Buddhist thought, impermanence and interdependence would seem to be the ones best able to illuminate the Buddha's teaching for us today. I grant you that Communist society in Russia did not provide us with the picture of a dynamic society. And yet, theoretically at least, Marxism is supposed to be a *dialectic*. It's still the old story of 'tomorrow is another day'. Five-year plans give the impression that society is on the move. But Communism had one idea in common with religions, and one that is seldom noted: the idea of time's new beginning. Perhaps Marxism has been our last transcendent philosophy, our last millenarianism?

## Space and Time: A Very Old Couple

**In the modern era revolutionary new ways of looking at time have
gone hand in hand with a new way of apprehending space.**

Yes, let's look at how our concept of space has evolved. It was round
about the fifteenth, sixteenth and seventeenth centuries that a new
approach to space slowly began to emerge. Up till then, as we were
saying, the earth was still huge, limitless. Not only was it the centre
of the universe but, in many people's eyes, it simply was the universe.
Period. For a medieval peasant the idea that he could go round the
world was absurd. Even the idea that he could go to the ends of the
earth was literally unthinkable. The first shift occurred at the time
of the great discoveries. Towards the end of the fifteenth century
people started realizing that it was possible to go round the world.
News of what Magellan had done created an enormous stir. The
earth now seemed like an isolated object, which would gradually
shrink in size till it became minuscule. A second shift can be seen
during the nineteenth century. Whereas up until then our means of
transport had scarcely evolved since Antiquity, and people in 1800
travelled at much the same speed as they had in the days of Julius
Caesar, things suddenly changed radically. The train, the automobile
and the aeroplane now made it possible to go round the world in
eighty days, and then in eighty hours or less. As the speed of travel
increased, the earth grew smaller and our perception of space altered.
But at the same time (and this was no coincidence) as Magellan was
circumnavigating the world, an obscure Polish canon by the name
of Copernicus was proving his contention that the earth is not the
centre of the universe. Hardly had the earth been conquered than it
ceased to be at the centre of things. In the same way, at the end of
the nineteenth century, the speed of transport was increasing in a
manner that had hitherto been inconceivable, yet the sun in its turn
ceased to be the centre of the universe. Our perception of the very
size of the earth is thus inseparable from our perception of its place
among all the other celestial bodies.

**And during the same period time became longer, and we went from thousands of years and millions of years to thousands of millions of years.**

And the two are related, you're quite right. Do you know in which year we stopped regarding the sun as the centre of the universe? In 1921.

**Scarcely one year before the first theory of the Big Bang was formulated.**

I don't believe that was a coincidence. I'm not presenting all this very well because, of course, it's not my field. All the same, one can't help noticing a disturbing simultaneity. Let's see if we can take things further. We began to lose interest in planet earth from the minute we left it and were able to observe it from the moon or a satellite. We discovered this little blue planet. So we were right after all: it really was round, isolated and probably unique of its kind, at any rate within the close vicinity. And it was very, very small, when seen from far away, for in the course of the twentieth century the universe has assumed proportions that border on the inconceivable. What does it mean to speak of a distance of 2,000 or 10,000 million light-years? Thus the planet changes in size as the true dimensions of the universe become known, and as new numbers come along to humble and bewilder us. 'In my bathroom this morning,' said Cioran (or words to that effect), 'I heard an astronomer on the radio talking about hundreds of millions of suns. I immediately stopped shaving: why bother to wash and get dressed any more?' Cioran is not alone: the sense of the infinite can be profoundly discouraging.

**That's one of the wounds of Narcissus that Freud talks about.**

Exactly. What a humiliation! We who thought that the earth was the centre of the universe, indeed was the universe, now discover that we don't even amount to a grain of sand on the limitless beach we call the universe. And just as we were experiencing this profound sense of humiliation, astrophysicists made an incredible discovery which, paradoxically, brought us into relation with that which defies comprehension: the universe may be unfathomable, but it's the same as us, it's composed of the same matter as us. We are made of the same elementary particles and the same atoms. What seemed lost in the distance, in a vast space, is rediscovered in an intimate relationship that might be called consubstantial. Our relationship with time is not so different from our relationship with space. When we talk of 12,000 million light-years, we're talking not only about distance but about an immense, stupefying, unimaginable length of time.

**Stephen Jay Gould says that the discovery of deep time in the nineteenth century was the greatest single scientific discovery of all. But do you see a causal link between this space that's getting bigger and this time that's getting faster?**

If the distance I have to cover, beyond the ancient boundaries of my village, is vastly greater than the distances for which my legs or my vehicle were designed, I have to think of faster means of travel, especially if there are obstacles in my path. I can just about imagine walking to China (some people have done so), but I shall never – without certain special technology – be able to reach America or land myself on the moon.

To conquer space, I must conquer time. I need to go faster and faster. Space and time are like Siamese twins. You can't summon one without the other coming along too. They are our two appointed companions, each of them takes us by the arm. And yet, if we are to believe the 'experts', this couple is thoroughly bizarre, for one of them – time – is unique, while the other – space – is multiple.

**How is that?**

Don't get me talking about things I know nothing about. The fact is that the scientists I know, or have read, have never been able to experiment with a second dimension of time. On the other hand, beyond the three usual dimensions we all know about, they now talk about space having ten or eleven dimensions. And some people predict even more. Whether from duty or inclination, scientists are much more speculative than they used to be. Having defined science in previous centuries as a rigorous activity that excluded a certain number of phenomena from its area of research, they now recognize that the frontiers between what can be scientifically known and everything else are much less clear-cut than they were a hundred years ago. Occasionally you even find them pulling a whole new universe out of a hat, without any experimental process having taken place – for how, after all, do you summon the stars to your laboratory? Not content with 'dark' or 'missing' matter, which they have known about for fifteen years or more and whose mass (which is inaccessible) is apparently nine times greater than the mass of our entire universe, they're now talking about a 'shadow universe' beyond that. And who knows what they'll think of next?

**Has 'dark matter' anything to do with antimatter?**

No, it's something different. We are relatively familiar with antimatter, which in any case represents only a very small part of the universe. Dark matter is not nuclear. It's of a different kind, of a different 'composition' from our matter. We can't know it, we can't analyse it. It is a reality that is radically foreign to us. We can no more enter into contact with it than we can with 'shadow' matter, which is the latest to be identified.

**Will this 'shadow universe' allow us to solve the great enigmas of science?**

How do you expect me to answer that? It is true that enigmas still remain. The Big Bang theory doesn't explain everything, apparently. I was having lunch recently with three high-powered scientists. After twenty minutes' conversation devoted precisely to these enigmas, we suddenly stopped talking. There was a long, surprising silence. We had reached the point where we couldn't speak any more. I was thinking of a sentence from the Persian poet Farid Oddin Attar, who wrote in the twelfth century: 'Sight and sun have the same root' (the word 'root' can also be translated as 'principle'). Michel Cassé has put it his own way: 'The sun's atom speaks to the atom of the eye in the language of light.'

During this silence I was wondering, and not for the first time, whether one or two of these ancient insights, which are sometimes magnificently expressed, did not relate to – indeed did not already intuitively sense – these enigmas that science faces today. For the first time, science and a number of different traditions are all in agreement that 'there is something else', without saying what exactly. Science – which has made huge discoveries in the course of this century – has also lost its arrogance. That's perhaps another paradox, but so much the better. I dream of founding a Centre for the Study of Paradox somewhere, which would approach reality *a contrario*, starting from the impossible. Paradox forces us to turn our thoughts inside out like a glove. In any event, it can be productive and amusing.

Having been rendered modest by its own advances, science recognizes these zones of silence too, and falls silent before them. An old Indian metaphor, about Krishna (the name means 'black'), has it that if we light a candle in the dark, the flame draws a circle of light which remains surrounded by the darkness. If you add one, then two candles, the circle gets bigger. Place 100,000 there, replace them with a sun, with a thousand suns, with a million suns, and the circle of light becomes prodigiously huge, but it is always surrounded by the black arms of Krishna. Such is the extraordinary elasticity of darkness.

**So the end of spaces would constitute a revolution in our way of experiencing space?**

My daughter is leaving for Montpellier by plane in fifteen minutes. She will be there in two hours' time. A hundred years ago it took us fifteen hours by train to cover that distance, and 200 years ago it took us a week. Space hasn't shrunk; what's changed is our capacity to traverse it. It's the shrinking of time that makes distances seem shorter.

Other forms of space have changed; theatrical space, for example. For a long time theatrical space was frontal and separate, conceived of as a spectacle performed by the lit for the unlit, by the active for the passive (in English, people used to talk about a 'two-rooms theatre'). This theatrical space has altered, actors and spectators have come closer together, have become one. Nowadays people talk about a 'one-room theatre'. Peter Brook sometimes wishes the audience and the actors would 'sleep in the same bed'. Not to mention synthetic images.

**Is virtual space still a kind of space?**

Good question. The synthetic image produced by the laser networking of a real object does not exist. It's no more than a mathematical garden. We can play with it, divide it in two, pass over and under it, get lost in new vertiginous whirls. Virtual space is well named. It has no real existence. Yet it is laden with multiple possibilities.

**Where did you first come across these synthetic images?**

I was interested in them from the beginning, about fifteen years ago. I was working at the time with a computer graphics designer and I asked him to make me an ancient vase, to light it (with imaginary projectors) and then to use his arsenal of buttons to transform it into a Sumerian vase from the third millennium BC. The young designer asked me: 'Is it a vase which has been discovered in the ground or under the sea?' I did like that question, I must say . . . Eight minutes later we were looking at a vase and were able to play around with it. But where were we? In which space and time? Freed from normal space, that's for sure. On the other hand, the time spent in front of the computer was real. Our watches could measure it. There's an interesting oddity: space is virtual, but time remained real. The old couple has separated.

**Isn't it a way of escaping from the world?**

One can get carried away with these games. Some of the people who let themselves be dragged into this place-without-darkness end up getting lost there. It allows them to experience extraordinary adventures, beside which their lives can seem very grey in comparison. Is that a reason to reject these games? No, of course not. Are the people who seek oblivion in this way different from those who sought oblivion in bars and taverns during the last century? Is our oblivion any worse than theirs?

**The end of spaces can be seen too in relation to globalization.**

People of my generation are astonished to learn that a crisis in South-East Asia can affect us. Previously, any crisis in a far-off place seemed, if anything, more likely to favour us. If a country was in difficulty somewhere, then things would probably go better for us. We need to break out of these mindsets. But we'll get used to it. That's not the most difficult part.

**The twentieth century has taken great delight in upsetting our relationship with time. The heroes of science fiction don't realize what barriers used to separate past, present and future. In *Back to the Future* the main character goes back to the past to help his father meet and marry his mother. These paradoxes that the cinema plays with show us, don't they, that time is a product of consciousness?**

Have you read *Le Voyageur imprudent* [*The Incautious Traveller*] by Barjavel? It tells the story of a time-traveller who returns to the age of the French Revolution. He gets into a fight with someone, then kills the person, who turns out to be his ancestor, and so he disappears at the same time. I'm also reminded of the American writer Paul Anderson, who wrote *Time Patrols*. He tells the story of how patrolmen would intervene in time to *preserve* the course of history. They must have been extraordinarily discreet not to intervene in the chain of cause and effect.

**This idea of travelling back in time is very recent.**

So it seems. We talked about the sixteenth century as a watershed, after which people in the West became fully aware of time and space. Western civilization settled into time like a river taking full possession of its bed. Soon people would call that time 'History'. If Malraux had one idea in his life, it was to say that the twentieth century is the century of Man in History. People in the past used to live more within the context of their own time and solely within their own time, in their own age, as narrowly defined. Whence, perhaps, their mental difficulty in seeing beyond it.

**Now we move more freely in time and we move more freely in space. To use the same image again, the twentieth century is the century when the river broke its banks.**

The best writer of science fiction is still Marcel Proust. You've only to look at the last page of *Remembrance of Things Past*, where the final word, precisely, is 'time'. Proust was obsessed by time at least as much as Prigogine. We ought to get them talking to each other. It seems to me that right up to his last page, to his last word, Proust is wondering, with anguish almost, whether he will have the time to finish his work, the time for time to be 'regained'. Time is such an integral part of his work, and he appears to have had an almost tactile sense of it, a sense that sustains and extends his thinking. We can see him attempting once again, and at the highest level, what theologians and philosophers have attempted throughout the ages: to gather all times into one time, to merge the objective into the subjective. Each part of his work, as a hard-won, daily victory over time, seems simultaneously to be part of some broader aspiration to eternity.

## The End of the Human Race is Not the End of the World

**So we can master space, as we have seen, and the twentieth century will have done everything to persuade us of the fact. But we are still time's slave.**

Yes, so it would seem, we can master space, or spaces. And we are time's slaves, most certainly. Everything we say or do or think is necessarily inscribed within time. And what if each sentence we utter were a wager with time, where time bets that we shall never be able to finish it? Sometimes this wager can be an almost poignant spectacle, on a par with the old, old fear that time may brutally and inexorably stop, that it is capable of destroying us at any fraction of a second. Looked at this way, the taut thread of our life would represent a very long series of victories over such a threat – until the moment of personal defeat that awaits each and every one of us. Remember what Lautréamont says, in the fifth 'chant' of *Les Chants de Maldoror*: 'But, it having been demonstrated that, by some extraordinary chance, I have not yet lost my life since that distant moment when, filled with trepidation, I began the previous sentence . . .' It's almost Proustian.

**In *The Sheltering Sky*, which Bertolucci adapted for the screen, the novelist Paul Bowles suddenly appears in person and says how he thinks he may have reached that moment in his life, in his time on earth, when he will have dreamt something for the last time, when he will have remembered certain events for the last time.**

Lévi-Strauss's *Mythologiques* end on the word 'nothing'. The author writes that after a certain time, whatever happens, there will be nothing left on earth. Nothing of what we have imagined, of what we have built, of what we have thought, of what we have remembered, of what we have dreamt. There won't even be any memory of this destruction left. Everything will have disappeared. 'Nothing.' The whole archive of human works, of human thoughts, will topple into the void. The universe, too, is inscribed within time. Like us it has a history, and like us it will have an end. This notion of the end of times and the end of spaces, of the end of the sense of time, is something it does one good to speculate about a little. The director of the Institute of Astrophysics in Paris, Alfred Vidal Madjar, dreams of making what he calls a cosmic year in the year 2000, that is, to chart the history of the world over one year.

**The original idea is said to have come from the astronomer Carl Sagan.**

If you situate the Big Bang on 1 January, you will have dinosaurs by November, I believe, and the arrival of *homo sapiens* a few minutes before the first stroke of midnight on 31 December. We are thus very young in the world, time's newcomers. But the most disturbing thing about this is to realize that if we go beyond the year, Lévi-Strauss's 'nothing' – the real end of time – is predicted for the following April. As far as our solar system is concerned, at least. But how are we going to move house? How are we going to change suns?

In 450,000 million years the sun will have burnt up all its energy and the earth will be uninhabitable. One solution would be to prolong the life of the sun artificially. Another would be to live somewhere else. But at the moment we're not capable of achieving such feats of technology.

Science lists the different scenarios for the end of the world: an asteroid colliding with the planet; global warming as a result of the damage to the ozone layer, leading to most of the inhabited parts of the world being covered by the sea; population explosion; water pollution; some disaster or other in one of the countless nuclear-waste sites; global warfare, etc. The future is far from being one long and peaceful river.

To be more precise, these would mean the end of our world, but not the end of the world. We can't even directly affect those planets which are closest to us in our solar system. So what about the planets engaged in other celestial ballets?

But by virtue of the principle which holds that the beating of a butterfly's wings in Asia can produce a catastrophe in America, shouldn't we be worried about the consequences that the disappearance of our world might have on the smooth running of the universe?

One needs to be careful about that cliché, which is theoretically true but which we have never actually seen in practice; and what's more, we mustn't forget the enormous distances and almost total emptiness separating galaxies and galaxy-clusters. We can distinguish three definitions of the end of time, which get progressively broader. First, the end of the human race; we're working on it. Second, the end of all forms of life on earth, thanks to us.

Apart from bacteria, according to the scientists.

Just getting rid of cockchafers takes some doing. Insects are very resistant. Coleoptera, it seems, have been found alive and well in the craters left by atomic explosions (though I don't think the same is true for H-bombs). And yet whole species, even species of insects, disappear before we even identify them. There are twentieth-century fossils already. Plutarch tells how, when Alexander was marching east, he took some Greek scientists and philosophers along with him. In one encounter these Greeks came up against some Hindu sages, the 'gymnosophists'. One question the Greeks asked was: 'Which animal is the most cunning?' The Indian reply came back: 'The one that man has not succeeded in identifying.'

**History does not relate whether Alexander's philosophers were impressed or disappointed.**

Another Greek question was: 'Which came first, day or night?' The Indian reply came back: 'Day. But it preceded night by only one day . . .' After the end of terrestrial life we shall pass to a final stage, when the destruction will spread beyond the earth to all the planets in the solar system, and even to the entire universe. Then God will discover that he made a mistake, that he shouldn't have created this world . . .

**But the religious vision of the end of time doesn't go like that. God doesn't think he's made a mistake! Creation has reached the final stage of its development, God's work is complete.**

So he'd only created it for a limited period? I don't understand.

**But yes. So that something might come into being. God grants a certain degree of freedom to his creatures, and then withdraws in order to allow them to experience this freedom. The time allotted to us to enjoy this freedom is also the time of God's withdrawal. Within this world from which God is absent is a world in which we search for him, in which he has left us free either to forget him or to rediscover him. And this period of time during which we are searching for God has an end. But the time in which we shall once more find ourselves in the presence of God is presented, of course, not as a punishment but as something to hope for. In this sense the Book of Revelation is not a book about sound and fury, as people usually think it is, but actually a book about hope.**

Which is no doubt why the Inquisitors used to save souls and destroy bodies. On the basis of these ethereal and angelic lucubrations, and in the name of a transcendental realm that is by definition unreal, legitimacy is conferred on the action which consists in destroying real immanence. What does it matter if I massacre this particular Indian community since I'm saving their souls! Justifying any thought or action in the name of some imaginary realm, however delightful this realm may be, is simply not acceptable. What is imaginary is not divisible into parts. As Borges says, theology is a form of the literary fantastic, whose quality can of course be appreciated, as in the case of what you have just been talking about, for example. I often find myself being fascinated by theological imaginings, but that's what they are, human imaginings. Justifying the worst kinds of human behaviour on the grounds of some secret divine plan is a form of madness. And a dangerous form. It's as though it were a matter of 'excusing God' for having created a world that is so manifestly imperfect, so steeped in blood that it obliges all living creatures to devour each other. So people imagine that God is hiding, that he's biding his time. But if he comes back and finds us in this state, worse off than we were to start with, where's the hope in that? If I were a believer, I'd be scared to death.

But fortunately, all that is just a form of madness. A religious form of madness that often goes further than other forms of madness and which remains an object of study that is both interesting and blood-curdling. It is by a 'divine fatwa' that Salman Rushdie, and others, have been condemned to death. In the name of a fantasy!

**The word of the prophets continues to issue like this from the mouths of people who have voluntarily adopted an extreme position as their way of coming to God.**

Of persuading themselves that they have come to him. One of the most baffling phenomena exhibited by the workings of the human mind is that it can end up believing – with total conviction, to the point of hallucination – in the reality of its own inventions. It constructs chimeras for itself and is then fiercely, sometimes violently, determined to proclaim that they exist, that they are true. This curious contradiction, in which subjectivity loses its way, can be found in the history of ideas, and even of science. But nowhere is it more spectacularly evident than in the history of religions.

Religions are human inventions that have evolved slowly over time. We have a fairly clear idea how they arose, how the first cults tentatively established themselves and then developed, how the first gods assumed various forms and functions, how they became fewer in number until finally there was just one. But there always comes a point in the course of this gradual evolution, when we end up believing in what we previously simply imagined. Rather as though we were to believe in the reality of dreams we once had.

**Have you yourself never been in a position to believe?**

As a child perhaps, since I was brought up as a Catholic. But not since the age of fifteen. Man invented the gods, then God: it's perfectly obvious. But the burning question remains: How is it that this high perversion of the human mind can have led – and is still leading – people to affirm transcendental realities of which, by definition, we can say nothing except that we have invented them? And there's an even stranger perversion: for, having affirmed that these 'realities' are baffling, that they are 'transcendental', beyond the reach of our understanding, we immediately start describing them, dissecting them minutely, establishing God's attributes, the hierarchy of angels and goodness knows what else.

**Einstein used to say of these questions about the origin and purpose of things that not only had science not disposed of them (as scientism had claimed), but that they remained at the heart of all intellectual endeavour. Anyone incapable of asking himself these questions, he thought, would be incapable of living. One should continually confront these ultimate questions of meaning, of transcendence, with the same patience as though one were trying to empty the oceans with a tumbler.**

With the same patience and to the same effect! However, in this area at least, Einstein is not necessarily an absolute authority. Here, for whatever reason, we are talking about religion. Well, religions do not ask questions. They answer them. They are the very negation of the necessary asking of questions. What could be worse than a catechism? Science itself invites us to think that there is something else. But it takes good care not to tell us what that something is.

**Another reality, another level of understanding things.**

At a given moment in every tradition there is, as we were saying, a 'sense of'. I don't quite know how else to put it. It isn't a scientific truth, nor a revelation, it's a sense of something other. The sense of hidden forces, of another dimension, of other worlds. In every philosophical or religious tradition we find this 'sense of'. As soon as it appears, the priests are there, ready and willing to interpret it. You must learn it by heart and recite it every Sunday. Buddhism has avoided this urge to appropriate. It is perhaps the only tradition to make a real effort in this direction (even if it is not always successful).

## In Praise of Slowness

**We were talking about how powerless we feel in the face of time, of this arrow that some unseen bowman has let fly and which seems to be gathering speed as it approaches its target. Do you believe that we can tame time?**

I read an extraordinary article just recently about learning how to take things slowly. There are institutions in Germany that teach people how to act slowly. They tell them: 'Pick up your glass, lift it to your lips . . . slowly, much more slowly!' In a similar way, the t'ai chi that I have been practising on and off for a number of years gives one the sense of situating oneself differently within time. The most precious thing, in fact, if it can be achieved, is to distance oneself from time, to escape its tyranny.

People often ask me: 'But how do you manage to do so many things?' It's a question I must hear at least once a day, indeed it wastes a lot of my time! My reply is always the same, and I'm not just trying to be funny: 'Because I do them slowly.' I'm not a man in a hurry. True, there are a number of things you can do to save time, like not driving in Paris, for example, and taking the metro or a taxi instead, where you can read, work, prepare for your meetings, daydream, reflect, discuss . . . There are various tricks, but really what's essential is not to be in a hurry. When someone asks me to do something and I think it'll take me two months, I ask for three. Very often I grab my diary and cross out two half-days at random in the following week – for appointments with myself. When the half-days arrive I can do what I like with the time available. The main thing perhaps is not to have a digital watch, is to tame time, to take one's time rather than to be taken by it.

## Do you practise t'ai chi with someone Chinese?

I do it pretty much all over the place, in the Jardin du Luxembourg, in China, when I'm there. I do it on my own. I have done a lot of exercises of this sort during my life, especially with Peter Brook and his group. We've done so many different ones over the past twenty-four years that I have created a little routine for myself: one for the morning, one for the evening.

## A sequence of them, then?

Yes, but it's not really t'ai chi. It's just based on it. Everything depends, I think, on the nature of the individual. I'm a bit wary, even with t'ai chi, of group movement that imposes the same rhythm on everybody. I am a child of the countryside, and I've always been fairly energetic, active, I've always needed physical exercise. When I don't take any for a day or so, I don't feel well. Other people might find the physical regimen I impose on myself exhausting (a lot of walking, gymnastics, etc.), especially at the age of seventy-seven. And, indeed, it could be bad for them. Whereas if I don't do it, I miss it. T'ai chi isn't enough for me. I need something more energetic. Everyone has to achieve this kind of personal wisdom, and not try to measure themselves against other people – and not subject other people to the rules they have set for their own lives.

## But if you train on your own, isn't there the risk of taking the easy option, of just repeating what you've done already?

I'm not trying to win any medals. The calming exercise, for example, which I often do in the evening before going to bed, is a mixture of yoga and t'ai chi. One can easily find the right formula for oneself. There are leisure centres where you can join a group. When I'm directing theatre workshops, whether in South America or in India or in France, I look for the best way of creating a bond between the actors. When you're creating a group of seven, or fifteen, twenty people, the best way of bringing them together is to do some exercises together. When there is someone from China in the group, I ask them to lead a t'ai chi exercise. If there is an Indian, I ask for a different type of exercise. When it's a Japanese person, a different one again. But generally they're entertaining exercises, intended to make people relax and get closer to each other. No one's sent to prison if they make a mistake.

**The way we relate to actual time can vary considerably. If you're sitting on a cushion meditating and you suddenly decide to look at your watch, you discover either that only a few minutes have gone by or that you've been sitting there for a whole hour.**

What the experience of Zen meditation offers above all – and t'ai chi is just one of several forms – is a way of penetrating time. It's a subjective experience, of course, but one that allows a quite different attitude to time. It's no longer a matter of trying to control time, but rather of taming it, making it familiar, making it one's own. All sensations connected with the passage of time disappear during meditation. Time is rather like the wind. You don't see the wind; you see the branches it stirs, the dust it raises, but no one has actually seen the wind itself. I often make this comparison. Obviously we see the effects of time, but no one can say they have ever seen time itself. We are each of us a house of time. Our body bears every trace of it, like storm damage. We are the witnesses, the proof, of time. But we don't all grow old in the same way, we don't all die at the same age. Also, we know how happiness can burn up time, how days of happiness fly past, and how time is made longer by unhappiness, which is heavy and slow, and drags. So we don't all live in the same subjective time, which is, in fact, the only time that matters.

**It was Bergson, wasn't it, who was the first to talk of duration, of subjective time, in an attempt to 'deobjectivize' time?**

The first person in the West, I believe. Despite the fact that time has been considered our great master ever since Saint Augustine, our culture has produced very little reflection on time. One has to look to the artists. In a painting by Poussin, or Magritte, the painter may be trying out different approaches to time. In Magritte we'll find elements that seem to be in contradiction: a house with a lighted window and yet also a sun riding high in the sky. In Poussin a sequence of successive actions will sometimes be presented as simultaneous. In one or two Shakespeare plays a character comes on to the stage and stays there, while another character arrives, leaves, and others come, bringing news. By the time the first character leaves, five years have passed. Between the first and second acts of *Othello* there is a blatant chronological impossibility. So professors say: Shakespeare got it wrong, he made a mistake. But that's absurd.

**He's simply gone down time's fast lane.**

Artists have played with time more than philosophers have wanted to admit. I adapted a marvellous poem by the Persian writer Saadi, which Juliette Gréco sings: 'I have scarcely entered your room, than the door opens on to the day.' I see you, I take you in my arms, the door opens on to the day. Night is dissolved as though in an instant. Time seeks vengeance for the pleasures we enjoy.

## Dreams are Our Real Victory over Time

How might we conquer time, remove ourselves from time, play with time? There's a story in the *Mahabharata* which shows us how we might. A master and his disciple are walking in the countryside and stop beneath a tree. It's warm, they sit down. The master says to his disciple: 'I see a well over there. Will you go and fetch me some water?' The young disciple goes to the well, 500 metres away, where he meets a girl. They take a fancy to each other. They start talking. The young girl explains that she lives in the nearby village. The young man offers to carry her water jar for her. They go to the village. As the story unfolds, we become increasingly aware of the presence of time. The girl presents the young man to her family. They invite him to eat with them. It's getting late. They invite him to spend the night. He stays there. He is very attracted to the girl. He spends the next few days with her. In the end they get married. The young man works in the village. They have children. Then the girl's parents die; life goes on quite normally and then, one day, he suddenly remembers . . . that he had gone to fetch some water! His wife's hair has already turned white. He remembers that he is supposed to be taking water to his master who's waiting for him beneath the tree. So he hurries out of the village, fills a bowl with water and reaches the tree, where he finds his master who says to him: 'Good . . . You nearly kept me waiting.' Perhaps that had all happened in the split second of his exchanging a glance with the girl. A whole lifetime. But had that life really been lived?

In the film *In a Train One Evening* by Paul Delvaux, there's something similar. At one point the train in which Anouk Aimée and Yves Montand are travelling stops in the middle of the countryside. Everything is white with snow. Nobody knows what is going on. He gets out and walks to the nearest village, where they are celebrating Christmas. The party is in full swing. He finds himself dancing with a nurse. Suddenly something snaps, and we realize that the train has been involved in an accident.

Dreams are the real victory over time. And not only in films . . .

Have you noticed how people with short lives manage to organize their time so terribly well, when they have less of it than other people? Isn't it almost as if people like Mozart and Rimbaud had a premonition of their destiny being squeezed into a smaller number of years and hence *their* capacity to 'manage' this time-capital to the best possible effect? In their case everything starts very early, gets done in record time and seems more or less complete by the time death comes. Is it, then, that we receive a fund of time-capital when we're born and know, in some unconscious way, how long we are going to live?

The most disturbing case is that of Rimbaud. He said all he had to say by the age of seventeen.

And left the West in search of improbable climes. But his correspondence shows us a man disillusioned, disappointed by the worlds he travelled through. As if, having written what he had come into the world to write, he had then had to 'manage' a redundant amount of time.

Rimbaud didn't leave just like that. He was a wanderer, who crossed France on foot, went to Austria, came back . . . It wasn't a definitive departure. Nor was he a literary amateur. He did well in his studies. His genius didn't just spring up from nowhere. He excelled at writing Latin verse. He was abandoning all that. His time was up. When he left, he had published only *Une saison en enfer*, which (apart from seven copies) remained in the warehouse of a Belgian publisher. *Les Illuminations* and the *Reliquaire* were to be published without him. He would know nothing about it. He would leave, then die. He was never to know that he was Rimbaud.

**Just as we each have fingerprints, perhaps each of us has a time to live, a particular rhythm of life, a given amount of time to deploy in living.**

For all that dreams are our little victory over time, they themselves often have to contend with time. In my dreams, more often than not, I am late for something. I am going to miss the train. Or the plane is waiting and I have lost my luggage or my passport. The world is leaving without me. And yet dreams – in which it is said that a hundred images flash by in a second – is just where we ought to feel we have no worries, where we are allowed a bit of leeway. But the power of time is such that we continue to feel it, to obey it, even when our consciousness believed it had given it the slip. The fact is, lurking within our body cells, the master never gives up. Time's thief has not ceased his work.

Spinoza says somewhere that in each instant, here and now, we are immortal. There's nothing we can do about it: we just can't feel time. Yet we can think of no greater victory than the victory we would like to achieve over this consubstantial adversary. In the majority of cases the victory is bitter, for it is obtained only at the price of oblivion. An oblivion, moreover, which is so absolutely necessary, as Umberto Eco reminds us; an oblivion – a filtering out – without which we just wouldn't be able to live.

A man I was very fond of, the Spanish writer Jose Bergamin, used to refer in this context to 'eternal instantaneity' in a book I had the good fortune to translate.* We want to know and feel, as far as we

* *Le Clou brûlant*, Paris, Plon (1972).

possibly can, what came before us. And to know also what there is far in the future, even beyond the tomb. Our life, Bergamin says, is 'a perplexing and ecstatic experience of temporality'. It is a series of historic moments (and for many people that's all it is), punctuated by moments of eternity – which only poetry, in all its forms, can bring us. When we're fascinated by some occurrence, we say in common parlance that 'time stood still'. If only that were true! The most profound, the most beautiful effect a theatrical performance could have would be for the spectators to cease to age as they watched it. I can think of no higher aspiration. That time might deign for a moment to sit down among the audience and cease a while from its perennial labour. That – *in the meanwhile* – all of us might be granted access to some secret glade. That time itself might escape time. We could formulate the same wish for our conversation, for this book. What would it cost us? Merely the passage – the waste perhaps – of a few more seconds, as we write, then read, these final words.

*Conversations held in Paris on 15 October and 5*
*and 27 December 1997*

# Signs of the Times
*Umberto Eco*

## *Introduction*

All those who have followed Umberto Eco on his intellectual journey in recent years will not be surprised to find, after the palaeontologist, the historian of religion and the philosopher, the author of *The Name of the Rose* and the *Faith in Fakes* asking questions about the meaning that can reasonably be attributed to the 'end of time'. For who could be better placed to try and diagnose the illness which seems to be besetting the West as its second thousandth anniversary approaches than this itinerant university professor, the holder of a Chair of Semiotics at the University of Bologna, who spends his life in airports, and whom one might well suspect of travelling not only to keep out of the way of those who want to pester him but also so that he can write? And what do you suppose this ceaselessly vigilant mind does when he returns home? Do you suppose he is preoccupied by the fate of mankind? Not a bit of it. Comfortably seated in front of his computer in his Milan apartment, the 66-year-old scholar sets off, once night has fallen, on the Web's impenetrable byways, and it is in these corridors of time that he makes his diagnosis of the mental state of the planet.

A disciple and friend of Roland Barthes, he sets out to exercise what the author of *Mythologies* called 'the semiologist's flair': the ability to identify messages where one might suppose that there were only gestures, to sense signs where it would be easier to see nothing more than objects. This method, which he applies to the study of the whole range of signs that contemporary society sends out, has given rise to the genre of 'theoretical sketches', about which there has been much entertaining discussion in the Italian press; they reached their literary and humoristic culmination in his book *How to Travel with a Salmon.*\* Our interlocutor has also long been familiar with Saint Thomas Aquinas's work and sees in the civilization of the medieval West a summary version of the human mind's aspirations and tribulations, and hence an inexhaustible subject for interpretation. This has also led him to have a great deal to say about television, about the *Playboy* website, about mobile telephones and all those other strange delights of the modern world.

It is therefore not surprising to hear him claim that the world is 'open', in the sense that every individual reinvents it through the interpretation he makes of it; and that our propensity to state that we live in the most dangerous of all ages as far as the future of our species is concerned is a morbid condition that has been shared by more or less the whole of the human community at all times or at nearly all times. So Eco the academic is playing for time, and endeavouring to turn mankind's attention away from the objects around it, towards itself as a subject characterized by an inability to reach sound judgements. And Eco the ethnologist and student of our times is applying in the pages which follow his semiologist's intuition to its best effect, and reveals to us, in the words of Robert Maggiori, 'flashes of intelligence in the mishmash of ready-made opinions, prejudices and stereotypical language'.

**Here in Paris, near the Centre Beaubourg, we have got a great clock that is counting down second by second the time separating us from the year 2000. Do you think that people in the West have an inner awareness of this countdown?**

There is nothing to show that people are worried about being told of the coming third millennium. It's the press, and only the press, which persists in working up a psychosis about it. People are paying no attention to it, other than to arrange to celebrate twice as much as normal by booking a hotel room in Samoa or Fiji. No, I don't have the impression that there is any particular preoccupation with the year 2000 among society in general. There has always been a

\* Trans. William Weaver, Harcourt Brace (1994); also *Comment voyager avec un saumon*, Grasset (1998).

man brandishing a placard on the corner of Fifth Avenue bearing the words, 'The end is nigh'. There have always been, and always will be, people expecting the world to end. We are naturally inclined to link extraordinary events with AD 2000; but such events could just as easily have happened at another time, a time which has nothing to do with this date.

## The Myth about the Panic Terror of the Year 1000

### What about AD 1000?

As Stephen Jay Gould points out, a great deal was said in the nineteenth century about the last night of the first millennium, and the terrified crowds weeping in the churches. It has since been shown that there isn't a single document to support this hypothesis. I was twenty years old when I read Henri Focillon's book *The Year 1000*, and I can remember how astonished I was to discover that there was no fear of the year 1000. There were bouts of millenarian panic before the end of the millennium, or after it, but not at that precise date. Gould, however, cites the recent research of Richard Landes that has led scholars somewhat to go back on this opinion. Landes concedes that there may have been manifestations of terror here and there, stirred up by heretical sects, but that we don't have the documents any more to prove it because the Church (that is to say, the official culture of the day) wiped out all traces of the phenomenon, so to speak. These localized episodes were not recorded in order to prevent unease in the community at large.

As Jean Delumeau has said, the Church has responded to any upsurge of millenarianism by adopting the brilliant solution of Saint Augustine. The period of a thousand years of happiness on earth, of which the Book of Revelation spoke – an eagerly awaited period whose coming all millenarian movements were urged to hasten by violent means – was already there! And to cut short any argument on the point, Augustine added that the figure of 1,000 should not be taken literally. A thousand meant only a very long time. Yes, Christ would come again, but take your time. Don't live your lives in fear. By this sleight of hand, Augustine was able to destroy the conceptual basis of any hoped-for millenarian utopia.

**So why didn't Saint Augustine's interpretation manage to get rid of millenarian movements once and for all?**

Let's say that Saint Augustine was victorious at the level of official theology, but his interpretation was not up to calming social tensions or restraining the emotional drives of society as a whole. Which is tantamount to saying that millenarianism is neither a theological nor an exegetical problem . . .

**Stephen Jay Gould has also linked millenarian tensions and social problems.**

Quite rightly. Millenarianism has always been a popular movement. There has never been a millenarian emperor. Millenarians have always been people who are dissatisfied with a given state of affairs and who want to change it. Apocalyptic movements are in fact revolutionary in nature. That's why the Church and the authorities in general have always mistrusted them, to the point, as we have seen, of suppressing manifestations of them and making no reference to them, as in the year 1000. I'd like here to insert a brief comment which I believe to be amusing. To do this, I need to go back to the debate about the first millennium. In 1996 some American specialists of the topic came together at a conference in Boston; it was Richard Landes himself who invited me, as I had once done some work on the *Apocalypse* of Saint Beatus of Liebana. A number of journalists rushed along, thinking that historians would be there who would be speaking about the terror of the year 2000. We tried to explain to them that the conference was about the preceding millennium, and that even then there wasn't really any evidence of these terrors. But they asked the same questions as you have: is there a fear of the year 2000? And my reply was the same: no, such fear is imaginary, and in reality people couldn't care a fig about it! The journalists then sank into the deepest gloom. If there weren't any fears to some degree connected with the transition to the third millennium, then there wasn't any scoop to be made, nothing to splash in big letters over tomorrow's papers. As a consequence, all that was left for the journalists to do was to make something up.

The moral of the story is interesting. The end of the first millennium didn't occur without giving rise here and there to a few reactions of fear, even if these were marginal. So much is probable. But the Church as the guardian of ideology and memory did its best to make sure that they weren't talked about. At the end of the second millennium it is obvious that these fears do not exist, except in a few marginal groups. But the media, who are today's guardians of ideology and memory, are doing their best to make sure that they are talked about. Because of the lack of archival evidence, we thought that there were no such fears during the night of 31 December 999. From a superabundance of archives, our descendants may come to believe that all of humanity was seized with terror on the night of the 31 December 1999 . . .

**Why is there such a difference?**

Because the Church's orders were: 'No publicity whatsoever!' The media's are: 'As much publicity as possible!'

## Paranoiac Visions

**Isn't there a potentially strange coincidence between civilization's present crisis and the turn of the millennium?**

The approaching end of the millennium is an opportunity for us to reflect on our history. If someone feels himself getting old, he thinks about drawing up his will and looking back over his life. The millennium is an interesting time in that it offers us the excuse to take stock, in the same way that a century ago, a voyage to Australia provided a pretext for putting one's papers in order. The year 2000 is a signal to us to examine ourselves; it's a memory prompt that will allow us to know at what point we fell ill and by what means we can get well again.

**Many epochs have considered themselves as living through the end of civilization . . .**

The end of a century always produces a feeling of exhaustion. As one gets closer to a date with two zeros in it, literature suddenly gets deluged by a wave of spleen. Think about the decadent movements of the end of the nineteenth century, the feeling that the Austro-Hungarian Empire was coming to an end, Nietzsche proclaiming the death of God . . . Such is the power of two zeros. I would point out to Jean-Claude Carrière that every generation has its *Kali Yuga*.

**This time, it's the magic of three zeros!**

Three zeros is even better than three sixes, 666, the year of the Beast. A feast day for numerologists!

**We've lost count of the books in which present-day occurrences are considered to be signs of the times and are made sense of in relation to coming catastrophes. To cite just one, the *Bible Code*.***

I was sent the proofs of this book with the request that I supply what in English is called a 'blurb', that is, a short piece in praise of the book to be printed on the inside back cover. In asking for my support, the publisher who sent me the proofs let slip that he hadn't grasped the fact that the precise point of my book *Foucault's Pendulum* is to make fun of books of that kind and of the people who see meaning in everything. By the way, I recently read that someone had applied the same code to another text with equally astonishing results. You can obviously make numbers mean what you like. What struck me, however, was not that someone had actually written or published *The Bible Code*. It also struck me that the author or publisher who read my *Foucault's Pendulum*, which, I admit, speaks about occultism, read it as though it were an occultist book! Such things are more common than you might believe. Those whom I had called the 'Diabolicals' in the book read it and rushed out to send me their own works.

* Michael Drosnin, *The Bible Code*, Simon and Schuster (1998).

**It was only to be expected that the Diabolicals, through whom you denounce what you call 'interpretative paranoia', should end up seeing you as a sympathizer.**

Obviously, otherwise I would not speak about interpretative paranoia in their case! But I cited this phenomenon in order to show that even associating an earthquake with the year 2000 is a symptom of interpretative paranoia. Do you know how many earthquakes there have been in the last millennium, even in years which do not end in two zeros?

**Nowadays, at a time when the signs of changes of the times or of civilization are proliferating, the Diabolicals are publishing countless treatises proclaiming the end of time.**

Ask yourself the question: is it the year 2000 or the fall of the Berlin Wall which creates such behaviour? At the moment when great ideologies collapse, man, who is by definition a religious animal, can only do one of four things. He can adopt a philosophical position – that's the aristocratic solution; or he can adhere to the official religion; or he can join a sect . . . The drawback of religion is that it generally leaves it up to you whether or not to follow its precepts, especially nowadays. In a curious way it is less protective than an ideology, such as Nazism, or Marxism of the Stalinist or Maoist varieties, which regulate every moment of your lives. On the other hand, a sect allows you to abdicate your free will in order to submit it to that of a guru, and to swap your ego for his. It is more in such circles that the end of time and the dawning of a new age are being talked about. But I should like to ask again whether we are sure that this phenomenon is linked to the end of the millennium. The ever-growing number of sects today seems to me to be a result of the collapse of the great ideologies.

**What is the fourth option?**

A sort of non-repressive sect that is less demanding than religion and more amusing than philosophy: the New Age, a complete syncretic movement, which accepts the truth of every position not requiring any rational warrant or any form of theology. Everything is taken on board, flying saucers as much as macrobiotics, Buddhism as much as pranotherapy. All you have to do is choose your own menu. It's 'do-it-yourself' religion. But this too I attribute to the collapse of ideology more than to the year 2000.

**What indications are there of the link between the fall of ideology and the development of the New Age movement?**

When the utopianism of 1968 ran into crisis, when the bell was tolled for 'red' terrorism in Germany and in Italy, when perestroika finally came along, the bookshop shelves, which had been filled with books on Marxism and on revolutionary mythology (with posters of Che Guevara and so on), came to be filled with books on what was then called the New Age. I even found Saint Augustine on the New Age shelves in a New York bookstore! This is a feature of the 1968 revolutionaries who have been converted to mysticism: because it has been shown that we cannot now change the world any longer, anything that might tend to prove the existence of another form of reality will be welcomed (too bad about the bourgeois scientific requirement of coherence: we'll freely associate radically different things). But all this tells us something too about the way in which many members of the 1968 generation experienced a revolution which has remained at the level of virtuality. Can we be certain whether the return to mysticism is a consequence of the crisis of 1968, or whether the events of 1968 are the first signs of crisis in 'scientific' Marxism and hence the first chapter of the New Age movement?

**That's an unexpected reversal of the normal interpretation.**

If you look for the roots of the 1968 movement in California, all the elements of the New Age movement will be found there: flower power, peyotl, Castañeda's *Don Juan* . . . * Many of the generation of 1968 are now Buddhist or New Age; some have become Catholics again. On Mount Athos I met a librarian monk who spoke excellent French; we spoke a bit about the Orthodox faith, and then we spoke about Paris. He at once asked me whether Julia Kristeva was still

* Carlos Castañeda, *The Teachings of Don Juan*, Penguin Books (1970).

married to Philippe Sollers. When I asked him how he could possibly know about such things, he told me that he had been present in the Sorbonne in May 1968 and that afterwards he had taken the road to Damascus and become a monk on Mount Athos. I then teased him a little about Orthodox liturgy. 'You're an intellectual,' I said, 'you know perfectly well that the icons you kiss during the mass are not real relics.' He replied that that wasn't where the problem lay: 'If you kiss the icons devoutly, then you will really experience their holy odour.' He hadn't forgotten his philological education; he didn't try to prove to me that they were authentic, he simply said that if I entered into the spirit of his faith, then they were true; which is not to say that they were authentic. I wonder whether he wasn't inspired by the same enthusiasm when he was on the barricades in Paris, as when he was drawn to the Holy Mountain (I'm using 'enthusiasm' here in its religious sense of 'zeal').

## All Men are Mortal

In your dialogue with Cardinal Martini,* you wrote that 'the preoccupation with the end of the world is nowadays more a feature of the secular than the Christian world. The Christian world turned this thought into an object of meditation, and the lay world pretended to ignore it while being haunted by it.' Can we speak about a lay apocalypse?

In his Apocalypse, John sees the sea become blood, the stars fall from the heavens, the locusts swarming up out of the bottomless pit, the armies of Gog and Magog being deployed, the Beast rising up out of the waters ... It's clear that today's secular world is not moved by this sort of description; we are moved instead by the wretched condition of one section of humanity, by acid rain, by holes in the ozone layer, by the proliferation of nuclear waste, by changes in the

* *Croire en quoi?* Translated from the Italian by Myriem Bouzaher, Paris, Rivages (1998).

climate, by glaciers melting, by certain species becoming extinct, by the incredible rate of scientific development, and so on. In the religious way of thinking, the end of time is an episode, a rite of passage which leads to the shining city, celestial Jerusalem. In a secular way of thinking, it's the end of everything, and that's why the thought of it tends to be repressed. This, as it happens, is regrettable, because meditation on death ought to be the central subject of any philosophy. But all too often we stop at 'Carpe diem! Eat, drink and be merry, for tomorrow we shall die.' If you raise the subject of death with lay people in Italy nowadays, they respond by saying, 'Let's not talk about it!' But why not? As it happens, I am a philosopher; thinking about death is my job! Why shouldn't I speak about my specialist area? In one of my letters to Cardinal Martini I tell the story I have told before of my meeting with an old Communist. At the time I was a young Catholic, and every evening at six o'clock in the town square, I used to meet up with this much older man, who was a fervent Communist. We used to have endless friendly but heated arguments. One day I asked him, in a provocative way, how he could, as an atheist, attribute any meaning to death. He replied: 'By asking for my funeral not to be a religious ceremony. In that way, I'll die, but I'll leave behind a message for others.'

I greatly admired this man, because he had an acute awareness of the continuity of history, as well as a sense of community. His own death took on meaning in his eyes in so far as he could use it to transmit something of value to others. It's a remarkable non-religious way of thinking about death. In secular society, you have to go to the educated classes to find such an ideal. On the other hand, even the lowliest believer, no matter how humble or uneducated, can be convinced that death is no more than a transition. Judaeo-Christianity made history out to be a journey, and in this history less attention is paid to the end of all things than to the sequence of transitions. The only thing to disappear completely on the day of the Last Judgement will be purgatory. And even then we won't lose much, because, according to the historian Jacques Le Goff, purgatory is a recent invention!

**What is the specific role of the Book of Revelation in Christian thought about the end of time?**

The function of the Book of Revelation is not to speak about the end of the world. It isn't about the depiction of earthly Jerusalem, but rather, celestial Jerusalem. All the thinking about the end of the world has its origins in a heretical interpretation of the Book of Revelation. This book recounts how the world will end, but that's not what it is about. Even if the text does ask questions about the future of earthly Jerusalem, its essential message is to let us know that celestial Jerusalem is already here. It has always been with us. The Book of Revelation is an ambiguous book which can give rise to both despair and hope.

**In the same way as you yourself made the connection in *The Name of the Rose*, there's a whole new flourishing genre of books which sets out to connect the tragic events we are now experiencing with certain passages from the Book of Revelation.**

I can prove to you that every age has interpreted certain events in the light of this apocalyptic text: events such as comets, cows with two heads, and so on, were all spoken of as signs foretelling a dramatic day of reckoning for the human race. Specialists are aware of this and write about it, but the general public refuses to believe it. Let's say that you have to console a friend who has been deserted by his wife. The man says to you: 'I can't go on living.' 'Come, come,' you say, 'all of us have been deserted, at least once if not more often, in our lives. It happens to everyone.' This argument has never consoled a sad lover. He thinks of his problem as graver than the ones you describe to him. In the same way, the argument that all men are mortal has never consoled a dying man! 'You're dying, old friend, but be reasonable, it happens to everyone!' If he has any strength left, he will slap you in the face. So what can you do to persuade people who believe that the end of the world is nigh that people from every past generation have seen it coming before they did? Do you say that it's a sort of recurrent dream, like the dream that our teeth are falling out or that we suddenly find ourselves naked in the middle of the street? No, they'd reply, this time it's more important than all the other times.

**Where does this need to think about the end of the world come from?**

It's a sort of optical illusion linked to the fact that we know men are mortal. Men are mortal, but should the world necessarily be so? Human beings are the only animals who know that they are bound to die. I have never met a dog capable of saying that all dogs are mortal. Man projects this fundamental idea on to the universe. If the man who is my father dies, won't the world in which I live die also? It's an intuitive move that cannot be prevented rationally, for a very simple reason: experience teaches us that men are mortal and that we will all die one day. But we don't have the same experience of the universe, because no one has experienced the end of the universe. Even if the world is no more than the aggregate of mortal beings, that doesn't mean that it is itself mortal.

The transference of our own experience on to that of the universe is a logical error about which Kant said a lot: we conceive of the idea of the world, the idea of God or the idea of liberty as though it is something which exceeds our sensory experience, but we make the mistake of applying categories to these ideas that are valid only within the limits of our sensory experience. One cannot apply to the world the laws which the world imposes on the objects of the world. We are taken in by the Greek idea (this reminds me of Plato) of the universe considered as a great animal. And by the way, what else is the Adam Kadmon of the cabbala? Any cosmogony starts from the personification of the constitutive elements of the universe which is considered to be a great animal. But the universe isn't an animal (any more than it is a mineral). Animals can become extinct without a certain 'condition of existence' which manifested itself through them also becoming extinct.

**Astrophysicists tell us that the universe has lasted so far about 13,000 million years and that it will perhaps last several hundreds of thousand million years. We're still right at the beginning.**

But as Jean-Claude Carrière has said, the end of the world is not the end of time itself. You and I are bound to die; the human race will also become extinct perhaps, if the sun dies out, and with it the galaxies with which we are familiar. But all that doesn't mean that the universe will die out. That for me is the positive message of the Book of Revelation: there will always be new heavens and new earths. In any case, our ideas about the universe are still very imprecise. Even if we know practically everything about the human body, we know practically nothing about the real dimensions of the universe or its age or the number of bodies which constitute it. So we turn to mythologies and occult theories, all irrational approaches to the problem.

**The search for origins has led science to push back further and further our intellectual horizons. Now you have reminded us that any human society works out its project of life inside certain temporal and spatial frontiers which it imposes on itself. Aren't we lacking such frontiers today?**

We have to resign ourselves to growing up. If this universe is without beginning and without end, and if it has no precise boundaries, then it becomes almost impossible to think about it in anthropological terms. We are then more likely to be in the position of being able to free ourselves from the obsessive idea that the universe must do as we do, and be born and die.

**But science has also revealed to us the historical dimension of the universe. Stars are born and die. The universe, too, will come to an end. This is the sense of what a scientist like Ilya Prigogine has set himself as a task: to rehabilitate the concept, rejected by classical physics, of time as irreversible.**

I don't want to get involved in issues which lie beyond my competence, but I have the impression that saying that time has directionality is not the same thing as saying that it has an end. Infinite evolution is conceivable. The problem of infinite evolution is very close to the old problem of the eternity of the world, which was discussed in the Middle Ages. Now Saint Thomas Aquinas, in so far as he was a saint, had a vested interest in showing that the world was not eternal, because such an idea makes the notion of a creator God almost superfluous. But because he was a saint (or a scholar of integrity, at any rate) he was forced to conclude that there is no rational way of demonstrating that the world is not eternal. One must believe it (says Saint Thomas) for reasons of faith. One cannot prove it. I have arrived at the same conclusions as Saint Thomas with regard to the directionality of time: one cannot prove that time comes to an end.

# Time is an Invention of Christianity

**You explore the issue of 'sick interpretation' in two of your novels and in some of your essays. One gets the impression that you are investigating here a sort of relationship of cause to effect which may have something to do with the problem of 'time's arrow'. Is this tendency to rush into the search for meanings linked in some way to the relationship the West has with anxiety-generating linear time?**

Quite right. Let's try to be clear on this point. I am not claiming that there is only one arrow of time. There may be more than we believe. Thinking along the same lines, I would not claim that there is one sort of geometry, Euclidian geometry, because there are many other sorts. All I would claim is that in daily life, when we have to hang a picture on a wall, we must follow Euclidian geometry and not Lobachevski's, and if we ask at what time the fast train from Paris which left at seven o'clock will arrive in Lyon, we have to think in terms of the time which our clocks obey and not in terms of Bergson's internal time consciousness. Now any tendency to interpretative paranoia – and as a consequence any esoteric or occultist thought, or any thought which claims to be part of the Great Tradition, or any New Age anti-modern thought (which sometimes styles itself as post-modern) – refuses to acknowledge the reality of the arrow of time, even if we regulate our daily affairs by a belief in it. Occultist thought has worked out a theory of correspondences, of resurgences, of reversals of cause and effect. Dante was a Rosicrucian because his writings manifestly foretell the coming of the Rosicrucian movements three centuries after his death! Occultists refuse to consider the fact that Rosicrucians had simply read Dante. They are always on the lookout for events that have already occurred. That is why many occultists refer themselves to Eastern patterns of thought which do not invest the arrow of time with the same meaning as we do. I'm obviously not an expert in Eastern philosophy like Carrière, but I do not think that an Indian or a Japanese engages in the sort of reasoning we find in Phaedrus's fable of the wolf and the lamb, in which it is said that the lamb, by drinking downstream of the wolf, disturbs him as he is drinking upstream. It's just that for certain Eastern religions and philosophies, relationships of cause and effect are only surface phenomena which have nothing to do with the metaphysics of an eternal cycle or an eternal return. So far so good. But Western occultist thought applies this indifference towards the arrow of time to the surface phenomena themselves, which seems crazy to me. This leads me to pronounce judgement: the lamb cannot disturb the wolf's water. Case closed. Contemporary science is the daughter of a Judaeo-Christian vision of the world. That vision may be wrong, but that's how things are. Those stories about the way science and Taoism are compatible with each other are all very fine, but please allow me to be a bit sceptical about them.

**Can you explain in a little more detail in what sense contemporary science is Judaeo-Christian?**

It would be sufficient to say that it was born in that milieu. If it had been born on Easter Island, one might think of other influences. But let's not joke about this; or rather let's not be too serious or too rigorous about it. Jewish Messianic thought (the expectation of something or someone who is still to come and who will alter the destiny of Israel) constrained Christian thought to invent history. The arrow of time does not exist in ancient mythology.

**So it was the Christians who let fly time's arrow?**

The arrow of time is indeed an invention of Christianity, but only in so far as Christianity is the heir of traditional Judaism. Although, for Christians, the Messiah has come, that's not enough: we have to think in terms of an earthly history (which goes from the present into the future, without any possible return) after which, on the second coming of Christ, celestial history will begin. This is, again, the message of the Book of Revelation. Hegel and Marx are unthinkable without Saint John the Divine. By contrast, the esoteric thought which emerges again after the Renaissance accepts the eternal return. According to this thought, everything that could be said had been said in the most remote past, and it was merely a matter of rediscovering a buried ancient wisdom. There was no progress of knowledge.

**Given the dominance of Western civilization, doesn't this vision of history which was begun by Christianity influence all the peoples of the earth?**

I am not sure about this. Look at the cargo-cult phenomenon in Polynesia and Melanesia. When the first European ships appeared on the horizon, bringing with them unknown goods, the natives thought that one day deities would disembark from them to bring them happiness. That to my mind is a typical millenarian attitude. The cargo-cult myth doesn't indicate that Melanesian and Polynesian populations began to believe in a version of history considered as constant progress. For the ancient Mexicans, for example, Cortez and his soldiers clearly were the incarnations of gods from across the sea, because it was from that direction, according to the mythology of these peoples, that the gods would come. Cortez took advantage of the Mexicans' credulity and remorselessly destroyed Montezuma's civilization. But this civilization died because of its own millenarian illusions, not because it harboured an idea of progress which was trampled under foot by Cortez's soldiers. The ancient Mexicans had no concept of progress.

**But modernity is constructed on the notion of progress: it's its great myth. Is this myth in the process of collapsing as our century draws to a close?**

I have stated that our Western civilization was born with the idea of a directionality in history that was closely linked to the idea of progress. But there are two ways in which progress can be understood. One is that we never go back on ourselves, that transformation is the law of nature as well as that of culture, and that even when we turn back to our past, we think about it in a way which produces something new. The other way of understanding progress is to think that everything which comes after is better than what existed before. The two ways are not the same. In making something different of the past, one can also produce monsters. The nineteenth century deified the idea of progress as infinite and irreversible improvement. Indeed, the Hegelian idea of cumulative progress is perhaps the great error of modern civilization. Our age has realized that progress is not necessarily continuous and cumulative. Progress can know phases of ascent and reversals. The nineteenth century marks both the moment at which this version of progress was widely celebrated and the beginning of a deep moral crisis. It brought forth a sort of fundamentalism about progress from which we must escape. Contemporary ecology perhaps represents most importantly and most momentously this questioning of progress.


## The Millennium Bug

**What do you make of the 'information technology apocalypse' which on 1 January 2000 poses a threat to the computers of the whole world?**

The real problem is not how to find a solution. As we have seen, that's a question of money. What plunges me into the deepest despair is how such a state of affairs could have come about; how so crude an error could have been committed by the geniuses who invented today's information technology, men who have radically transformed our ways of thinking, working and communicating. They weren't cavemen with a fuzzy conception of present and future, but men of our time, who know their history, who had learned that centuries usually come one after another. How could they not have realized, and I'm not speaking of 2,000 years but of less than thirty (only thirty!) years ago, that their software would not work after the year 2000? There are only two possible explanations.

The first is that they knew perfectly well what they were doing, but that their major concern was not to think about the problems of people on the eve of the year 2000, but rather to sell a product fit for the 1980s. As the memories of the computers of the time were more limited in capacity than those of today, and as two figures took up less space than four, they gave birth to the Bug by not giving thought to the future. Twenty years was a stretch of time which did not correspond to the scale of the investment they were making (mentally and financially). Supposing that someone said to us: 'Be careful of your investments, because if you buy them in dollars, it could happen that in a thousand years the dollar will be worth nothing.' Our reply would be naturally to make a priority of worrying about our children or, as the case might be, our grandchildren, and not about what was going to happen in a thousand years' time. For a short term investment, twenty years are the same as a thousand years.

**So no one believed that those machines would last as long as the third millennium. But what is your second explanation?**

The information technologists were so used to an economy founded on short-term production that they didn't think that what was on the market at the beginning of the 1980s would still be working in December 1999. They were so convinced that machines would be replaced every two years that they didn't bother to sort out the question of the calendar! But if that's what they really did think, they made a fatal error. They forgot that all the hardware and all the software can be replaced, but the component of memory remains the same, whether it is of the date of Hiroshima or of the day I deposited £10 in my bank account. From the 1980s up to the present, banks have changed machines and software programmes several times, but every new programme has had to ingest the previous one. They thus overlooked the fact that the previous memory featured the counting system that they originally set up.

**So you're speaking about an inability to think in a long-term way. Might it not be said that this inability has always been in evidence in the past?**

Indeed. Isn't the greatest act of stupidity in history Napoleon's sale of Louisiana to finance his expedition to Russia? If he hadn't sold Louisiana, the United States would now be a French-speaking country! What is more, Louisiana was the area most under cultivation, and wasn't restricted to the present state of Louisiana but occupied the whole length of the Mississippi. But this story only allows us to reproach Napoleon for not having foreseen that the United States would become the most powerful nation on earth. The problem of the Millennium Bug seems to me of a different order. It has become the symptom of a difficult relationship between memory as the treasury of the past on the one hand, and, on the other, the future as that for which we feel ourselves to be responsible. If there is a problem to be faced on the threshold of the year 2000, it is about the loss of historical memory.

## Funes or Memory

**How can you speak about the loss of memory at the very time when the Internet is placing at our disposal a sort of global human memory, an immense virtual library?**

This is my chance to broach the subject of what I have described as the contemporary crisis of memory. Let's come back for a moment to the notion of progress. For centuries we had the impression that our culture was defined by the uninterrupted accumulation of knowledge. We learned the solar system of Ptolemy, then that of Galileo, then that of Kepler, and so on. But this is not true! The history of civilizations is a sequence of abysses into which tons of knowledge go missing. The Greeks were already incapable of recovering the mathematical knowledge of the Egyptians; this state of affairs gave rise to the blossoming of occult philosophies founded on the notion of recovering ancient wisdom which has been lost. Then the Middle Ages lost Greek science, all of Plato (except for one dialogue) and half of Aristotle . . . We could go on and on in the same vein. If we did, we would note that throughout history an amount of knowledge had been lost during every age.

**Are you suggesting that all we set out to do is to rediscover what has been forgotten?**

No! Quite the contrary! Although it is sometimes possible to recover some fragments of lost knowledge, most often we are not able to. What I'm saying is that the function of social and cultural memory is to act as a filter; it's not to preserve everything. Sometimes we approve of these filterings-out (unless we're historians of science, we're not unhappy to have lost Mesopotamian mathematics, if there was such a thing); sometimes we view them as acts of censorship, whether they were carried out by the Inquisition, by Stalinists or by American adherents of the doctrine of political correctness, who try to eliminate from historical textbooks everything that could be considered as injurious to a racial minority, for example. In any case, the function of memory, whether it is individual or collective, is not only to retain; it is also to filter out.

**So culture is made up of both memory and oblivion?**

It's a question of a very delicate sort of dialectic, a difficult balancing act. Let's begin with memory. Without memory, there is no survival. If you were dealt a great blow to the head and the areas of the brain which preside over your memory were damaged, you would no longer have an identity. Societies have always relied on memory for the same reasons. Beginning with the old man of the tribe who, seated under a tree in the evenings, told stories about the exploits of his ancestors. He was transmitting these legends to younger generations; that's how the group kept its identity. Every civilization discovers its identity when a great poet composes its founding myth. And when some act of censorship wipes out a section of a society's memory, it undergoes an identity crisis. And let me repeat that when, by the same process, the voyage of Christopher Columbus is erased from history textbooks through an excess of political correctness (because to speak of the 'discovery of America' would be to insult the original natives), part of society's memory is thereby cut off as if by amputation and alienated. Memory must be respected, even if it is cruel.

**But you said that memory is an art of bringing together acts of remembering with acts of forgetting.**

Yes. To remember is to select. If I remembered everything that happened yesterday, if I were like Borges's character Funes . . .

**Who remembers every leaf on every tree which he has seen during his lifetime, every letter of every sentence of all the books he has read . . .**

I'd have had it. Funes, you remember, cannot act any more, cannot even move. What characterizes the transmission of memory is the filtering out. And with the filtering out, comes generalization. I have just come back from a journey to Istanbul, and have several reminiscences of it in my memory. But if I tried to relate everything that happened to me during the journey, I'd notice that I had already forgotten half of it. I've fortunately allowed everything that didn't seem to me to be worthy of my attention to fade away. And I have generalized, I have made abstractions. I have retained some very precise details, but also some vague impressions. I remember taking several taxis, for instance. If I remembered every journey that I'd made across town, I'd be carrying a lot of baggage. I only remember two of them, one with a driver who couldn't find his way to a certain place, and one with another who had clearly cheated me over the fare, as I realized afterwards. But that's all. It happens perhaps that during psychoanalysis one can fish things out of the unconscious which one had set aside and which hadn't been erased. But that's exactly what the unconscious is for; it's a dustbin into which we throw what we don't have use for at present. Now, society and culture do the same thing. It would be mad if a book of Roman history had recorded everything that Julius Caesar did before going to the Senate on the day he died.

**So that's the nature of Funes's illness: he can't get rid of anything.**

I shall stop you there because the Internet, or the World-Wide Web, is already (or will soon be) an immense Funes. Up to now society filtered things out for us, through textbooks and encyclopedias. With the coming of the Web, all possible knowledge and information, even the least useful, is there at our disposal. Hence the question: Who is doing the filtering out? I use two search engines on the Internet called Altavista and Yahoo. The big difference between them is that Yahoo was actually designed to filter information, and Altavista gives you everything without making a selection.

Imagine that you are looking for information on the cultivation of coffee. If you type in 'coffee' in Yahoo, it can give you filtered information (very appropriate to coffee!) about all the websites in which coffee is in fact spoken about in a scientific way. On the other hand, Altavista gives you a list of the 14 million websites in which the word 'coffee' is used. Now the programme which is destined to become dominant in the future is more likely to be Altavista, and not Yahoo; our society is gearing itself up to possessing an electronic brain constructed on the model of the brain of Funes *el memorioso*. The inability to filter out entails the impossibility to discriminate. To my mind, to have 14 million websites is the same as having none, because I am not able to select. In the future, I will be crushed by the memory of everything that has been said about coffee. We have increased our memory storage capacity, but we haven't yet found the new parameters of filtering out.

**So you're in favour of bringing back oblivion?**

To a certain degree, yes, but you've touched on a delicate point. I once wrote a little half-serious, half-flippant essay about the possibility of introducing an *ars oblivionalis*, an art of forgetfulness (it's a problem I also touch on in *Foucault's Pendulum*). It was soon realized that it is impossible to invent a technique of forgetting, because it is impossible to forget by an act of the will. There is even a Renaissance book on the art of memory – Gesualdo's *Plutosophia* – which has a chapter on the means of forgetting: it's quite laughable. Generally speaking, forgetting is accidental and involuntary. It can be caused by there being too much information to digest. If during a reception, you are introduced to fifty people, you will forget their names very quickly. This means that forgetting is connected to chance and cannot be programmed. If I want to remember your name, I begin by repeating it to myself several times, and that will probably work. But if I want to forget it and say to myself over and over again that I want to forget it, then I am certain to remember it. The moral of the story is this: when confronted by the Web, you have at your disposal neither a rule for selecting information nor a rule for forgetting what isn't worth remembering. You only possess selection criteria in so far as you are prepared intellectually to face the ordeal of surfing the Web. I'll explain what I mean.

Last summer I was in my library in the country and needed some information about Immanuel Kant. I called up the Web and found an incredible amount of information about this philosopher. As I was well trained in philosophy, I was able to eliminate the cranks, the fanatics, the websites which only gave information at a pre-university level, and I was slowly able to select the, let's say, ten sites which contained viable information. But I'm more or less a specialist, with a lifetime of study behind me. So what happens to other people, all those innocents who search the Web for what it's important to know about Immanuel Kant? They're certainly more lost than the small boy in a tiny village who can find nothing to consult other than an old history of philosophy, written by a Jesuit, in the eighteenth century, in the house of the local *curé.*

**Doesn't the position you have taken encourage people to put up with a degree of ideological censorship, whether religious or political?**

I personally don't support this type of censorship. But I can well understand that in the absence of a strong political party or a strong Church, people will have recourse to sects in order to find an authority that will take on the job of filtering out information for them. Freedom of choice in respect of a wide range of information is a positive thing for those who are rich (I am referring here to the intellectually rich, to those who are capable of critical discrimination) but not for the poor. So we're moving towards a new distinction of class, not founded on money, but on the ability to use one's critical sense and to select information.

**What solutions do you propose for dealing with this globalization of memory?**

The first part of the response to it might be a form of training in how to select; it would be an altogether new discipline, yet to be invented. In the interim, I foresee an uncomfortable situation for which we must all prepare ourselves. Confronted with total Funes-like information, everyone has to make a selection. In the past, it was known that there were privileged ways of doing this, let's say the Catholic way, the Marxist way, the reactionary way, and so on. One could foresee how information would be selected depending on the textual reference point, whether this was the Bible, Diderot's *Encyclopédie, Das Kapital,* Saussure's *Cours de linguistique générale* . . . Nowadays everyone chooses in an altogether private and unpredictable way. Five thousand million inhabitants of this planet will produce 5,000 million different ideological selection procedures. The result could well be a society composed of juxtaposed individual identities (which seems to me a mark of progress), without the mediation of groups (which seems to me a danger). I don't know whether such a society would be able to function properly. I would argue that a degree of gregariousness is necessary . . .

**Not to speak of the fact that individuals demand criteria and hierarchies in order to give coherence to their vision of the world.**

Absolutely! No one is able in his personal life to construct such criteria. That's why we accept the filter that collective memory provides. Because it helps us. Imagine that we are asked to forget everything we have learnt about astronomy. Each one of us, in the course of our lives, would then have the task of reconstructing the planetary system by observing the path of the sun; it would be mad! We need a previous culture to have filtered this knowledge and to have given us a coherent description of the planetary system. Even if it's false, it's not serious. We lived for millennia trusting in the Ptolemaic system; the earth continued to go round and we carried on living. Things more or less worked. Since Galileo, we have understood a bit more, and that allowed us eventually to travel to the moon. But we had been able to live perfectly well with a false system, as long as it was coherent. Generation after generation accepted it by making little critical adjustments and adding epicycles. It is unthinkable to ask everyone to construct such a system in the course of their lifetime! Today, even if every one of us was given the sum total of memorized knowledge, even if it was believed that every one of us would be capable of constituting for ourselves our own memory in the midst of this labyrinth, such a memory would always be inferior to social memory and we would end up with a society of 5,000 million inadequate memories. That's tantamount to saying that we would have a society of 5,000 million different languages, every one of them pidgin!

**It would be the Tower of Babel!**

Even worse! I'd like to say something very unkind about autodidacts. I have known great artists and intellectuals who were self-taught. Among them there were great geniuses, but they always lacked something. You discovered that they knew everything, let's say, about Cervantes, but they didn't know in which century, let's say, Lope de Vega belonged. Whereas someone who had a normal education would at least know where to place Lope de Vega, even if he or she didn't know a thing about him. The strength of normal education, with its sometimes Draconian selectivity, is to provide us with a sort of Mendeleyev periodic table, with pigeonholes in which to classify our knowledge as we absorb it. In the Tower of Babel, there were people speaking seventy languages; that can be solved with a good team of interpreters. But the Web may become a tower which will produce millions of different encyclopedias.

**So civilization develops out of a few common propositions.**

I'd like to give you a perhaps extreme but, it seems to me, revealing example. In the context of contemporary historical writing, what is the difference between a revisionist and negationist? The revisionist is broadly in agreement with the general accepted judgement about events in the past, but sets out to correct individual details about them. For him, there weren't 6 million deaths in the concentration camps, but 5.5 million; or else he challenges the fact that there were gas chambers in this particular camp, and so on. There's even revisionist historical writing which is not about the Shoah, but about other events such as the Civil War in Spain. The revisionist does not deny that what happened did happen, nor does he deny Franco's responsibility for it; he simply makes a different assessment of his role, arguing, for example, that Franco was not fascist but only anti-communist . . . and he can go on arguing for ever on the basis of facts and criteria which are accepted by both sides of the argument.

On the other hand, the negationist is someone who has 'revised' the history of the Second World War in its entirety. He does not acknowledge the general accepted judgement about it; he denies it categorically. He denies that the gas chambers existed. If the historical community places documents before him, he decides that its manner of validating the documents isn't the same as his. According to him, the historical community is either wrong or it is being manipulated. That is to say, he connects all the elements which are accessible in the historical encyclopedia in a personal way, he rejects some and gives more importance to others; he does not follow the criteria of the historical community, but his own. Now this perverse logic, which has up to now belonged only to a minority of fanatics, might one day become the logic of the Web. Everyone would produce his or her own criteria for selecting information. This would be *à la carte* history ... The day that every common norm disappears because everyone will be able to concoct his or her own interpretation of historical and scientific events, there won't be any common basis left on which to construct the history of the human race.

**To come back to the question of memory, there is the further problem today of storage and conservation, as memory has more and more material to store.**

Let's suppose that, in spite of the Web, we manage to produce a standard memory in an accessible format: an encyclopedia of encyclopedias. How would it be preserved for future generations? In book form? No; that was possible in Diderot's time, but was no longer possible half a century later, simply because towards the middle of the nineteenth century paper was no longer made from rag, it had begun to be made from wood and cellulose, posing the problem of acidity. In short, a fifteenth-century incunable is still as fresh as if it had just come out of the printing shop, whereas a modern book has an average life expectancy of seventy years – not to mention the books produced in the 1940s and 1950s which are already crumbling away like communion wafers! And I'm not even speaking about the information on the Internet, but how we are going to preserve the information stored in our libraries. By microfilming them? That would be very expensive; every book would have to be opened page by page, and there are libraries which possess millions of books. And even if we succeeded in microfilming all those pages, one may suppose that the books in question would not be available for public access and would be reserved for the use of scholars brave enough to read microfilms. A second solution would be chemical treatment; this would also be very expensive and would necessitate treating the books page by page. A third solution would be scanning; the transposition of the books into a magnetic medium. But magnetic media are not guaranteed to be everlasting; on the contrary, they are known to be more fragile than the medium of paper. So dates would have to be established for the retranslation of information into a 'fresher' medium. Finally, even if people decided to have recourse to these techniques, it would never be possible to treat all books, and a choice would have to be made. Who would make this choice? How would the committee responsible for this be chosen? Who would dare take the decision that Smith, J. would survive, but Smith, K. would be destroyed? In any case, the selection would have to be artificial. The true filtering out of memory, which I spoke about just now, follows the rhythm of the seasons and generations; it is society as a whole which discusses the matter and decides in the end what should survive. It is all this that stops me sleeping, not the prediction that the world will end in the first few days of the year 2000!

## The Myth of the Tabula Rasa

**Aren't you afraid that the accumulation of all these memory banks will stop us inventing new ways of thinking?**

Quite the contrary! They can be of use to us by still preserving some landmarks and by keeping us from sinking into the illusion of absolute novelty. There's no such thing as absolute novelty. You can't transform the French language from one day to the next, and even if you could, other people wouldn't be able to understand you. You can only do what normally artists and writers do in their line of work, that is, make up a new word or a new syntactic construction; and then, a century or two later, someone may notice that a change had occurred. But this change could only become generally accepted if traditional grammar continued to be taught in schools. The surrealists, it is true, abruptly proposed new French usages; but what would have happened if the language of the surrealists had been taught in schools without reference to traditional French usage? If someone suddenly put forward a new world vision that applied globally to the whole field of knowledge, we would be incapable of assimilating it. Knowledge, or science, is reformist; it is not revolutionary. It progresses through discreet changes, by little adjustments here and there, while the whole remains stable. The innovative part of science and art must always remain in contact with the conservative part. There are no October revolutions in science, no *tabula rasa*.

**Yet at the end of this century, we have the feeling that we are seeing a new questioning of all the knowledge inherited from past centuries.**

You seem to have got the impression that someone is sawing through the branch on which you are sitting; but you're only thinking on one level. I don't deny that the ideological upheavals which are occurring are great, but no one has questioned the chemical composition of aspirin! We're encouraged to believe that the Big Bang may never have taken place, but no one has suggested that the solar system is organized in a way other than the one described by astrophysicists.

**But aren't we more uncertain about everything than people of other centuries were?**

I'm not even certain that that is the case. The seventeenth century was more uncertain about things than us. For European intellectuals, the whole world was falling apart in respect of astronomy, mathematics, chemistry and medicine. It's not by chance that art and literature became baroque, and that architects began to design spaces and walls that didn't seem able to remain standing. But what is happening to us nowadays is different: back then, the disillusion only affected a small class of scholars and intellectuals. Whether deliberately or not, peasants and priests didn't know about the extent of the damage to the old order of which the scholars were aware. There were clearly centuries which were less well off than we are.

**But one could still believe that the heavens had always existed, that the clouds were immortal, that the ocean would for ever pound the rocks. Some things seemed to be permanent.**

But that's true today as well! There are a certain number of certainties which command the support of the majority of us. Let's leave cranks and revolutionary sects out of account: we know that our way of building houses is valid since they have remained standing for a certain number of years, and since only earthquakes can cause them to collapse. Moreover, no one has suggested that we adopt a new musical notation . . .

**Stephen Jay Gould has reminded us that in the eighteenth century scholars realized that the history of the world had to be calculated not in thousands of years, but millions, if not thousands of millions.**

So you see, our century is not the only one to have experienced the edifice of knowledge quaking. In our case, I grant you, everything is going faster. At the end of the 1950s, I was working in a publishing house which was producing a popular book about the history of inventions. I remember typesetting the page which spoke about man existing for 40,000 years. Gould is now speaking about 200,000 years. That's how fast knowledge is moving on!

## 'If I Were an Elephant, I Would Have Tusks'

**Jean-Claude Carrière has drawn our attention to the disappearance of certain grammatical tenses. Do you see in this a sign of the times changing, as he does?**

I very much liked his analysis of verb tenses. I am particularly sensitive to the problem of the existence or non-existence of the imperfect in various languages. For forty years I have been thinking about Gérard de Nerval's *Sylvie*, which is the text of my life, and I recently did a survey of several English translations. Now, *Sylvie* is based on the continual transition from the perfect to the imperfect tense, and vice versa. How can one translate this oscillation into English, a language which only possesses the imperfect tense? Jean-Claude Carrière gives an example: '*je lui disais*' goes into English as 'I was telling him' and not 'I told him', which is the perfect tense: '*je lui dis*'. The 'durativity' and 'iterativity' of the imperfect tense is rendered in English not morphologically by the verb being conjugated but through the use of a different syntactic construction. That's why even languages without the imperfect can render this rather vague sort of temporality, a temporality that was much employed by Proust. The problem of the subjunctive seems to me more worrying. There are several languages in which it looks likely to die out. You French do not use those lovely verbs which end in 'ussent' or 'assent' any more. I once risked using one at an evening reception when an opportunity presented itself, and I was looked upon as though I was an oddity of nature! It's also used less and less in Italian, but '*se io andasi*' is still said in the subjunctive. In French this is translated by '*si j'allais*' and not '*si j'allasse*', as in the good old French of the eighteenth century. The indicative is used, and the subjunctive has been lost. In English, the subjunctive is still used, but not by recent immigrants. Recent generations are losing all the nuances which are found in the transition from the subjunctive to the conditional tense.

### Why do you think that the loss of the subjunctive is so serious?

Because only the subjunctive expresses the tense of the hypothetical, of the possible, of the non-real. 'If I went to Paris this evening, I would go to the Comédie Française.' 'If I went' must be acknowledged to be a subjunctive. In fact I'm not going, but I could go. If that condition was given, then, as the following conditional says, I *would go* to the Comédie Française. By the use of the subjunctive my thought is suspended in virtuality. If I were an elephant, I would have tusks. This proposition is true, even if I am not an elephant. The subjunctive is needed to underline this potentiality. Mastery of the subjunctive allows one to establish a difference in speech between what is virtual and what is real. In this sense the passing of the subjunctive threatens to weaken this difference even further. I may be going too far, but I wonder whether this doesn't correspond to our growing tendency in this age of information technology to confuse the virtual and the real.

Beppe Grillo, a very humorous Italian singer, a sort of Savonarola figure railing at contemporary civilization, recently said: 'Just think, there are people who use their credit card to masturbate by telephone, listening to a voice which hails from Wyoming, while if they bothered to look across the landing, they'd see a girl there who has for years only been waiting for a sign from them to come running.' We've reached a point of extreme confusion between the virtual and the real, if it is more exciting sexually to masturbate by credit card than to make a pass at a girl across the landing. I don't want to be moralistic and say that it's a tragedy of the times. There have been other times in which the gap between the imaginary and the real has been very narrow. The Greeks and the Romans mixed reality and fiction without drawing a clear line of demarcation between them; they saw dryads and naiads in rivers and waterfalls. The people of the Middle Ages saw unicorns in the forests, and believed so firmly in witches that witches really came to exist. But in the course of time, modernity accustomed us to drawing a clear line between the imaginary and the real.

**Are you one of those who believe that people sometimes end up by no longer noticing the difference between virtual reality and 'real' reality?**

It's more complicated than that. I'll give you an example. One of my female students wrote an article about a Japanese phenomenon: a woman called Yoko who has become a famous star throughout Japan. Now Yoko doesn't exist: she was produced by a computer, by putting together elements which were thought to represent the highest degree of beauty in a twenty-year-old girl. Yoko makes appearances on television and chats with the other guests. People sometimes say that they sense she is not real when she dances. But when all is said and done, she could very well pass for a real girl. She is very popular, and lots of people write to her. Now I would claim that, with the exception of a few madmen, people are very well aware that Yoko doesn't exist, but they have decided to take her seriously, to make believe. I can sense your objection: aren't there Stendhalians among us who discuss Mathilde de La Môle and la duchesse Sanseverina in their conferences as though they were real creatures? Don't James Joyce fans go to Dublin to follow the route Leopold Bloom took on 16 June 1904, street by street? Granted; and yet what is designated in the case of Yoko as virtual is not what in the past was called the collective or romantic imagination. The proof is that no one wrote letters to Molly Bloom (or Little Red Riding Hood, for that matter), but people are writing to Yoko. I think that the crisis of the subjunctive has something to do with all this.

**Isn't television violence part of the same problem?**

No; that's not a matter of a confusion between the virtual and the real, but a question of imitation. Everyone knows that if two suicides are reported on the front page of the papers one day, then there will be a third on the next. A bonze who douses himself in petrol and sets fire to himself in a public square will certainly have a few imitators. Television violence can certainly have a seductive effect and can create a sort of mimetic violence in turn. But insofar as it claims to be real, or at least realistic, it's not likely to mislead us, to make us believe that it doesn't have any consequences. Now there's another sort of violence which is virtual and which has been cor-rupting children for years, and which seems to me to be very worrying. I'm speaking of the violence contained in those cartoons where one sees characters (like Tom and Jerry, for instance) falling off skyscrapers, being crushed by heavy weights, being broken into bits or flattened to the thickness of a piece of paper, and two seconds later getting up again as though nothing had happened, as though none of the thousand deaths they have had to endure have had the slightest consequence. That's where the real confusion of the virtual and the real is to be found! It's found also, *a fortiori*, in video games, in which people are killed and are then resurrected at once only to have to die again.

**When one is a public figure, as you are, doesn't one also enter, in a different way, a sort of virtual world?**

One mustn't exaggerate! The degree to which I am famous bears no comparison to the celebrity of a cinema or television star, or that of an actor who may get taken for the character he plays. People may have seen my photograph on the cover of a book or in a newspaper, and I've taken part on Bernard Pivot's programme from time to time as an author, but that's as far as it goes. It is true, however, that this modest notoriety has led me to have some curious experiences which I wrote about in an article.

If people happen to recognize me in the street or on a train or in a bar, I sometimes hear them saying to each other aloud: 'Look over there, that's Umberto Eco!' They say this just as they are walking by me, and they are perfectly well aware that I can hear them. But oddly, they don't think that they are being impolite, and they are not embarrassed to speak about me in front of me. Now this attitude goes against all the rules which they learnt in childhood ( you mustn't point at that gentleman, you mustn't speak about his funny hat if he is within earshot, etc.). So they behave in the same way as they would to a character who they think is both real and imaginary, or a real person who has something in common with a fictitious character. But take note! This is the inverse of the phenomenon of Yoko. In that case, a character – invented, and hence not real – is taken to be real. In this case, a person – who is real and known about through the media – is treated as though he is unreal, no more than an image. To be known about through the media is, in a certain way, to belong already to the virtual world.

## The Time of Repentance

**Let's speak for a moment about the century that is about to come to an end. How is it different from the ones that went before it? More especially, won't our century have been the most murderous of all time?**

I'll be giving the impression that I take up contrary views on everything, but I don't think that our century has been more bloodthirsty than the rest, in spite of its great crimes – the Shoah, the nuclear apocalypse or germ warfare. More people were killed in past centuries, with less emotion, less remorse and more matter-of-factness. If you study the figures of world population in a given age, you will notice, for instance, that the anti-Jewish pogroms at the time of the Crusaders' entry into Jerusalem were, relatively speaking, even more horrendous massacres than those of the twentieth century. What strikes us about the massacres of our century is the industrial efficiency of their organization, and the fact that there are still people about who claim not to have known anything about them, not to have had any direct responsibility for them, and only to have dealt with the paperwork. The massacres of the past required a more direct form of cruelty; one had to plunge one's hands into someone else's guts and end up covered with blood. In our century we have known a different form of cruelty – I would venture to say a more cowardly form, with no grandeur about it. That's all. Shakespeare did not wait for our century to dawn in order to define life as 'a tale told by an idiot, full of sound and fury'. Frankly, I can't convince myself that the Saint Bartholomew's Day Massacre was less cruel than a bombardment with napalm.

On the other hand, going against generally held opinions once again, I should like to claim that our century has been more moral than many others. To have a moral sense does not mean that one avoids doing evil: it means that one knows that a given action is evil and that it would be better not to commit it. In this sense, hypocrisy is a constant feature of moral conscience, because it consists in recognizing the good and appreciating it for what it is, even if one is doing evil at the time. Well, our century has perhaps been hypocritical, but it has been moral in equal measure. It is in this century that a sense of global solidarity has developed for the first time. Even if people do not practise it, they feel it to be a duty. Among other things, the great rites of modern remorse bear witness to this general awareness, in a certain way. In the past, peoples engaged in massacres, but didn't repent of them.

**Isn't one of the sources of modern anguish to be found in the feeling that humanity is now able to destroy itself?**

Our century thinks a lot about the great crimes it has committed. I believe that everyone is ready to admit that the exploitation of children and genocide are crimes. Yet the great threat of the future, I mean the power to destroy the planet that we humans have for the first time in our history, is a subject which, while giving rise to much speculation in the media, does not really disturb anyone's sleep. Which of us is ready to give up our car? I have the impression that the extraordinary repentance in which our century has been engaged is therefore an excuse to prevent us from assuming responsibility in the face of the threats which loom over the future. On such problems there is no reflection by society as a whole.

**You seem more worried about the problem of ecology than about the nuclear threat.**

We have come to realize that an atomic conflict would not be worth it, which is why the nations in question have done their best to reduce the risk of nuclear war. As for the rest, one has to trust the good sense of statesmen (I say this with a certain fatalism, although I took part in the great struggles of the 1950s and 1960s for nuclear disarmament). Yet while the president of the United States appears to do his best to reduce the risk of nuclear conflict, he simultaneously gives encouragement and financial support to the industrial activity in his country which threatens the ecological balance of the planet. Humanity doesn't seem to have grasped what is really at stake, or rather it does so only in so far as it pursues purely symbolic objectives. Smoking is banned everywhere in the United States, but those dying of heart attacks because of obesity are, I believe, more numerous than those who die of lung cancer.

**Do you see this casualness as a suicidal form of behaviour?**

Personal suicide is an experience which every one of us is able, more or less, to conceive of. Even if I have no intention of committing suicide, I know exactly how to set about it. But to speak of planetary suicide presupposes that there is such a thing as a collective will. The destruction of the planet would seem logically not to be a voluntary act, but a tragic consequence of the way we alter nature without negotiating with it. An accident, not suicide.

## For an Ethics of Negotiation

**Rational animals possess the means of altering and hence of destroying the world in which they live, move and have their being.**

The process of destroying the environment began with the discovery of fire, or even earlier, with the first flint being struck to change its shape. Once man acts on the world, he deforms it and slowly destroys it. For this reason I am against any radical ecological thought, according to which even man should be eliminated to save Gaia, the Earth.

Earth is the planet together with all the species living on it: the bees who build their hives, as much as the men who construct the skyscrapers. Naturally, the difference between the bees and us is very clear; the planet had millions of years to get used to the constructions of the bees, whereas we humans change our building techniques with every season and have the annoying tendency of never stopping. So what must we do to enter into a pact with our planet? Since we need the earth (we can't get off it), we must experiment to find out to what degree it can put up with us. We therefore have to negotiate: first of all with the earth, and then among ourselves. It's a good thing to hide the smell of our sweat by the use of aerosol deodorants, but if these aerosols produce a hole in the ozone layer, then we must find another means of avoiding bad smells. I'm quoting a simple case; everyone knows that it has been possible to negotiate to have the aerosol replaced by the deodorant stick, and that we have all slowly reached agreement on this point.

**Could you give an example of a negotiation which did not end in agreement?**

All the others! Petrol-driven cars, for example. It is obvious that they are killing us (not only killing the earth, but also ourselves). Such a realization would require us to move on to electric cars without delay. Nothing is apparently simpler; consumers no longer demand speed from their motors, producers give up their powerful and expensive racing cars, and the whole petro-chemical industry begins to undergo conversion to something else. But that's still science fiction. No one is ready to negotiate. Take the case of those two tape recorders (*Umberto Eco here points to our two tape recorders located on a low table in his sitting-room*); they were made in such a way as to break down after a very short period of time, a year or two.

**Let's hope they last to the end of this conversation at least . . .**

It's also planned that they will be rapidly superseded by new models which will be released in six months' time. If these also break down, it will cost more to repair them than it cost to buy them. But in fact, it's not at all necessary to produce new models of tape recorders. You are pleased with that one, and it does the job you require of it.

Yet think of all those thousands of millions of old tape recorders which will be a heavy factor in the ecological balance of the planet ... It would be so easy to decide to produce tape recorders that last twenty or more years! Let's get all of us together around a table, engineers, manufacturers and consumers, and engage in intelligent negotiations to find a solution which everyone will be forced to respect. I've still got somewhere the old Telefunken radio that my family bought in 1938: that proves that it's possible to manufacture radios that work for sixty years. So why do present-day radios break after a year or two, and why do the components fall to pieces?

**Perhaps the people who design these disposable objects think too much in the short term.**

That brings us back to the problem of the Millennium Bug. The engineers who produced the computers which cannot work beyond the year 2000 indeed thought of their invention as belonging to the short term, like all late-twentieth-century inventions. But why is the principle of short life, which is valid for computers which go out of date regularly because of new developments in information technology, applied also to tape recorders? A form of negotiation based on common sense will have to lay down that all decisions resulting in the overall reduction of pollution must be profitable to all parties, including the manufacturer of tape recorders. It is true that for the time being he runs the risk of selling fewer spare parts. So he will make us pay more for them – a small consolation, as the machines will be sturdier. It is difficult to settle these sorts of negotiations, which require that industrialists show a little vision.

**It is difficult to ask of a man who counts his till every evening to show a little vision.**

Negotiations of this sort go against our basest instincts. Take the classic case of fire. A fire breaks out in a theatre and the audience rushes towards the emergency exits. Because everyone tries to get out before the others, a great jam forms so that 80 per cent of the people die. If they queued up and adopted an attitude of greater solidarity in the face of the disaster, then they would file out of the burning theatre and nearly everyone would escape, with the result that only 5 per cent or so would be victims. Why prefer a risk of 80 per cent to a risk of 5 per cent? For very basic reasons: because everyone hopes to have luck on their side and be part of the minority who are saved. It's irrational, but it's human. At the precise moment when danger is immediate and mortal, recourse to negotiation seems impossible and everyone thinks of themselves as cannier than the others. So among the wishes I would like to make for the next century is the hope that there will be a new ethics of negotiation.

**Can we hope that the economy will come up with a sort of survival marketing? It would be in the interest of industries to produce objects that would guarantee respect for the environment.**

It's possible; I'm not entirely pessimistic about this. In certain cases, thinking by intellectuals and moral pressure from the media can help bring about change. My generation does not respect trees as much as today's children who have been taught to do so. They have a different attitude towards cigarettes, fur coats, and so on. Here in Italy, people are ready to make the effort to put their rubbish into three different dustbins: one for plastic, one for paper and one for glass. That's not yet compulsory in France, but it's only a question of time before it is. It will be difficult, there will be ditherings, wrong turnings and accidents, but it is possible that people may soon reach the decision that it is better to pay more for a longer-lasting tape recorder. After all, the widespread obsession with having new things is less than fifty years old. There are reasons to believe that we are becoming a less spendthrift civilization. This present trend is not, however, bound to continue. We are coming back, you see, to one of our previous questions: we must accept the idea from now on that progress is not linear.

**Shouldn't society establish a certain number of prohibitions that would be non-negotiable?**

But prohibitions are themselves the result of long negotiations! The prohibition of incest, for example, was established once it was realized that consanguinity led to harmful consequences – unless these were the result of one of God's whims . . . Even the prophet who forbade his people to eat pork spoke in the context of negotiations that had already taken place. That doesn't mean that all negotiations end in agreement. There would never be any divorces or wars if negotiations always succeeded.

**In what way do you consider negotiation to be such a central principle?**

In my last book, *Kant and the Ornithorhynchus*, I tried to extend my discussion of this principle beyond the commercial domain, and even beyond that of politics and religion. I believe that from now on we will be negotiating about the very meaning of the words and language we use; our very way of using language to speak about the world is thus founded on negotiation. And negotiation may be involved in the way in which we recognize objects and states of the world as such. I am here speaking about contractual realism. We can even negotiate about the possibility of saying, 'It is raining.' In principle, if I stick my hand out of the window and it is wet when I withdraw it, I have an empirical basis for saying that it is raining, but it is necessary to negotiate within the general meteorological system to be able to distinguish rain from dew or someone watering their plants on the fourth floor, above me. We can negotiate also about the degree of tolerance acceptable in the pronunciation of a phoneme. Today, you are negotiating with me to allow me to produce French phonemes, and you accept them up to a point. For my part, I must try hard to grasp that '*nom*' is not pronounced as if it were written '*nome*', but rather '*non*'. I've said '*nome*' several times, but as we are in negotiation, you have accepted this. If you had been the director of the Comédie Française, you would have reacted differently.

**That would depend on the character you were playing!**

Yesterday evening I saw Bob Wilson's production of Ibsen's *The Lady from the Sea* as adapted by Susan Sontag. It was in Italian, but the two leading actors, Philippe Leroy and Dominique Sanda, were French. They spoke pretty good Italian, but one could sense that they were not Italian, and so the effect threatened to be somewhat comical, a bit as though you were to play the role of Phèdre with a Corsican accent. What did Wilson do to deal with this problem? He employed other, this time Italian, actors, and had them all speak in a somewhat mechanical and artificial manner. In this way Dominique Sanda spoke like the others. That seemed to me to be a good case of phonetic negotiation.

**Would you say that the twentieth century had created favourable conditions for the emergence of new modes of thought? Or is it just the century of the triumph of science?**

I am going to go against the commonly held view once again, and think that I can say in all seriousness that apart from atomic energy and television, all the great inventions we know about, including computers (but also radio, electricity, aviation and the car, of course) date from before the twentieth century, at least in so far as their fundamental principles are concerned. It was possible to glimpse the emergence of a society founded on technology from the nineteenth century onwards. The present technological revolution can only be understood as the continuity of what was initiated in the nineteenth century.

Indeed, the great revolution of our century is not technological but social. A new type of relationship between people has emerged in this century. The simple fact that racism and intolerance are frowned upon today is proof of it. It involved a total reversal of human relations and relationships. While, in the nineteenth century, the aeroplane, the car and electricity were being invented, the relations between fathers and sons and husbands and wives were more or less the same as they had been in the Middle Ages. Children still worked, almost as much as they did in the eleventh century. Education was only accessible to the rich. What was to become the technological miracle of Western societies had already been set in train, but English society still tried Oscar Wilde for homosexuality. No real change in behaviour had in fact occurred.

Nowadays, the fact that a black person can become mayor of New York is in itself the indication of a considerable social upheaval. The fact that, at the United Nations, the republic of Bongo-Bongoland enjoys the same rights as the United States of America, at least in principle, is a typical phenomenon of our times. In a different context, the fact that paedophiles are publicly denounced relates to a more mature sense of the dignity of children than in the time of Socrates, who was a paedophile and didn't bother to hide it.

**But the seeds of a concern for the rights of man were already to be found in the writings of eighteenth-century philosophers.**

Locke's *Letters Concerning Toleration* date from the seventeenth century. But Locke, like the philosophers of the following century, approached the question in an abstract way and excluded from the discussion all the people whose opinions were judged to be dangerous to the well-being of the state. Voltaire was very tolerant, but did you know that his fortune was invested in the slave trade? It's not more surprising to learn that Voltaire was a slave-trader than to find out that a modern European state makes a great deal of money out of selling arms to the Third World. The difference is that today the press can point the finger at the contradictions in our societies. During his lifetime, no one thought of telling Voltaire that his praise of toleration was not in harmony with his investments in the slave trade. It's true that the nineteenth century was the century of Marx and Engels's *Communist Manifesto*. But, you see, a cry of revolt, an unheard-of act of provocation, was necessary at the time to denounce the sufferings of the workers and to proclaim their rights, while today such values have become universal and irrefutable. That may be one of the reasons for the defeat of communism: Marxism is in crisis not because (or not only because) it was badly applied in the East, but because what it demands is no longer shocking to the West.

**So you see a principle of solidarity emerging with the twentieth century?**

The global threats which bear down on our lives have perhaps brought us into greater solidarity with each other, and have given us the feeling that we are sailing together on the same ship. This feeling is absolutely new. The sense that all men have the same degree of dignity is new; it did not exist in the nineteenth century. But, I repeat, the emergence of a new moral conscience does not necessarily correspond to new moral behaviour, of course; there is always a gap between the values that are publicly proclaimed and everyday practice. Yet, if one judged civilizations by such gaps, one would have to say that Christianity hasn't changed the moral conscience of the West because people are still killing their neighbours, still stealing, still not respecting their neighbours' wives, and so on.

**The divisions between ideologies fell with the fall of the Berlin Wall. Can society today survive without ideology?**

It still lives with an ideology, if you take that term in its widest meaning as a body of ideas which offer us lines of action and a certain vision of the world. Our century has seen the fall of the great ideologies which implied involvement in the construction of society. That's a cause of confusion among many young people. Hence a degree of reversion to religion, whether official or heretical, for the purpose of rediscovering a common sense of destiny above all else. Take the example of the Journées Mondiales de la Jeunesse rally in Paris, which took place on the Pope's initiative during the summer of 1997. I don't think that it was inspired by deep religious sentiment. Half the young people who came up to Paris could equally well have taken part in another rally. But through it they found a chance to demonstrate their support for certain acceptable ideals and an opportunity to come together in a sort of fraternal union. Many of our contemporaries, by the way, are looking for new forms of commitment through voluntary work, a very important phenomenon of the end of this century. It is impossible to deny that the generation born in the 1960s is going through a very deep crisis. I've got people around me who are in the process of falling apart at the age of thirty or forty. Nothing they have done is able to give meaning to their lives. They also don't have a higher *raison d'être* based on community with others to keep them from falling into the abyss. It's a terrible crisis. Is it to do with the year 2000? I would say: no. But because the year 2000 is there as an invitation to reflect on the end of the century, let's take advantage of the situation.

**Is our age in search of new utopias?**

I'd be more inclined to say that our age is afraid of new utopias. As you know, I am an avid reader of classical utopias, from Thomas More to Charles Fourier, and I believe that the fact that these utopias were thought of at a time when they could not be turned into reality is interesting from a philosophical or political point of view. It is our century's misfortune not only to have tried to turn these utopias into reality, but also to have done so as scientifically as possible. The architects' model cities have been failures, and the perfect communist societies have come to nothing ... but all this was already to be found in the books of utopian writers. Read Thomas More's *Utopia* again and try to imagine putting it into practice: you've got Orwell's *1984*. The idea of living in such a society is a nightmare.

The twentieth century is the age of the industrialization of utopia. What makes the Shoah particularly horrible is the fact that it was part of a global utopian plan. I spoke about the pogroms during the Crusades. But the Crusaders had no theory, no plan of extermination; what made them act was a primitive sort of anti-Jewishness and a certain contempt for human life in general. Their little experiments in genocide were accidents on the road to Jerusalem, accidents which were sometimes linked to the simple need to obtain provisions. On the other hand, the genocide of the Jews by the Nazis was an integral part of a plan to bring about the perfect society, a 'purified' society.

## Tragic Optimism

**Our age has seen the end of hope in Christianity, and then the end of the secular hope in a shining future. Are there any reasons for us to look forward in hope, or must we now give that idea up altogether?**

The whole of my religious and philosophical position can be summed up in a phrase of Emmanuel Mounier, the man who developed the doctrine of personalism in the 1930s, who had a great influence on me when I was young. He spoke of 'tragic optimism'. We are living with a whole row of Damocles' swords hanging above our heads. We are quietly waiting for there to be an atomic war between India and Pakistan, or for pollution to kill 10 million Europeans. And yet things keep going on ... For Mounier, hope was linked to faith, which is not so in my case. But I remain a believer in specific optimism, which consists in putting into practice a series of little improvements. It's a sort of optimism based on trust in the human community. Why write books when it's not known whether there will be anyone there to read them in a thousand years? Why have children when it's not known whether they will have children in turn? This is why the risk of planetary destruction is indeed the major risk. Pessimism, which is much more tragic, in fact begins when one believes that there may come a day when human beings will cease to exist. But in that case, as Gould suggests, we might then be able to place our hopes in bacteria . .

**What are we first and foremost? The heirs of a great tradition, or primitive peoples at the dawn of a great history?**

All we have stated so far is that our identity is based on a long collective memory.

**The palaeontologist Yves Coppens talks about the transition from inanimate to animate matter, then from animate to thinking matter, and he seems to have in mind something else beyond this, another stage . . .**

That's Teilhard de Chardin's theory of the process by which men came into being.

**Do you think that mankind is only now beginning to learn how to use the powerful instrument of thought, and to appreciate its powers?**

No! Mankind had already learned how to use thought in the time of Touthmôsis! We have extended life expectancy and have produced new chemical prostheses which can make man taller. There are probably more cultivated people about today than ever before. The brain of an average taxi driver is better trained than that of a peasant in ancient Mesopotamia. From this point of view, there is progress, in the same way that today's athletes are able to break records and set new ones which would have been inconceivable at the beginning of this century. In quantitative terms, there is an increase in human potentiality. But just look how much Aristotle understood without the benefit of our means of acquiring knowledge and our encyclopedias! There's real reason to be impressed by the capacity of a single brain! The difference between then and now is that then it was a matter of individual geniuses. A greater number of human beings now accede to knowledge. The same could be said of them as is said of athletes: they are better fed and trained.

**So you don't believe in progress in philosophy?**

Thomists already said that there is no progress in metaphysics, but they only meant by that that it would not be possible to find better answers to metaphysical questions than those of Thomas Aquinas. Philosophy has however nothing to do with answers: its task is to formulate questions to which there are precisely no answers (or no simple and immediate answers). In this sense, I agree, the great philosophical questions are always the same.

**Hegel said that the whole of Western philosophy is a commentary on Plato and Aristotle. Do you agree with this?**

Absolutely. I would be incapable of mentioning a single problem that has been conceived of since their time. Nowadays bioethics raises many questions. Should we create clones or not? To reply, we turn to myths of nature, we speak of the good and the bad, of good and evil. The problems are always the same! The reason why the questions are asked has changed, but the fundamental problem is the same. Infinite progress does not exist, nor is there, as traditionalists wish to believe, a circle which we will for ever travel round and round. We are faced with spiral shapes or explosions.

**We agreed on the statement that the year 2000 was an excuse for taking stock. Could you give a rough version of your reckoning of 2,000 years of Christianity?**

You have mentioned my letters to Cardinal Martini. In one of them, we speak about the fact that non-believers can also possess ethical principles. If I am a believer, I find it sublime that God asked his only son to sacrifice himself for the salvation of all mankind. That's what is specific to Christianity: it isn't the fact that Christianity spent 700 or 800 years debating whether Christ is endowed only with a divine nature, or only a human one, or both, or how many persons and wills he incarnated. Such questions seem to me to belong to a futile theological game, whereas what was really at stake was the understanding of the following mystery: How could God have done that for us? But if I think that God does not exist, then the question becomes even more sublime: I have to ask myself how a section of humanity possessed enough imagination to invent a God who was made man and who allowed himself to die for the love of humanity. The fact that humanity could conceive of so sublime and paradoxical an idea, on which mankind's intimacy with the divine is founded, inspires me with great admiration for it. There's no doubt but that this same humanity has done some terrible things, but it was able none the less to invent this really extraordinary story, even if God himself does not exist.

In the past it invented gods who ate their own offspring, adulterous gods or evil, bulimic deities, who ate human beings. And then it dreamed up the ideal of the sacrifice of love. That's not at all bad! In this sense, the invention of Christianity is a fine justification for our species, and for its right to exist. Thereafter, the fact that some popes were swines, that Christians killed more infidels than infidels Christians, or that they burnt heretics, all these things are just some of the inevitable side-effects. As I said, there is always a gap between what we think we should do and what we actually do.

*Conversations held in Paris and Milan*
*on 16 November 1997 and 8 June 1998*

# Conclusion
*Stephen Jay Gould*

As philosophers frequently tell us, not out of cynicism but with a view to revealing a basic principle of humanistic enquiry, lies furnish precious clues to anyone trying to assess the history and meaning of cultural events. After all, it is enough for the truth of facts to be just that – the truth of facts; but lies have to be invented by particular people for specific reasons. From that point on, lies become unique phenomena, whose history can be told, while truths can be discovered by different people again and again many times over. (I am writing this paragraph in New York, during a shameful week for America, in the course of which President Clinton has had to admit publicly that he lied about his sexual liaisons at the White House: a historical episode that can serve as an illustration of this basic principle about lies and truth, as well as an illustration, as it happens, of Marx's famous satirical comment, according to which great events usually take place twice, the first time as tragedy – Nixon and Watergate – and the second time as farce – Clinton and Sexgate.)

If we apply the same reasoning to events which are in fact unimportant but which seem to us to be disturbing and laden with meaning, we get the same disjunction between subjective and objective reality (in one case the lie presented as a truth, in the other, the unimportant event suddenly invested with dramatic meaning). This allows us to confer on a human event a particular psychological and sociological significance. The world-wide interest in the transition to the next millennium is a perfect illustration of what I am saying. The mechanism of the heavens produced several real cycles (days, lunar months, years) which have been recognized in practically all calendars. But we have also, at least in Western calendars, constructed longer cycles (centuries and millennia, in particular); their definition is absolutely precise, but the length assigned to them is absolutely arbitrary. Nothing in physical or biological nature functions in cycles of ten or a hundred; so all our fears about the ends of centuries, all the debates about the 'panic terror of the year 1000' or the events which are due to happen in 2000 flow from our decision to have recourse to a decimal arithmetical system, and to use a notation in arabic numerals which causes certain dates to alter in all their visual components (the four figures of the date all change only once every thousand years, as in the case of 1999 to 2000). It might just be possible to argue that the decimal system is natural because it has a biological base: we have ten fingers. But if we do have ten, this is merely an accident of history, for the first terrestrial vertebrates had between six and eight fingers, and the reduction to five fingers, which took place subsequently, cannot be considered as inevitable in evolutionary terms.

Take this strange property of numerical notation. Add to it two human characteristics: first a psychological need to cling on to a degree of regularity in an apparently chaotic world, a wish to discover meaning and find comfort in this vale of tears. Second, the specific myths which our societies have worked out to try to respond to this need, for instance, the eschatological belief, based on Chapter Twenty of the Book of Revelation, according to which Jesus will soon come again to reign over the earth for a thousand years of happiness. Now you are in the position to understand the deep meaning for humans of the unimportant transition which will occur in 2000 (or 2001, to mention another trivial debate which is also charged with human emotion).

Our fascination with the millennium illustrates, above all, one of the most fundamental and paradoxical features of human nature, which has manifested itself for good or ill throughout our history. Human beings are creatures in search of structures. We need to locate an order in our environment, whether that order does or does not possess the meaning and causal basis which we are led to postulate of it. That's why Umberto Eco's remark is so profound: 'Men cannot conceive that things occur by chance . . . they have a holy terror of chance.'

In their search for the order which they so much need, human beings reveal themselves to be tellers of tales. In other words, they feel the need to find meaning in a series of historical events (or, in certain cultures, to explain that which has apparently no meaning at all) by fabricating a coherent story, generally a fable destined to palliate their petty woes (in millenarian stories, the future Golden Age which will begin with an apocalyptic Big Bang). And since the natural world doesn't conform to the scheme which their pet stories predict, they often end up by concocting false explanations of the regularities or irregularities of human history.

This deep tendency in human nature – the need to discover instances of regularity and to fit them together with the help of stories – should not necessarily be looked upon as an act of dishonesty, even if it leads to flagrant fictions which (when combined with the fervour of the 'true faith') often culminate in acts of mutilation and destruction. Such acts occur when we try to impose our own pet stories on people who believe in other fables. (I shall quote again from Umberto Eco's wise words: 'There are millions of human beings who have died because of these frenzies of interpretation.') These explanatory routes, although limited and capable of leading us astray, are our own. It is up to us whether to follow them to the point of enlightenment or destruction. If we come to understand our crankiness, including our strange obsession with that insignificant event which is the transition to the next millennium, we may succeed in profiting from it by moving towards greater insight. Giordano Bruno (burnt in a public square in 1600 as expiation for the crime of having questioned one of the most powerful of all historical fables) rightly said that our theories about the order of nature can operate either as 'vehicles' or as 'chains'. There is no human struggle more noble than the one through which we set out to break these chains and go forward in the vehicles of understanding. Not perhaps towards the mythical and inaccessible splendour of the millennium, but at least towards a decent and peaceable existence based on respect for human diversity.

## Conclusion
*Jean Delumeau*

My first reaction to the contributions of my three interlocutors in this book of 'conversations' is one of admiration and affection for their sense of humour. I think that this is the right attitude to adopt towards the year 2000. 'Keep cool,' Umberto Eco suggests. I hope that this advice will be heeded. Like Stephen Jay Gould, I am 'prudently optimistic' in the face of the future, and like my three companions, I look upon the so-called fear of the year 2000 as an invention of the media. I am convinced that the great majority of our contemporaries are not afraid that the world is about to end.

I am also at one with Jean-Claude Carrière and Umberto Eco when they say, against the widely held opinion of people who have not read the Book of Revelation, that it was composed less to instil fear than to inspire hope.

I should also like to underline the importance of the diagnosis made by one or other of the contributors on our age. We have reached, at least in the West, the point of the 'proliferation of individuals', the 'plurality of individual entities', the dissolution of group identity. Hence, in part, our difficulty in living without the solidarity which people had in the past, and their collective support systems. The century which is coming to an end has been the century of exile from our traditional forms of security. As the familiar landmarks fade away, we are invaded by the virtual as if by a 'new drug' (Jean-Claude Carrière).

The twenty-first century will begin with sharply contrasting attitudes. On the one hand, Chesterton's remark that 'since men have stopped believing in God, it isn't the case that they believe in nothing; rather, they believe in everything' has been proved right; on the other, a growing number of enigmas is opening up before us in spite of the dazzling progress in our knowledge, or rather because of it. 'Knowledge entails ignorance,' as Jean-Claude Carrière put it.

Yet the third millennium is an invitation for us to rehabilitate the irreversibility of time. Space may be plural, but time is unitary. In this flow which never returns back to its source, how can one not observe with

Stephen Jay Gould that the emergence of human consciousness can be regarded as 'the most sensational invention in the history of human evolution'. This is his answer to the question he had elsewhere humorously asked: 'Why bother about a strange species which has only been around for 200,000 years, while bacteria are 3,500 million years old?'

Of course, I part company with Stephen Jay Gould when he claims that the emergence of human consciousness was a 'chance invention'. But I am at one with him when he says: 'I am ready to bet that the universe is not determined, and that contingency is not the result of our ignorance of the determinist nature of things. I am ready to bet that somewhere out there there is an indeterminacy, some essential freedom.' In a similar way, the astrophysicist Trinh Xuan Thuan, who, it is true, 'bets' on there being a 'regulating force' in the universe, thinks for his part that everything was not determined by the Big Bang. According to him, physical laws provide a general framework on which nature can 'embroider'. The unforeseeable exists. A degree of balance is maintained between determinism and freedom and, as a consequence, no one can exist as an autonomous reality.

In the conversation with Stephen Jay Gould, there is a question which recalls Einstein's view that science has not settled the problem of the origin of the world and its final destiny. I am ready to take on board Einstein's diagnosis and ask questions which seem to me still not to be outdated at the end of this century: What if creation had a meaning? What if, in the midst of the tide in which we are swept along, every human existence also had a meaning? What if there were something beyond time? These are questions to which science does not have to reply, but upon which light may be cast by a word from elsewhere; I refer to a revelation which, while not contradicting science, is to be written in a different register from that of science.

Christianity believes itself to be the herald of such a revelation; and this belief brings me back to the year 2000. What does this anniversary mean, or rather, what should it logically signify? Indubitably, the only sense it has is to mark 2,000 years, in round figures, of Christianity. What other reason, apart from this, do we have for remembering the year 2000? It's obviously all about the third millennium of the Christian era. But a problem is posed by the wholly predictable fact that on this anniversary we will frequently drink champagne without thinking of the true meaning of the year 2000, just as many who go on holiday at Whitsun do so without knowing what the feast corresponds to. Is

Christianity behind us? Will the end of the millennium mark the moment at which it dies, the end of its history? These questions have worried me for a long time, providing, as they do, the theme of one of the books through which I have made a name for myself – *Will Christianity Die?* *

Historians are not futurologists. But they can draw up a balance sheet of the past on the one hand and, on the other, identify the features of it which may have an impact on the future. When we are accounting for 2,000 years of Christianity, we must remind our contemporaries (who are sometimes inclined to forget the fact) that in spite of its undoubtedly grave acts of betrayal of the message whose bearer it was, Christianity has an impressive credit side to its account, and in many different spheres: spirituality, culture, education, art, help for the least well off . . . I am also one of those who think that it is not fortuitous that both modern science and 'human rights' were born on Christian soil, even if at some points in the past (although no longer) it is true that conflicts over these matters broke out between progressive thinkers and religious authorities. In the light of this balance sheet, I have no hesitation in saying that if Christianity is destined to die, it will be a shame.

But don't let us be too much in a hurry to report the news of its death. The death of God was prophesied and trumpeted about before the end of the nineteenth century. Well, it seems that this prophecy has turned out not to be true. Who, in 1900, would have guessed that, a hundred years later, religion would be front-page news, and that in France, for instance, the guest cells of monasteries would be full, booked up for months in advance by people – well-educated in many cases – eager to partake of the contemplative life?

It's a historical fact that Christianity has shown an extraordinary ability to revitalize itself and adapt to both time and place. The diversity of the artistic forms, systems of thought, modes of organization and liturgy to which it has given rise cannot but impress any observer of the past and present. And who possesses the key to the future and can say that Christianity has come to an end, and that its ability to renew itself and to adjust to changing states of affairs is now exhausted?

From the point of view of Christian history, we are certainly at the end of an age; the age of conformism and, more generally, of religion inherited from the family. But perhaps we are entering into a new form of Christianity, characterized by adult baptism.

* *Le Christianisme va-t-il mourir?*, Hachette (1977).

# Conclusion
*Jean-Claude Carrière*

A conclusion about the end of time: that's a joke. A conclusion is the work of man, and belongs to our rhetoric, of which it is the last fruit. The universe has no conclusion; nor has history.

As a general rule, visions of the future, whether sombre or inviting, lead us to speak almost exclusively about our own time, about the time in which we are presently living. We have proved no exception to the rule. We have spoken less about the end of time than about the ways of envisaging it, here and now. We spoke in the sublime conviction that we are living in a special, privileged, exceptional bit of time. For about 200 years, since the beginning of the Great Acceleration, every generation has claimed to coincide with the end of an era, that nothing would any more be what it was before, that a total revolution was taking place. We all want to have known the time of all times, the hinge of destiny, the real break with the past, the transition with no going back.

There's another rule which I seem to have obeyed; and I am far from being the only one to have done so. How many ecstatic prophets are there around us, even if we only take this century! The latest lot are the cyber-prophets. Possessed of a vision, categorical: tomorrow, all communication will be free. And everything's there, oh yes, everything, in this shared pool of information. The old world is crumbling away (once again); long live virtual enlightenment! Here a triumph, there a triumph. And now our problems are solved, our anxieties stilled, our old mistakes can no longer be made. In short, the spider has a great future opening up for it on the Web. Of course, all this will pass. It's already beginning to pass, one can sense it passing. Some people are reverting to solitude and the old, slow ways. A new tactic: one can cancel one's subscription to happiness.

And the end of time will also pass. That's more than probable. For the idea of annihilation is basically linked to the superficial impression that 'enough's enough, it can't go on like this'. An old impression, perhaps connected to the sense of having made a grave mistake. We deserved the end of time. It served us right. A sense which acceleration obviously makes sharper, for any engine which goes faster and faster can only blow up in the end. A sense which will lessen little by little and maybe disappear with the acceleration itself. Soon, who knows?

When the end of time shall have become nothing more than the memory of an illusion, and since 'Time' with a big 'T' remains for ever tantalizingly out of reach, what will be left of the times in which we lived, our petty and diverse times, which sometimes succeed each other and sometimes pile up one on the other? What will be left of those times which we have attacked because we were not able to think up a single weapon against the other 'Time'? We don't know. Perhaps we'll live longer, in a century or two's time. This will change our relationship, if not with time, then at least with duration. There's even talk, further off in the future, of a sort of immortality: we will be kept alive thanks to multiple prostheses. This will mean, as I have already said, that if death disappears, then so will birth, unconditionally outlawed as it is by immortals. It is forbidden to be born! Stop life! It would be the end of evolution, the end of that time which, by acting on matter, slowly made us what we are. A disturbing vision, very common in science fiction, the death of death (at least for some), the radical alteration of our relationship with the only time which matters to us, the time of our lives.

I sometimes imagine another end to time, to our time. In a neighbouring galaxy, on a very big planet, an intelligent species has succeeded over the course of millennia in adapting itself to gravitation and developing a civilization which certainly would seem very grand to us. Unfortunately, the occupants of that planet didn't succeed in ridding themselves of the terrible faults which throughout the universe accompany intelligence. They are greedy, acquisitive, brutal and basely full of hate. That's why the higher authorities of the galaxy (which the people from the big planet call 'gods') decide to extinguish all life on that heavenly body and to start again from nothing somewhere else. A total weapon, the authentic thunderbolt of the gods, is made ready. It is unleashed. But at that moment, through prayers and sacrifices (this part of the story needs to be fleshed out) the inhabitants of the big planet succeed in moving the authorities to pity. All right, they can be spared, they'll be given a reprieve. But the weapon is flying through space. It cannot be recalled or stopped. Couldn't it at least be thrown off course? It can, says a young expert who is an inhabitant of the planet. He knows a way. Everyone gets to work. The weapon gets closer and closer and, at the very last moment, it just misses and flies off into space. Sighs of relief all round. The exterminating weapon hurtles onward, leaves that solar system, enters ours, and smashes into the earth like an avenging fury. Nothing is left of us, not even a single atom, not even, as the Persian poet put it, 'the leg of a lame ant'.

And 'Time' goes on, having witnessed similar things. And life returns again to the big planet which has been spared. With life, commerce, everyday business to transact and everyday problems to deal with, fears all come back. Not to mention pale-faced individuals with burning eyes who go about crying 'The end of the world is nigh!'

## Conclusion
*Umberto Eco*

You asked all of the people you interviewed to write a few words in conclusion, having taken note of the other conversations. Now, as it happens I gave my second interview last, and so, to a certain extent, was already able to take into account what my colleagues had said. So I hadn't anything new to say. But on reading the three other conclusions, I notice that Stephen Jay Gould highlights (and I thank him for doing so) one of my remarks about men not being able to conceive of things occurring by chance, of having a holy terror of chance, and as a consequence making up stories which explain what has happened. I am obviously in agreement with what I said, but reading through the latest version of my interview I can't find where I said it. There's a simple explanation: in re-reading my replies, I had suggested to my friends (the composers of this book of several voices) to leave out one or two questions which didn't seem to hang together with the rest and which, in my view, broke the thread of the conversation. Such things happen in interviews. Anyway, the final version doesn't contain the remark that Gould quotes.

So I'm forced to come back to it. It was merely a matter of answering the question whether the end-of-the-world mood didn't favour the conspiracy theory which has haunted people's imaginations over the last few centuries. My answer was a cautious negative. In a famous essay, Karl Popper clearly shows that conspiracy theory is already present in classical mythology. The fall of Troy, which was the consequence of a commercial conflict between Greece and Asia Minor, was depicted there as the result of a plot hatched by the gods. Popper traces this theory back to the very first attempts to explain unexpected or extraordinary events. So one can consider conspiracy theory to be a mythological version of the causal explanation of chance. Men have recourse to it when a phenomenon cannot be explained in a causal way, because the human mind cannot stop itself looking for an explanation of phenomena which have no obvious intentional cause. In this sense, our century (with the support of the last) has produced quite a few conspiracies – one only has to think about the *Protocols of the Elders of Zion* and the 'Jewish conspiracy'; and it goes without saying that we will hear about others in the course of the third millennium. But, as I have already said, I don't see anything specifically millenarian in that.

So everything's explained. But take note of this: this little editorial accident represents a fine allegory of the filtering function of memory, in the way that culture leaves something out only to recover it later – and in the way that language is sometimes capable of throwing time's arrow off track, since I am here producing a cause whose effect had been a remark by Gould; for the readers of this book, Gould's quotation comes before, not after, the sentence which he quotes, but I am writing only after his quotation of the sentence . . .

But all that has nothing to do with the year 2000, nor with my conclusions. I now suggest to our readers that we play a game we haven't yet played in this book: not to speak about the end of the world, and the fact that this spectacle will not occur, but rather to speak about certain phenomena which have nothing to do with that conspiracy, and which only the logic of chance could bring about in the coming centuries – perhaps even before 2100.

1. The end of the Europe of nation states. The nation state is, when all is said and done, a recent invention (a few centuries for France and Spain, a century and a half for Italy and Germany). The less stable European states are already in the process of collapsing. In the telematic universe which is being set up, two towns, however far apart they might be from each other, are in immediate contact; that is how permanent commercial and cultural exchanges will be set up in the four corners of Europe, with a network of associated towns, while the unit represented by nation state will progressively lose power.
2. The cause and simultaneous consequence of this evolution will be the end of white Europe. Europe will be a 'coloured' continent. Now why should a citizen of Barcelona consider himself as belonging to a different family from a citizen of Berlin if they are both 'coloured'? When I say 'coloured', I am not thinking (or I am not only thinking) of skin colour; there may also be 'coloured' religions. Why not a Sunni Christianity, an Anglican Avicennism, a Buddhist Sufism?
3. The end of the experiment of fraternity. To confront the growing world population it will be necessary to take measures like the ones

the Chinese have taken: only one child per family. Notions such as sister and brother will become buried in the memory, rather like the fairies and ogres of our childhood stories. Not to speak of the figure of the nanny – which child living today has met a nanny? Fraternity will, of course, survive as a metaphor, but it will be difficult to explain to a child what it means to love a sister or a brother.

4. The end of representative democracy. A leader chosen for his communication skills will be elected to govern each great 'global territory'; powerful groups will support candidates who have exactly the same qualities and the same programme as the opposing candidate; thus the citizen's vote (which will be motivated not by political choice but by the requirements of a society of the visual spectacle) will become a formality which decides nothing (I've a tiny suspicion that we've already got there).

5. The end of ethics. Any moral doctrine consists in putting forward a model of behaviour which one must try to imitate. Hence the 'modelling' function of the saint, the sage, the guru, the hero . . . Now, it so happens that television tends more and more to put forward as models normal people, so that it takes no effort to become like them. The case of Princess Diana is a perfect example. Today, the aim is to stage one's own normality in the world of the media. So ethical success (the Good) will soon have no link any longer with the pursuit of virtue, only with the struggle to be seen. Recently a test performed on a group of young Italian girls who had gone in for the Miss Italy competition revealed that a considerable number of them thought that Monica Lewinsky was a positive role model because she had succeeded in making herself as visible in the media as a president of the United States.

I am not Nostradamus and offer no guarantee that these visions will become reality in the course of the coming millennium. But because the ability to pick up the challenges of chance (without throwing the blame on to the conspiracies of others) is among the secular virtues, why don't we begin to prepare ourselves for what may be the important dates of the third millennium instead of enquiring into the end of the world?